CAMBRIDGE LIBRARY COLLECTION

Books of enduring scholarly value

Cambridge

The city of Cambridge received its royal charter in 1201, having already been home to Britons, Romans and Anglo-Saxons for many centuries. Cambridge University was founded soon afterwards and celebrates its octocentenary in 2009. This series explores the history and influence of Cambridge as a centre of science, learning, and discovery, its contributions to national and global politics and culture, and its inevitable controversies and scandals.

Capell's Shakespeariana

Edward Capell (1713–81) published his landmark edition of Shakespeare's works in ten volumes during 1767–8. It was the first edition to be prepared from a completely new transcript from the surviving Folio and Quartos rather than a marked-up copy of the previous edition, and thus he inaugurated a new direction in textual editing of Shakespeare's work. In 1779 Capell gave away the library of books used in the preparation of his edition, and the most valuable part of the collection, comprising 245 volumes including his copies of the quartos, went to Trinity College. Capell insisted his books were kept together, as they still are in the Wren Library at the College. This catalogue was prepared in 1903 by the renowned bibliographer and specialist in early modern drama, W. W. Greg, who became Librarian of Trinity in 1907. It offers a fascinating insight into Capell's sources and methods.

Cambridge University Press has long been a pioneer in the reissuing of out-of-print titles from its own backlist, producing digital reprints of books that are still sought after by scholars and students but could not be reprinted economically using traditional technology. The Cambridge Library Collection extends this activity to a wider range of books which are still of importance to researchers and professionals, either for the source material they contain, or as landmarks in the history of their academic discipline.

Drawing from the world-renowned collections in the Cambridge University Library, and guided by the advice of experts in each subject area, Cambridge University Press is using state-of-the-art scanning machines in its own Printing House to capture the content of each book selected for inclusion. The files are processed to give a consistently clear, crisp image, and the books finished to the high quality standard for which the Press is recognised around the world. The latest print-on-demand technology ensures that the books will remain available indefinitely, and that orders for single or multiple copies can quickly be supplied.

The Cambridge Library Collection will bring back to life books of enduring scholarly value across a wide range of disciplines in the humanities and social sciences and in science and technology.

Capell's Shakespeariana

Catalogue of the Books Presented by Edward Capell to the Library of Trinity College in Cambridge Compiled by W.W. Greg M.A.

Walter Wilson Greg

CAMBRIDGE UNIVERSITY PRESS

Cambridge New York Melbourne Madrid Cape Town Singapore São Paolo Delhi

Published in the United States of America by Cambridge University Press, New York

www.cambridge.org
Information on this title: www.cambridge.org/9781108004404

This edition first published 1903
This digitally printed version 2009

ISBN 978-1-108-00440-4

CAPELL'S SHAKESPEARIANA

London: C. J. CLAY AND SONS,
CAMBRIDGE UNIVERSITY PRESS WAREHOUSE,
AVE MARIA LANE.
Glasgow: 50, WELLINGTON STREET.

Leipzig: F. A. BROCKHAUS.
New York: THE MACMILLAN COMPANY.
Bombay and Calcutta: MACMILLAN AND CO., Ltd.

CATALOGUE OF THE BOOKS PRESENTED BY EDWARD CAPELL TO THE LIBRARY OF TRINITY COLLEGE IN CAMBRIDGE COMPILED BY W. W. GREG M.A.

CAMBRIDGE
PRINTED FOR TRINITY COLLEGE
AT THE UNIVERSITY PRESS MCMIII

Cambridge:

PRINTED BY J. AND C. F. CLAY,

AT THE UNIVERSITY PRESS.

EDWARDI CAPELL

MANIBVS

PREFACE.

THE books catalogued in the present volume were collected by the Shakespearian scholar Edward Capell and formed the principal part of his library during the years which he spent in the preparation of his edition of Shakespeare's dramatic works. After the publication of this his life's work and the completion of his commentary, the appearance of which however was delayed, Capell parted with his library, the most valuable portion being presented to Trinity while the remainder was dispersed. The conclusion of the Seniority relating to the gift is preserved in the books of the College under the date June 26, 1779. It runs "Agreed by the Master and Seniors, that the thanks of the Society be presented to Edward Capel, Esq. for the valuable Collection of the old Editions of Shakespeare, and of the several manuscripts and printed books, relating to the same Author. J. Peterborough, M.C." The further conclusion relating to the keeping of the books will be found quoted in the entry concerning the MS catalogue (p. 163).

Edward Capell, son of the rector of Stanton in Suffolk, was born on June 11, 1713. He was educated at the grammar school of Bury St Edmunds and at Catharine Hall, Cambridge. In 1737 he became deputy-inspector of plays and in 1745 groom of the privy chamber; both appointments being due to the patronage of the Duke of Grafton. In 1760 he published his volume of 'Prolusions.' In 1768 appeared his edition of Shakespeare in ten volumes, dedicated to the grandson of his former patron. The commentary was not finally published till 1783. In the meanwhile Capell had died at his chambers in Brick Court in the Temple on February 24, 1781. He also published 'Two Tables elucidating the Sounds of Letters' in 1749 and 'Reflections on the Originallity of Authours' in 1766.

The system on which the books have been catalogued will I think explain itself. Each work is entered under the author's name whenever the ascription can be made with a reasonable degree of certainty, whether or not the name appears in the work itself. Otherwise books are entered under their titles, except in the case of those published under pseudonyms, which are treated as real names. Initials have not been allowed as headings. In all cases in which any possibility of doubt exists, cross references will be found in the index. With regard to information concerning printers, etc. I have only given notes in cases of particular interest. A list of printers and stationers will be found at the end. In one detail I have deliberately sacrificed consistency to expediency. I have, namely, in giving the names of authors of commendatory verses and the like, followed the original or modernised spelling as appeared more convenient in each individual case.

Finally it is my pleasant duty to acknowledge the kind and valuable help I have throughout received from Mr Aldis Wright, at whose original suggestion the present work was undertaken. I also owe certain suggestions and corrections to my friend Mr A. W. Pollard of the British Museum, to whom the proofs were submitted.

W. W. G.

November, 1903.

ERRATA.

p. 1, l. 9. *for* Blovnt *read* Blount.
p. 2, l. 16. *for* Blovnt *read* Blount.
p. 49, l. 8. *for* $_{2}T^{4}$ *read* $2T^{4}$.
l. 11. *for* 'adwertisement' *read* 'aduertisement'.
p. 67, l. 7. *for* HORMANUS *read* HORNANUS.
p. 90, l. 1. *for* Hvmphrey *read* Humphrey.
p. 111, l. 22. *for* SALVIANUS, Massiliensis *read* SALVIANUS, *Massiliensis.*
p. 114, l. 26. *for* SAVIOLO, Vicentio *read* SAVIOLO, Vincentio.

CAPELL'S SHAKESPEARIANA

ADLINGTON, William.

The eleuen Bookes of the Golden Asse...1596. *See* APULEIUS, Lucius.

ALEXANDER, William, *Earl of Stirling*.

The Monarchicke Tragedies; Crœsus, Darius, The Alexandræan, Iulius Cæsar. Newly enlarged By William Alexander, Gentleman of the Princes priuie Chamber. Carmine dij superi placantur, carmine manes. *London Printed by Valentine Simmes for Ed: Blovnt.* 1607.

4°. ($7\frac{1}{4} \times 5\frac{1}{4}$). R. 15.

Collation: A–2D⁴2E²; a²B–M⁴N²; A–K⁴L², unpaged. K 4 in the third alphabet blank. Wanting A 1 in the first (? blank). The general title is on A 2, followed by argument and personae to the 'Alexandrian Tragedy,' which begins on B 1. 'Julius Caesar' has a separate titlepage with same imprint on P 2. The rest of the volume (sig. a etc.) is the edition of the 'Monarchic Tragedies' of 1604 with omission of the first sheet, A. It begins with commendatory verses by Robert Ayton, which are followed by the argument and personae to 'Croesus' (some copies have four leaves to sheet a, the additional matter being verses to King James). Then follows the tragedy of 'Croesus' while 'Darius' has separate titlepage dated 1604. In the present copy the 1604 portion has been placed immediately after sheet A of the new portion, in order to get the plays in the order mentioned on the titlepage. This arrangement is frequently met with but leads to absurdities, since the 1604 portion must either be placed, as here, between the personae to the 'Alexandrian Tragedy' and the play itself, or else, as in the copy in the British Museum, in the middle of sheet A.

BM 31.

Aurora. Containing the first fancies of the Authors youth, William Alexander of Menstrie. *London, Printed by Richard Field for Edward Blount.* 1604.

4°. ($7\frac{1}{4} \times 5\frac{1}{4}$). R. 15.

Collation: A–M⁴, unpaged. M 4 blank. Epistle dedicatory to Lady Agnes Dowglas, Countess of Argyle. This and the 'Paraenesis' are inserted in the middle of the 'Monarchic Tragedies' at the end of the 1604 portion, but appear to be really distinct publications.

BM 30.

A Paraenesis to the Prince By William Alexander of Menstrie. *London, Printed by Richard Field for Edward Blovnt.* 1604. 4°. ($7\frac{1}{4} \times 5\frac{1}{4}$). R. 15.

Collation: A–C⁴D² unpaged. D 2 blank. The author's initials appear at the end of the poem.

BM 31.

ALLOT, Robert.

Englands Parnassus: or The choysest Flowers of our Moderne Poets, with their Poeticall comparisons. Descriptions of Bewties, Personages, Castles, Pallaces, Mountaines, Groues, Seas, Springs, Riuers, &c. Whereunto are annexed other various discourses, both pleasaunt and profitable. *Imprinted at London for N. L. C. B. and T. H.* 1600.

8°. ($6\frac{1}{2} \times 3\frac{3}{4}$). Y. 4.

Collation: A–2K⁸, paged. Wanting A 1 and 2 and 2K 8 (? all blank). The last has been erroneously said to contain an epilogue. Dedicatory verses to Sir Thomas Mounson, signed R. A. (*i.e.* Robert Allot, the editor). Verses to the reader signed R. A. Table of headings. Errata. The stationers were Nicholas Ling (whose device appears on the titlepage), Cuthbert Burby, and Thomas Hayes. In some copies the name of the last appears at length on the titlepage. Allot's full name also appears in some copies at the end of the dedicatory verses (Haz. I. 321).

Sinker 621. BM 3.

APULEIUS, Lucius.

The eleuen Bookes of the Golden Asse Containing, the metamorphosie of Lucius Apuleius, enterlaced with sundry pleasant & delectable tales, with an excellent narration of the marriage of Cupid and Psyches, sette out in the fourth, the fifth, and the sixt Bookes. Translated out of Latin into English by William Adlington. *London Printed by Valentine Symmes.* 1596. **B. L.** 4°. (7 × 5⅛). T. 3.

Collation: A–2D⁴, paged. Wanting, 2D 2. Epistle dedicatory to Thomas, Earl of Sussex, signed by the translator. Address to the reader. Life of Apuleius. Author's preface translated in verse and prose. This is the fourth edition; the first appeared in 1566.

Sinker 803. BM 48.

ARIOSTO, Lodovico.

Ariostos seven Planets Gouerning Italie. Or his Satyrs in seven Famous discourses, shewing the estate 1. Of the Court, and Courtiers. 2. Of Libertie, and the Clergy in general. 3. Of the Romane Clergie. 4. Of Marriage. 5. Of Soldiers, Musitians, and Louers. 6. Of Schoolemasters and Schollers. 7. Of Honour, and the happiest life. Newly Corrected and Augmented, with many excellent and noteworthy Notes, together with a new Addition of three most excellent Elegies, written by the same Lodouico Ariosto, the effect whereof is contained in the Argument. Qui te sui te sui. *London Printed by William Stansby for Roger Iackson, dwelling in Fleete-streete neere the Conduit.* 1611.

4°. (7⅛ × 5½). S. 28. 2.

Collation: A–Q⁴; paged. Address to the reader. Argument. Seven Satires. Three Elegies with head-title and fresh pagination. This is a reprint with additions of 'Ariostos Satyres in seuen famous Discourses' which appeared in 1608 as translated by Gervis Markham, but in reality by Robert Tofte.

BM 50.

⌜Orlando Furioso in English heroical Verse by Iohn Haringtõ Esquire. Principibus placuisse viris non vltima laus est. Horace] [Colophon] *Imprinted at London by Richard Field dwelling in the Black-friars by Ludgate.* 1591.

F°. (9¾ × 7). I. 1.

The word 'Esquire.' is printed on a slip of paper pasted on the titlepage, which is engraved. Collation: ¶^{8}A–P^{6}Q^{4}R–2N^{6}2O^4, paged. Wanting ¶ 1, containing engraved titlepage signed Coxonus (*i.e.* T. Cockson) in some copies (Sayle 2228) but by W. Rogers in others (Haz. H. 11) and table of contents on verso. Last leaf containing colophon misplaced at the beginning. Epistle dedicatory to Queen Elizabeth signed by the translator. 'A preface, or rather a briefe apologie of poetrie.' Address to the reader signed Io. Har. At the end, 'Allegory of the Orlando Furioso,' Life of Ariosto by John Harington, alphabetical table of contents, table of principal tales and list of errata. Inserted at the beginning is a large engraved portrait of Queen Elizabeth, 'Printed and Are to be sould by P. Stent without Newgate.' The first fifty stanzas of Book 32 were translated by Sir John Harington's younger brother Francis. Each of the 46 books is preceded by a full-page engraving, some of which are a good deal worn in the present copy. First edition.

Sinker 740. BM 50.

Orlando Furioso in English heroical Verse, by S^r. Iohn Haringtō of Bathe Knight. Now secondly imprinted the yeere . 1607. Principibus placuisse viris non vltima laus est. Horace. [Colophon] [*Imprinted at London by Richard Field, for Iohn Norton and Simon Waterson.* 1607.]

F°. (10½ × 7¼). G. 3. 2.

Engraved titlepage as above; title partly re-engraved. Collation: ¶^{8}A–P^{6}Q^{4}R–2N^{6}2O^4, paged. Wanting 2O 4 containing colophon. Contents etc. as before but without errata at end. Most of the plates are very much worn in this copy. Second edition; a third with the addition of Sir John Harington's 'Epigrams' appeared in 1634.

ASCHAM, Roger.

Toxophilus, The schole of shootinge conteyned in two bookes. To all Gentlemen and yomen of Englande, pleasaunte for theyr pastyme to rede, and profitable for theyr use to folow, both in war and peace. The contentes of the first booke..... [Colophon] *Londini. In ædibus Edouardi Whytchurch. Cum priuilegio ad imprimendum solum.* 1545.

B. L. 4°. ($6\frac{7}{8} \times 5\frac{1}{8}$). T. 4. 1.

Collation: A⁴a⁴A–Y⁴, folios numbered. Wanting A1 containing frontispiece etc. Frontispiece, with Latin commendatory verses by Walter Haddon on verso. Epistle dedicatory to Henry VIII, signed by the author Roger Ascham. Address 'To all gentle men and yomen of Englande.' Title with table of contents to the two books. The second Book begins with new foliation at sig. N3. The two leaves a3 and 4 containing Title and Table have been placed at the beginning to supply the place of the frontispiece. This is the first edition; subsequent ones appeared in 1571 and 1589.

Sinker 90. BM 58.

BACON, Francis.

A Declaration of the Practises and Treasons attempted and committed by Robert late Earle of Essex and his Complices, against her Maiestie and her Kingdoms, and of the proceedings as well at the Arraignments & Conuictions of the said late Earle, and his adherents, as after: Together with the very Confessions and other parts of the Euidences themselues, word for word taken out of the Originals. *Imprinted at London by Robert Barker, Printer to the Queenes most excellent Maiestie. Anno* 1601.

4°. ($7\frac{1}{8} \times 5\frac{3}{8}$). S. 28. 1.

Collation: A–Q⁴ unpaged. Wanting A1 blank. There is a woodcut of the royal arms on verso of titlepage, which occurs again on K3ᵛ at the beginning of the 'Confessions'. The official account prepared by Bacon.

BM 474.

BANDELLO, Matteo.

La prima [seconda, terza] Parte de le Novelle del Bandello. *In Lucca, Per Vincentio Busdrago,* 1554. *e di nuovo In Londra, per S. Harding,* M.DCC.XL.

La quarta Parte de le Novelle del Bandello. *In Lione, Per Alessandro Marsilii,* 1573. *e di nuovo In Londra, per S. Harding,* M.DCCXL. 4°. ($9\frac{1}{4} \times 8\frac{1}{2}$). K. 1–3.

The original edition of Parts i—iii is in quarto, Part iv in octavo. The four parts contain a total of 214 novels, of which 28 appear in Part iv.

Certaine Tragicall Discourses written oute of Frenche and Latin, by Geffraie Fenton, no lesse profitable then pleasaunt, and of like necessitye to al degrees that take pleasure in antiquityes or forreine reapportes. Mon heur viendra. *Imprinted at London in Fletestrete nere to Sainct Dunstons Churche by Thomas Marshe. Anno Domini.* 1567.

B. L. 4°. ($7\frac{3}{8} \times 5\frac{3}{8}$). R. 8.

Title within woodcut border. Collation: $*^8 2*^2$ A–$2P^8 2Q^2$. Epistle dedicatory to Lady Mary Sidney, signed and dated, Paris, June 22, 1567. Commendatory verses from Sir John Conway, M.H., George Turberville, and Peter Beverley. Argument. Thirteen histories. Table of contents at the end. The first edition. Entirely translated from the novels of Bandello, through the French of Belleforest.

Sinker 314. BM 617.

BARCLAY, Alexander.

Stultifera Nauis.... 1570. The Ship of Fooles. *See* Brant, Sebastian.

BARKER, William.

The Fearefull Fansies of the Florentine Cooper...1599. *See* Gelli, Giovanni Battista.

BARKSTED, William.

Mirrha the Mother of Adonis: or, Lustes Prodegies. By William Barksted. Horrace. Nansicetur enim pretium, nomenque Poetæ. Whereunto are added certain Eglogs. By L. M. *London Printed by E. A. for Iohn Bache, and are* *to be sold at his shop in the Popes-head Palace, nere the Royall Exchange.* 1607. 8°. ($5\frac{1}{8} \times 3\frac{3}{8}$). *. 15. 1.

Collation: A–E[8] unpaged. Wanting E 2–8 containing the 'Eglogs'. Ornament at head, middle and foot of each page of 'Mirrha'. Commendatory verses signed I.W., Robert Glover, Lewes Machin, William Bagnall. The 'Eglogs' have separate titlepage, without imprint, on E 2: 'Three Eglogs, The first is of Menalcas and Daphnis: The other two is of Apollo and Hyacinth. By Lewes Machin.'

BEAUMONT, Francis, and FLETCHER, John.

Comedies and Tragedies Written by Francis Beaumont And Iohn Fletcher Gentlemen. Never printed before, And now published by the Authours Originall Copies. Si quid habent veri Vatum præsagia, vivam. *London, Printed for Humphrey Robinson, at the three Pidgeons, and for Humphrey Moseley at the Princes Armes in St Pauls Church-yard.* 1647. F°. ($13\frac{1}{4} \times 8\frac{7}{8}$). ✱. 3. 1.

Collation: Portrait unsigned prefixed, $A^4a–c^4d–e^2f^4g^2B–K^4L^2$ $2A–2S^4$ $3A–3X^4$ $4A–4I^4$ $5A–5R^4$ $5S^6$ $5T–5X^4$ $6A–6K^4$ $6L^6$ $7A–7C^4$ $7D^2$ $7E–7G^4 8A–8C^4$*$8D^2 8D–8F^4$, paged (except in preliminary matter and beginning afresh with each new set of signatures.) Wanting portrait and leaves a 1–2, b 1 and 4, c 1, d 1–e 2, all containing commendatory verses. Text in double columns. The engraved portrait of Fletcher is signed Guliel. Marshall, and has Latin verses subscribed, signed J. Berkenhead. Epistle dedicatory to Philip Earl of Pembroke, signed jointly: John Lowin, Richard Robinson, Eylærd Swanston, Hugh Clearke, Stephen Hammerton, Joseph Taylor, Robert Benfield, Thomas Pollard, William Allen and Theophilus Byrd. Address to the reader signed by the editor, Ja. Shirley. Stationer's address signed Humphrey Moseley and dated 'At the Princes Armes in St Pauls Church-yard. Feb. 14th 1646.' Verses to the Stationer signed Grandison. Commendatory verses signed: H. Howard; Henry Mody, Baronet; Thomas Peyton, Agricola Anglo-Cantianus; Aston Cokaine, Baronet; Jo. Pettus, Knight; Robert Stapylton, Knight; George Lisle, Knight; I. Denham; Edw. Waller; Rich. Lovelace; Will. Habington; Ia. Howell, P.C.C.; Tho. Stanley; Roger L'Estrange; Robert Gardiner; John Web; George Buck; Joh. Earle; I. M.; Jasper Maine; William Cartwright (2 copies); Rich. Corbet D.D.; Ben: Johnson; Rob. Herrick; I. Berkenhead; Edw. Powell; G. Hills; Jos. Howe of

Trin. Coll. Oxon.; T. Palmer of Ch. Ch. Oxon.; Alex. Brome; John Harris; Henry Harington; Ric. Brome; Ja. Shirley; H. Moseley. 'Postscript.' Table of contents. The collection consists of all the plays of Beaumont and Fletcher which had not yet appeared in print, with the exception of the 'Wild Goose Chase', which was published by way of supplement to the present volume in 1652.

The Coronation A Comedy. As it was presented by her Majesties Servants at the private House in Drury Lane. Written by John Fletcher. Gent. *London, Printed by Tho. Cotes, for Andrew Crooke, and William Cooke, and are to be sold at the signe of the Greene Dragon, in Pauls Church-yard.* 1640. 4°. ($7\frac{1}{8} \times 5\frac{1}{4}$). S. 4. 9.

Collation: $A^2B–I^4K^2$, unpaged. Personae. Prologue. Epilogue at the end. This play, though published with Fletcher's name as above, and later included in the folio of 1679, was claimed by Shirley.

BM 635.

Cupids Revenge. As it was often Acted (with great applause) by the Children of the Reuells. Written by Fran. Beaumont & Io. Fletcher Gentlemen. The second Edition. *London: Printed for Thomas Iones, and are to be sold at his Shop in Saint Dunstanes Churchyard in Fleet-street.* 1630. 4°. ($7\frac{1}{8} \times 5\frac{5}{8}$). S. 3. 6.

Collation: $A^2B–L^4$, unpaged. Wanting A 1 and L 4 (?blank). Personae. Epilogue at the end. The first edition appeared in 1615.

BM 117.

The Elder Brother: a Comedie. Acted at the private house in Blacke Fryers, with great Applause, by His late Majesties Servants. Printed according to the true Copie. Written by Francis Beaumont, and John Fletcher. Gent. The second Edition, Corrected and Amended. *London, Printed for Humphrey Moseley, and are to be sold at his Shop at the Princes Arms in S^t. Paules Church yard.* 1651. 4°. ($7\frac{1}{8} \times 5\frac{5}{8}$). S. 3. 5.

Collation: $A–H^4$, paged. Personae. Couplet headed 'Lectori'. Prologue. Epilogue at the end. The third edition really, two having appeared in 1637. On the verso of the titlepage and of the next leaf are some verses inscribed in an old hand.

The Faithfull Shepherdesse. Acted at Somerset House before the King and Queene on Twelfe night last, 1633. And divers times since with great applause at the Private House in Blacke-Friers, by his Majesties Servants. Written by Iohn Fletcher. The third Edition, with Addition. *London, Printed by A. M. for Richard Meighen, next to the Middle Temple in Fleet-street.* 1634. 4°. ($7\frac{1}{8} \times 5\frac{5}{8}$). S. 3. 7.

Collation: A–K⁴, unpaged. K 4 blank. Wanting A 2, containing the verses of Field, Jonson, and Chapman. Commendatory verses signed: Fr. Beaumont, Nath. Field, Ben Ionson, G. Chapman, Shack. Marmyon. Dialogue 'by way of prologue' (by Sir W. Davenant). The first edition appeared undated in 1609 or early in 1610.

A King, and no King. Acted at the Blacke-Fryars, by his Maiesties Seruants. And now the third time Printed, according to the true Copie. Written by Francis Beamont & Iohn Fletcher Gent.

The Stationer to Dramatophilus.

A Play and no Play, who this Booke shall read,
Will iudge, and weepe, as if 'twere done indeed.

London, Printed by A. M. for Richard Hawkins, and are to be sold at his Shop in Chancerie Lane, neere Serjeants Inne. 1631. 4°. ($7\frac{1}{8} \times 5\frac{5}{8}$). S. 3. 3.

Collation: A–M⁴, paged. Wanting A 1 (? blank). Personae. The first edition appeared in 1619.

BM 118.

The Knight Of the Burning Pestle. Full of Mirth and Delight. Written by Francis Beamount and Iohn Fletcher. Gent. As it is now acted by her Majesties Servants at the Private house in Drury lane. 1635.

——————— Quod si
Iudicium subtile, videndis artibus illud
Ad libros & ad haec Musarum dona vocares:
Bœotum in crasso jurares aëre natum.
Horat. in Epist. ad Oct. Aug.

London: Printed by N. O. for I. S. 1635. 4°. ($7\frac{1}{8} \times 5\frac{5}{8}$). S. 3. 8.

Collation: A–K⁴, unpaged. A 1 blank. Address to the readers. Preface headed 'Prologue'. Personae. Epilogue at the end. Two editions, the second and third, were published in this year; the first had appeared in 1613.

BM 118.

The Maides Tragedie: as it hath beene divers times Acted at the Black-Friers by the Kings Maiesties Servants. Written by Francis Beaumont, and Iohn Fletcher Gentlemen. The fourth Impression, Revised and Refined. [Woodcut.] *Printed by E. G. for Henry Shepherd, and are to be sold at the signe of the Bible in Chancery lane.* 1638.

4°. ($7\frac{1}{8} \times 5\frac{5}{8}$). S. 3. 1.

Collation: A–K⁴L², unpaged. Personae. 'The Stationers Censure' in verse. The first edition appeared in 1629.

BM 118.

Monsieur Thomas. A Comedy. Acted at the Private House in Blacke Fryers. The Author, Iohn Fletcher, Gent. *London, Printed by Thomas Harper, for Iohn Waterson, and are to be sold at his shop in Pauls Church-yard, at the signe of the Croune:* 1639. 4°. ($7\frac{1}{8} \times 5\frac{1}{4}$). S. 4. 5.

Collation: titlepage unsigned, A²B–M⁴N², unpaged. Wanting N 2 (? blank). Epistle dedicatory to Charles Cotton, signed Richard Brome. Commendatory verses signed by the same. First edition.

BM 635.

The Night-Walker, or the Little Theife. A Comedy, As it was presented by her Majesties Servants, at the Private House in Drury Lane. Written by John Fletcher. Gent. *London, Printed by Tho. Cotes, for Andrew Crooke, and William Cooke.* 1640. 4°. ($7\frac{1}{8} \times 5\frac{1}{4}$). S. 4. 4.

Collation: A²B–K⁴, unpaged. Epistle dedicatory to William Hudson, signed A. C. (*i.e.* Andrew Crooke). Personae. First edition.

BM 635.

Philaster or Love lies a Bleeding. Acted at the Globe, and Blackfriers By his Majesties Servants. The Authors being Francis Beaumont, and Iohn Fletcher. Gent. The fourth Impression. *London, Printed by E. Griffin for William Leak, and are to be sold at his shop in Chancerie Lane neere the six Clarkes Office* 1639. 4°. ($7\frac{1}{8} \times 5\frac{5}{8}$). S. 3. 2.

Collation: A–K[4], paged. Stationer's epistle. Personae. This is really the fifth edition, the first having appeared in 1620.

BM 118.

The Tragœdy of Rollo Duke of Normandy. Acted by his Majesties Servants. Written by John Fletcher Gent. *Oxford, Printed by Leonard Lichfield Printer to the Vniversity. Anno* 1640. 4°. ($7\frac{1}{8} \times 5\frac{1}{4}$). S. 4. 1.

Collation: A–I[4]K[2], paged. Personae. The second edition. The first edition had appeared in London the previous year under the title of 'The Bloody Brother'.

BM 635.

Rule a Wife And have a Wife. A Comoedy. Acted by his Majesties Servants. Written by John Fletcher Gent. *Oxford, Printed by Leonard Lichfield Printer to the Vniversity. Anno* 1640. 4°. ($7\frac{1}{8} \times 5\frac{1}{4}$). S. 4. 2.

Collation: A–I[4], paged. Prologue. Epilogue at the end.

BM 635.

The Scornefull Lady. A Comedy. As it was Acted (with great applause) by the late Kings Majesties Servants, at the Black-Fryers. Written by Francis Beaumont. and John Fletcher. Gentlemen. The sixt Edition, Corrected and amended. *London, Printed for Humphrey Moseley, and are to be sold at his Shop at the Princes Armes in St Pauls Church-yard.* 1651. 4°. ($7\frac{1}{8} \times 5\frac{5}{8}$). S. 3. 4.

Collation: A–H[4], unpaged. Personae. There were two editions this year, both styled the 'sixt', the present one being distinguished by having a printer's device on the title. The first edition appeared in 1616.

The Tragedy of Thierry King of France, and his Brother Theodoret. As it was diverse times acted at the Blacke-

Friers, by the Kings Majesties Servants. Written by Fracis [*sic*] Beamont. and John Fletcher Gent. *London, Printed for Humphrey Moseley, and are to be sold at his Shop at the Princes Armes in St. Pauls Church-yard.* 1649.

4°. (7⅛ × 5¼). S. 4. 8.

Collation: 2 leaves unsigned, A2–4, B–E⁴, unpaged. Wants E 4 (? blank). Double columns. Prologue. Epilogue. Personae. This is a re-issue of the second edition (1648), A 1 being replaced by a half-sheet unsigned. The first edition appeared in 1621.

The Two Noble Kinsmen: Presented at the Blackfriers by the Kings Maiesties servants, with great applause: Written by the memorable Worthies of their time; Mr. John Fletcher, and Mr. William Shakspeare. Gent. *Printed at London by Tho. Cotes, for Iohn Waterson: and are to be sold at the signe of the Crowne in Pauls Church-yard.* 1634.

4°. (7⅛ × 5¼). S. 4. 6.

Collation: titlepage unsigned, B–M⁴N², paged. Wanting N 2 (? blank). Prologue. Epilogue at the end.

[Another copy.] 4°. (7⅛ × 5¼). S. 27. 1.

Also wanting N 2.

BM 635.

The Wild-Goose Chase. A Comedie. As it hath been Acted with singular Applause at the Black-Friers: Being the Noble, Last, and Onely Remaines of those Incomparable Drammatists, Francis Beaumont, and John Fletcher, Gent. Retriv'd for the publick delight of all the Ingenious; And private Benefit Of John Lowin, And Joseph Taylor, Servants to His late Majestie. By a Person of Honour. Ite bonis avibus— *London, Printed for Humphrey Moseley, and are to be sold at the Princes Armes in St. Paules Church-yard.* 1652.

F°. (13¼ × 8⅞). *. 3. 2.

Collation: A² a² B–P², paged. Epistle dedicatory "To the Honour'd, Few, Lovers of Drammatick Poesie," signed: John Lowin, Joseph Taylor. Commendatory verses signed: Richard Lovelace, Norreys Jephson, W. E., H: Harington, James Ramsey. Personae with parts assigned.

Wit without Money. A Comedie, As it hath beene Presented with good Applause at the private house in Drurie Lane, by her Majesties Servants. Written by Francis Beamount, and John Flecher. Gent. *London Printed by Thomas Cotes, for Andrew Crooke, and William Cooke.* 1639. 4°. (7⅛ × 5¼). S. 4. 3.

Collation: titlepage unsigned, B–I⁴, unpaged. Wanting I 4 (? blank). Personae. First edition.

BM 119.

The Woman Hater, or the Hungry Courtier. A Comedy, As it hath been Acted by his Majesties Servants with great Applause. Written by Francis Beaumont and John Fletcher. Gent. *London, Printed for Humphrey Moseley, and are to be sold at his Shop at the Princes Armes in St. Pauls Church-yard.* 1649. 4°. (7⅛ × 5¼). S. 4. 7.

Collation: 2 leaves unsigned, A2–4, B–E⁴, unpaged. Double columns. Prologue and epilogue in verse. Personae. Prose prologue. This is a re-issue of the third edition (1648), A 1 being replaced by a half-sheet unsigned. The first two editions appeared in 1607.

BELL, ADAM.

Adam Bell, Clim of the Cl[ough] and William of Cloudesle. [Woodcut, with names printed above the figures.] *London, Printed by A. M. for W. Thackeray, at the Angel in Duck-Lane,* [sic.] B. L. 4°. (7½ × 5½). Q. 14. 4.

Collation: A–C⁴, unpaged. Wanting C 4 (? blank). The date cannot be earlier than about 1660, when Thackeray started as bookseller. The first edition of the ballad was probably that printed by Byddell in 1536, known only from a fragment of two leaves. (Haz. I. 33.)

BELLEFOREST, FRANÇOIS DE.

XVIII Histoires Tragiques. Extraictes des euures Italiennes de Bandel, & mises en langue Françoise, Les six premieres, par Pierre Boisteau, surnommé Launay, natif de Bretaigne. Les douzė suiuantes par Fran. de Belle-Forest,

Comingeois. *A Paris. Pour Gilles Robinot tenãt sa boutique au Palais, en la galerie ou on va à la Chancellerie.* 1564. *Auec Priuilege.* 16°. ($4\frac{1}{2} \times 3$). *. 21.

Collation: a–z⁸ A–2I⁸, paged. 'Extrait du Privilege du Roy' dated, Paris, Jan. 17, 1563; 'Achevé d'imprimer' Sept. 20, 1564. Epistle dedicatory, from Boisteau to Matthieu de Mauny, Abbe des Noyers. Address to the reader. Belleforest's continuation begins with head-title at sig. t 6, preceded by commendatory verses by Belleforest 'Au seigneur de Launay Breton' (*i.e.* Boisteau). Epistle dedicatory by Belleforest to Charles Maximilian, duc d'Orleans. Table of the whole eighteen histories at the end. The six novels translated by Boisteau appeared in 1559, and the same year saw the publication of the continuation by Belleforest containing the other twelve. The two parts were first printed together at Lyons in 8° the same year as the present edition. In the subsequent volumes Belleforest drew from many other sources besides Bandello, while throughout he enlarges greatly upon his original.

Le Cinquiesme Tome des Histoires Tragiques, Le succez, & euenement desquelles est pour la plus part recueilly des choses aduenues de nostre temps, & le reste des histoires anciennes. Par F. de Belleforest Comingeois. *A Lyon, Par les heritiers de Benoist Rigaud.* M. DCI.

16°. ($4\frac{3}{4} \times 2\frac{7}{8}$). *. 20.

Collation: A–2P⁸, paged. Epistle dedicatory to Anthoinette de Turaine, Contesse de Clinchamp, signed and dated, Paris, July 25, 1570. Commendatory verses by Justus Ludovicus a Tornone in Latin. Italian verses headed 'De gli Spiriti Francesi à la Francia' and 'Il libro, de se stesso.' Commendatory verses by Jaques Moysson, and A. du Verdier. Table at end. The volume contains eight histories. The first edition of vol. v. appeared at Paris in 1570. The final edition of the 'Histoires Tragiques' is that published at Rouen in 1603–4, in 7 vols. 16°.

The Hystorie of Hamblet. *London Imprinted by Richard Bradocke, for Thomas Pauier, and are to be sold at his shop in Corne-hill, neere to the Royall Exchange* 1608.

B. L. 4°. ($7 \times 5\frac{1}{4}$). S. 33. 3.

Collation: A–H⁴ I², unpaged. Wanting A 1 and I 2 (? blank). Argument. Preface. Translated from the third 'Histoire' of the fifth volume of Belleforest's collection. The present copy, which is supposed to be unique, came into Capell's hands from the collection of the Duke of Newcastle (see R. Farmer's 'Learning of Shakespeare,' ed. 2, 1767, p. 59). Capell had previously possessed a fragment (*Id.* p. 57).

BOCCACCIO, GIOVANNI.

Il Decameron Di Messer Giovanni Boccaccio. Del MDXXVII. 4°. ($8\frac{1}{2} \times 6\frac{1}{4}$). O. I.

On the verso of the facsimile titlepage of 1527 occurs the imprint "Londra per Tommaso Edlin. MDCCXXV." With engraved portrait and frontispiece. The reprint known as Consul Smith's edition.

The Modell of Wit, Mirth, Eloquence, and Conuersation. Framed in Ten Dayes, of an hundred curious Pieces, by seuen Honourable Ladies, and three Noble Gentlemen. Preserued to Posterity by the Renowned Iohn Boccacio, the first Refiner of Italian prose: And now translated into English. *Printed by Isaac Iaggard, for Mathew Lownes*, 1625.
F°. ($11\frac{1}{8} \times 7\frac{1}{8}$). F. 9. I.

Title within ornamental border originally used in 1593 for Sidney's 'Arcadia'. Collation: A–V^{6}2A^{8}2B–2N^6, folios numbered. 2N 6 blank. Wanting A I (? blank). Epistle dedicatory to Philip Herbert, Earl of Montgomery. Table of contents in double columns. Woodcuts in text.

BM 239.

The Decameron containing An hundred pleasant Nouels. Wittily discoursed, betweene seuen Honourable Ladies, and three Noble Gentlemen. The last Fiue Dayes. *London, Printed by Isaac Iaggard*, 1620. F°. ($11\frac{1}{8} \times 7\frac{1}{8}$). F. 9. 2.

Title within border formed of woodcuts used also in the text. Collation: A^4¶–2¶^{4}3¶^{2}B–2Z^{4}3A^6, folios numbered. A I blank. Epistle dedicatory to Philip Herbert, Earl of Montgomery. Address to the reader. Table of contents in single columns. Woodcuts in text.

BM 460.

Thirteene most pleasaunt and delectable questions, Entituled, A disport of diuerse noble personages, written in Italian by M. Iohn Bocace Florentine and poet Laureat, in his booke named Philocopo: Englished by H. G. *Imprinted at London by A. I. and are to be sold in Paules churchyard, by Thomas Woodcocke.* 1587. [Colophon] *Imprinted at London, by Abell Ieffes, and are to be solde in Paules churchyard by Thomas Woodcocke, dwelling at the signe of the Beare.* 1587.

B. L. 8°. ($5\frac{1}{4} \times 3\frac{1}{2}$). *. 12.

Collation: A–L^8, unpaged. Epistle dedicatory from H. G. to William Rice, dated Mar. 6, 1566. Verses to the reader. Argument. Translated from the fifth book of the 'Philocolo'. The first edition appeared under the title 'A Pleasant disport' &c., in 1567. The present edition is the fourth that is known. Both H. Grantham and H. Gifford have been suggested as the translator.

Sinker 1093. BM 239.

BODENHAM, John.

Bel-vedére or the Garden of the Muses.

Quem referent Musæ viuet dum robora tellus,
Dum cœlum stellas, dum vehet amnis aquas.

Imprinted at London by F. K. for Hugh Astley, dwelling at Saint Magnus Corner. 1600. 8°. ($5\frac{5}{8} \times 3\frac{3}{4}$). *. 1. 1.

Collation: A^8, two leaves unsigned, B–R^8, paged. Wanting A 1 (? blank). Address to the reader. Coat of arms of the Bodenhams. Commendatory verses to Iohn Bodenham the editor, signed A. M. (*i.e.* Anthony Munday?); other verses signed A. B., W. Rankins, R. Hathway. Dedicatory verses to the universities of Oxford and Cambridge respectively (two leaves unsigned and printed on recto only). At the end, prose 'Conclusion' followed by alphabetical table of headings.

Sinker 820. BM 240.

BORDE, Andrew.

Scogin's Jests: Full of witty Mirth, and pleasant Shifts; done by him in France and other places. Being A Preservative against Melancholy. Gathered by Andrew Board, Doctor of Physick. This may be Reprinted, R. P. *London: Printed for W. Thackeray at the Angel in Duck-lane, near West-Smithfield, and J. Deacon at the Angel in Gilt-spur-street.*

B. L. 4°. ($7\frac{3}{4} \times 5\frac{3}{8}$). Q. 8. 3.

Collation: $A^2B–F^4$, paged. Prologue. Epigram by Scogin. Table of contents. The date is after 1660. (*See* Bell, Adam.) There is not the least evidence for fathering the 'Scogin' jests upon Borde.

BRANT, SEBASTIAN.

Stultifera Nauis, qua omnium mortalium narratur stultitia, admodum vtilis & necessaria ab omnibus ad suam salutem perlegenda, è Latino sermone in nostrum vulgarem versa, & iam diligenter impressa. An. Do. 1570. [Woodcut.] The Ship of Fooles, wherin is shewed the folly of all States, with diuers other workes adioyned vnto the same, very profitable and fruitfull for all men. Translated out of Latin into Englishe by Alexander Barclay Priest. [Colophon] *Imprinted at London in Paules Churchyarde by Iohn Cawood Printer to the Queenes Maiestie. Cum Priuilegio ad imprimendum solum.* F°. 𝔅. 𝔏. (11 × 7½). F. 13.

Collation: ¶–2¶^{6}A–2V^{6}2X^4; A–G^6; A–D^6, folios numbered in first alphabet. Epistle dedicatory from Alexander Barclay to Thomas Cornissh, Bishop of Bath, in Latin. Latin verses by Iacobus Locher. Latin epistle of the same to Sebastian Brant, dated, Friburg, Feb. 1, 1497. Commendatory verses in Latin by the same to Brant. More Latin verses by the same. Latin verses by the same to Johannes Bergmannus de Olpe. Latin verses by Brant to Locher. Latin prologue by Locher. Same in English. Introductory verses in Latin and English. Prose Argument in Latin and English. Latin verses by Locher, and by Brant. Copy of English verses. Text of the 'Ship of Fools' with woodcuts. At the end is the note 'Thus endeth the Ship of Fooles, Translated out of Latin, French and Duch, into Englishe, by Alexander Barclay Priest, at that time Chaplen in the Colledge of S. Mary Otery in the Countie of Deuon. Anno Domini . 1508.' More Latin verses by Locher. English verses by the translator. Table of contents in Latin and English. The second alphabet contains, with head-title, 'The Mirrour of good Maners. Conteining the foure Cardinal Vertues, compiled in Latin by Dominike Mancin, and translated into English by Alexander Barclay priest, and Monke of Ely. At the desire of the right worshipfull syr Giles Alington Knight.' Latin and English in parallel columns. At the end verses, in Latin and English, by Petrus Carmelianus. The third alphabet contains, with head-title, 'Certayne Egloges of Alexander Barclay Priest, Whereof the first three conteyne the miseryes of Courtiers and Courtes of all princes in generall, Gathered out of a booke named in Latin, Miseriæ Curialium, compiled by Eneas Siluius Poet and Oratour' (*i.e.* Æneas Silvius Piccolomini, afterwards Pius II.) five in number, in double columns. Two editions of the translation of Brant appeared in 1509 from the presses respectively of R. Pynson and Wynkin de Worde, the latter of whom printed another edition in 1518. The present edition appears to be the fourth. Of the Eclogues, i–iv were printed by R. Pynson, the fifth by W. de Worde early in the century; i–iii were twice reprinted about the middle of the century, while the present is the first edition containing all five.

Sinker 210. BM 260.

BRETON, Nicholas.

[The Arbor of Amorous Deuices: Wherein young Gentlemen may reade many pleasant fancies & fine deuices: And thereon meditate diuers sweete Conceites to court the loue of faire Ladies and Gentlewomen: By N. B. Gent. *Imprinted at London by Richard Iones, at the Rose and Crowne, neere S. Andrewes Church.* 1597.] 4°. ($7\frac{1}{4} \times 4\frac{3}{4}$). S. 8. 3.

Collation: A–F⁴, unpaged. Wanting A 1, 4, D 3, 4, E 2–4, and A 3 badly, D 1, 2, E 1 slightly defective. Address to the readers, signed "R. I. Printer." Only one edition of the work appears to be known, but it was entered on the Stationers' Register as early as Jan. 7, 1593–4. The author was Nicholas Breton. The above title is given by Mr Hazlitt (H. 57) apparently from the Beauclerk sale-catalogue (1781) lot 3241. The present copy is the only one now known.

Sinker 470.

Grimellos Fortunes, With his Entertainment in his trauaile. A discourse full of pleasure. *London Printed for E. White, and are to bee solde at his Shoppe neere the little North doore of S. Paules-Church at the Signe of the Gun.* 1604. 𝔅. 𝔏. 4°. (7×5). S. 36. 3.

Collation: $A^2B–D^4E^2$, unpaged. Address to the reader signed B. N. (*i.e.* Nicholas Breton). The text is in dialogue.

BM 1129.

BROKE, Arthur.

[The Tragicall Historye of Romeus and Iuliet, written first in Italian by Bandell, and nowe in Englishe by Ar. Br. *In ædibus Richardi Tottelli. Cum Priuilegio.*] [Colophon] *Imprinted at London in Flete strete within Temble* [sic] *barre, at the signe of the hand and starre, by Richard Tottill the* .xix. *day of Nouember. An. do.* 1562. **B. L.** 8°. ($6\frac{3}{8} \times 4$). X. 4. 2.

Collation: four leaves unsigned, A–K[8], L[4], folios numbered. Wanting the first three leaves, containing titlepage, prose address to the reader, signed Ar. Br. Verses to the reader and an argument in verse precede the poem. Indexed throughout by Capell with the corresponding passages in the 'Histoires Tragiques' ed. 1564. 16°. The poem is based on Boisteau's version of Bandello's novel ('Hist. Trag.' No. 3. Bandello, II. 9). First edition.

Sinker 228.

The Tragicall historie of Romeus and Iuliet. Contayning in it a rare example of true constancie: with the subtill counsels and practises of an old Fryer, and their ill euent. Res est solliciti plena timoris amor. *At London, Imprinted by R. Robinson,* 1587. **B. L.** 8°. ($5\frac{1}{4} \times 3\frac{1}{2}$). *. 8. 2.

Collation: A–N[8], folios numbered. A 1 blank. Verses to the reader. Argument in verse. Second edition.

Sinker 704.

BULLOKAR, William.

Bullokars Booke at large, for the Amendment of Orthographie for English speech: wherein, a most perfect supplie is made, for the wantes and double sounde of letters in the olde Orthographie, with Examples for the same.... Heerevnto are also ioyned written Copies with the same Orthographie. Giue God the praise, that teacheth alwaies. When truth trieth, errour flieth. Seene and allowed according to order. *Imprinted at London by Henrie Denham.* 1580.
B. L. 4°. ($7\frac{3}{4} \times 5\frac{1}{4}$). Q. 10. 4.

Collation: A–R[2], 2 leaves unsigned, paged. Author's preface signed W. B. Prologue in verse. The last sheet contains specimens of the amended orthography printed from blocks on recto of leaves only.

Sinker 342. BM 293.

BURTON, William.

Seuen Dialogues Both Pithie and Profitable...1606. *See* Erasmus, Desiderius.

BUTLER, Charles.

The English Grammar, Or The Institution of Letters, Syllables, and Woords, in the English tung. Wher'unto is annexed An Index of woords Lik' and Unlik'. By Charles Butler, Magd. Master of Arts. Arist. Polit. lib 8, cap. 3. Grammatica addiscenda pueris, utpotè ad vitam utilis. *Oxford, Printed by William Turner, for the Author:* 1634.

4°. ($6\frac{3}{4} \times 5\frac{1}{4}$). S. 32. 4.

Collation: $*^4 2*^2$A–K^{4}a–c^{4}d^2, paged A–K only. Epistle dedicatory from the author to Prince Charles. Address to the reader, signed C. B. M. (=Charles Butler Magd.) and dated, Wotton, Sept. 1, 1633. Another address. Commendatory verses in Latin signed S. W. Sheets a—d contain the 'Index of Woords' (homonyms) mentioned on the titlepage. Printer's address to the reader at end. Prefixed is a sheet ($*^4$) containing cancelled preliminary matter, namely titlepage as above but without the peculiarities of orthography and dated 1633, the first address to the reader, also in ordinary orthography, and S. W.'s verses. Some copies only have the earlier titlepage, some only the later, but the two issues differ in the preliminary matter alone.

BM 299.

CAPELL, Edward.

Prolusions; or, select Pieces of antient Poetry,—compil'd with great Care from their several Originals, and offer'd to the Publick as Specimens of the Integrity that should be found in the Editions of worthy Authors,—in three Parts; containing, I. The notbrowne Mayde; Master Sackvile's Induction; and, Overbury's Wife: II. Edward the third, a Play, thought to be writ by Shakespeare: III. Those excellent didactic Poems, intitl'd—Nosce teipsum, written by Sir John Davis; with a Preface.

Impius hæc tam culta novalia miles habebit?
Barbarus has segetes? Virg. Ecl. I.

London: Printed for J. and R. Tonson in the Strand. 1760. [Colophon] *From the Press of Dryden Leach, in Crane-court, Fleet-street. Oct.* 6*th*. 1759. 8°. (7 × 4½). S. 39.

Dedication to Lord Willoughby of Parham, subscribed "the Editor" (*i.e.* Edward Capell).

CAXTON, William.

The Ancient Historie of the destruction of Troy.... 1617. *See* Le Fèvre, Raoul.

CERVANTES SAAVEDRA, Miguel de.

[The History of Don-Quichote. The first parte. *Printed for Ed: Blounte*] 4°. (6⅞ × 5⅛). S. 16.

The engraved titlepage to the second part has been inserted instead of that properly belonging. The only difference is in the words 'The second parte' which have at some time had a piece of paper pasted over them. Collation: ¶⁴A–2O⁸, paged. Wanting ¶4 (second leaf of preface). Epistle dedicatory to the Lord of Walden, signed by the translator, Thomas Shelton. Author's preface to the reader. Sonnets in praise of Don Quixote. Table of contents. Text in four books. More poems on Don Quixote. The first part originally appeared in 1612; this is the second edition, *c.* 1620.

BM 345.

The second Part of the History of the Valorous and witty Knight-Errant, Don Quixote of the Mançha. Written in Spanish by Michael Ceruantes: And now Translated into English. *London, Printed for Edward Blount.* 1620. 4°. (6⅞ × 5⅛). S. 17.

Collation: A–2I⁸2K⁴, paged. Wanting 2K4 (? blank). Epistle dedicatory to George, Marquess of Buckingham, signed Ed: Blount. Author's prologue to the reader. Table of contents. Errata. Text not divided into books.

BM 345.

CHALONER, *Sir* Thomas.

The praise of Folie.... 1549. *See* Erasmus, Desiderius,

CHAPMAN, George.

Hero And Leander... 1637. *See*. Musæus.

The Whole Works of Homer.... n. d. *See* Homer.

CHARLES II.

A Character of Charles the Second written By an Impartial Hand, and exposed to publick View For Information of the People. *London, Printed for Gabriel Bedell, and are to be sold at the Middle Temple Gate in Fleetstreet*, 1660.

4°. ($9\frac{7}{8} \times 7$). I. 1. 2.

Collation: portrait prefixed, A^4, paged. Engraved portrait signed G. Faithorne facing title. According to Wood the author was George Morley, D.D., who later in the same year became bishop of Winchester, but the attribution is not substantiated. The BM catalogue ascribes it to Sir Samuel Tuke, on what authority does not appear.

CHAUCER, Geoffrey.

The workes of Geffray Chaucer newly printed, with dyuers workes whiche were neuer in print before: As in the table more playnly dothe appere. *Cum priuilegio.* [Colophon] *Imprinted at London by Rycharde Kele, dwellynge in Lombarde strete nere vnto the stockes market at the sygne of the Egle. Cum priuilegio ad imprimendum solum.*

B. L. F°. ($12\frac{1}{4} \times 8$). C. 2.

Title within woodcut border. Collation: $A^8B\text{–}V^6X^4 2A\text{–}3Q^6$, folios numbered. Double columns. Wanting 3Q6 (? blank). Epistle dedicatory to Henry VIII. Table of contents. Preliminary verses. After the 'Canterbury Tales' is a half-title to 'The Romaũt of the Rose' within same border (sig. 2A 1). After the colophon appears a Latin epitaph on Chaucer by Stephanus Surigonus. Copies of this edition are also found bearing in the colophon the names of 'Wyllyam Bonham', 'Thomas Petit', and 'Robart Toye.' They are all alike undated. Mr Hazlitt places it before the edition of 1542, thus making it the second collected edition, and suggests the date 1538; Prof. Skeat and the BM catalogue place it after, making it the third, which seems more likely, the former dating it 1550, the latter 1545. The only dated book by Bonham, it may be remarked, appeared in 1542. In any case it is a reprint of Thynne's text first printed in 1532.

Sinker 111. BM 367.

COLLINS, John.

A Letter to George Hardinge, Esq. on the Subject of a Passage in Mr. Stevens's Preface to his Impression of Shakespeare.... *London: Printed by B. Sibthorp, for G. Kearsly in Fleet-Street,* M, DCC, LXXVII. 4°. ($9\frac{1}{2} \times 7\frac{3}{8}$). I. 3. 2.

MS. note on titlepage: 'Seen through the Press by Mr. H—go: Note on p. 18. added, and the Post-Script new-molded by him. E. C.' The postscript is preceded by a 'Sonnet To Mr. Capell'. Attributed in the BM catalogue and doubtfully by Lowndes to the Rev. John Collins of Hertfordshire.

COMMINES, Philippe de, *Seigneur d Argenton.*

The Historie of Philip de Commines Knight, Lord of Argenton. *Imprinted at London by Ar. Hatfield, for I. Norton.* 1596 F°. ($11\frac{1}{2} \times 8$). E. 4.

Title within ornamental border bearing the initials H D (*i.e.* H. Denham). Collation: $A^6a^2B–X^6Y^4Z^8 2A–2L^6$, one leaf unsigned, paged. Sig. 2K5 appears in duplicate; the first is presumably intended as a cancel though no alteration is apparent. Epistle dedicatory to Lord Burley, signed by the translator, Thomas Danett. Life of Philip de Commines with a reply to the accusations of Jacobus Meyerus. Table of contents. The history, preceded by the author's preface to the Archbishop of Vienne. After Bk vi there follow eight chapters headed 'A Supply of the Historie of Philip de Commines from the death of King Lewis the 11. till the beginning of the wars of Naples, to wit, from 1483. till 1493. of all the which time Commines writeth nothing'. Bks vii and viii follow, after which there are a number of genealogical tables. The single leaf inserted at the end contains errata. This is the earliest known edition, though a translation was entered to Thomas Marsh as early as 1565–6.

Sinker 663.

CONTENTION.

The First part of the Contention betwixt the two famous houses of Yorke and Lancaster, with the death of the good Duke Humphrey: And the banishment and death of the Duke of Suffolke, and the Tragical end of the prowd Cardinall of Winchester, with the notable Rebellion of Jacke Cade;

And the Duke of Yorkes first clayme to the Crowne. *London Printed by Valentine Simmes for Thomas Millington, and are to be sold at his shop vnder S. Peters church in Cornewall.* 1600. 4°. ($6\frac{7}{8} \times 4\frac{3}{4}$). T. 8. 3.

Collation: A–H⁴. Wanting all after G 1. Another edition is said to have appeared the same year, printed by W. W. for Thomas Millington. This may however be due to confusion with the 'True Tragedy of Richard Duke of York'. The first edition had appeared in 1594.

Sinker 808.

The Whole Contention between the two Famous Houses, Lancaster and Yorke. With the Tragicall ends of the good Duke Humfrey, Richard Duke of Yorke, and King Henrie the sixt. Diuided into two Parts: And newly corrected and enlarged. Written by William Shakespeare, Gent. *Printed at London, for T. P.* 4°. ($7\frac{1}{2} \times 5\frac{5}{8}$). Q. 12. 4.

Collation: A–2A⁴2B², with one leaf inserted before sig. R, unpaged. Wanting 2B 2 (?blank). Part ii begins at sig. I 1 with the head-title 'The Second Part. Containing the Tragedie of Richard Duke of Yorke, and the good King Henrie the Sixt.' 'Pericles' begins with separate titlepage dated 1619 (*q.v.*) on inserted leaf. In this copy 'Pericles' is bound up in front of the 'Contention'. This is either the third or fourth edition of the 'First Part of the Contention,' the third of the 'True Tragedy of Richard Duke of York' which first appeared in 1595, and the fourth of 'Pericles.'

BM 1388.

COOPER, Thomas.

Thesaurus Linguæ Romanæ & Britannicæ, tam accurate congestus, vt nihil penè in eo desyderari possit, quod vel Latinè complectatur amplissimus Stephani Thesaurus, vel Anglicè, toties aucta Eliotæ Bibliotheca: opera & industria Thomæ Cooperi Magdalenensis.... Accessit Dictionarium historicum & poëticum.... In Thesaurum Thomæ Cooperi Magdalenensis, hexastichon Richardi Stephani.... *Impressum Londini.* 1573. F°. ($12\frac{3}{4} \times 8\frac{3}{4}$). B. 2.

Collation: ¶⁶A–6V⁶7D–7O⁶7P–7Q⁴, unpaged. Double columns.

Wanting ¶ 1 (? blank), also 7P 3, 4 and 7Q 3. To supply this deficiency the last six leaves of Bynneman's edition of 1584 including colophon, have been bound in after 7P 2. Latin epistle dedicatory to Robert Dudley, earl of Leicester, from Thomas Cooper. Address to the reader in Latin and another in English. Commendatory verses in Latin from Alexander Nowellus, Thomas Wykus (2 copies), Thomas Valens (2 copies), Ia. Calfhillus, and in Greek by Richardus Stephanus (3 copies). The 'Dictionarium Historicum & Poeticum' begins with head-title on 7D 1. On the titlepage is the cut of the Dudley crest as in James Sandford's 'Garden of Pleasure' (*q.v.*). Based on Sir T. Elyot's 'Dictionary,' the first edition of which appeared in 1538.

Sinker 829. BM 406.

COPLEY, Anthony.

Wits, Fits, and Fancies: Or, A generall and serious Collection, of the Sententious Speeches, Answers, Iests, and Behauiours, of all sortes of Estates, From the Throane to the Cottage. Being properly reduced to their seuerall heads, for the more ease of the Reader. Newly Corrected and augmented, with many late, true, and wittie accidents. Musica mentis, medecina Mæstus. *London Printed by Edw: Allde, dwelling in little Saint Bartholmewes, neer Christ-Church.* 1614. B. L. 4°. (7 × 5¼). T. 2.

Collation: A^2B–$2B^4 2C^2$, paged. Address to the reader. The original edition appeared in 1595 and bore on the title the initials of the author, Anthony Copley.

BM 1620.

CORYATE, Thomas.

Coryats Crambe, or his Colwort Twise Sodden, And Now serued in with other Macaronicke dishes, as the second course to his Crudities. *London Printed by William Stansby* 1611. 4°. (8 × 6). P. 2. 1.

Title within woodcut border. Collation: a–b^4, 1 leaf unsigned, *A–D*^{4}, D 3, 4, 1 leaf unsigned, D 1, 2, 1 leaf unsigned, a–b^4c–g^8h^4 *H* 1–3 i–l^4, unpaged. The book consists entirely of dedicatory epistles, orations, commendatory verses and the like. On sig. a 4 (second l. c. alphabet) occurs a large woodcut of the Prince of Wales' badge with the initials H. P. (*i.e.* Prince Henry). The present copy differs from the three preserved in the BM, which have collation a–b^4, 1 leaf unsigned (necessitated by the catchword, but only preserved in one copy), *A–D*^{4}, D 3, 4, 2 leaves unsigned, *E–G*^{4} (G 4 blank, only preserved in one copy), *H* 1–3.

BM 411.

COTGRAVE, John.

The English Treasury of Wit and Language, collected Out of the most, and best of our English Drammatick Poems; Methodically digested into Common Places For Generall Use. By John Cotgrave Gent. Varietas delectat, Certitudo Prodest. *London, Printed for Humphrey Moseley, and are to be sold at his Shop at the sign of the Princes Armes in S. Pauls Church-yard*, 1655. 8°. ($6\frac{1}{2} \times 4\frac{1}{4}$). X. 2.

Collation: A^{4}B–V^{8}X^4, paged. Address to the reader, signed. Table of headings. The Shakespearian quotations have been marked by Capell.

COTGRAVE, Randle.

A French-English Dictionary, Compil'd by Mr Randle Cotgrave: With Another in English and French. Whereunto are newly added the Animadversions and Supplements, &c. of James Howell Esquire. Inter Eruditos Cathedram habeat Polyglottes. *London, Printed by W. H. for Humphrey Robinson, and are to be sold at his shop at the signe of the three Pigeons, in Pauls Church-yard.* 1650.

F°. ($12\frac{1}{2} \times 8\frac{1}{2}$). B. 8.

Collation: a–d^{4}B–4V^{4}4X^2, two leaves unsigned, A–2F^{4}2G^6, unpaged. Last leaf blank. Epistle dedicatory 'To the Nobility and Gentry of Great Britain', signed Iames Howell. French grammar &c. Epistle dedicatory to William Cecil, Lord Burghley, signed Randle Cotgrave. French address to the reader signed 'I. L'oiseau de Tourval, Parisien Δ.' The unsigned sheet begins Part ii, with separate titlepage: 'Dictionaire Anglois & François, pour l'vtilité de tous ceux, qui sont desireux de deux Langues. A Dictionary English and French; Compiled for the comodity of all such as are desirous of both the Languages, By Robert Sherwood Londoner. *London, Printed by Susan Islip.* 1650', within ornamental border.

Address to the reader in French, signed 'R. S. de Londres'. Address and note to the reader in English, the former signed. At the end, forms of address, irregular verbs, vocabularies etc. The original edition of Cotgrave's dictionary appeared in 1611. The present appears to be the third edition. Sherwood's portion first appeared in the edition of 1632.

CRASHAW, Richard.

Steps to the Temple, Sacred Poems. With The Delights of the Muses. By Richard Crashaw, sometimes of Pembroke Hall, and late fellow of S. Peters Coll. in Cambridge. The second Edition wherein are added divers pieces not before extant. *London, Printed for Humphrey Moseley, and are to be sold at his shop at the Princes Armes in St. Pauls Church-yard.* 1648. 12°. ($5\frac{3}{4} \times 3\frac{3}{8}$). Z. 5.

Collation: $A^4 B–F^{12} A–C^{12}$, 2 leaves unsigned, paged. Preface. Motto. 'Steps to the Temple.' Table. 'The Delights of the Muses' with separate titlepage (T. W. for H. Moseley...1648) at sig. F 12, and fresh pagination. Table at the end (unsigned). Second edition, the first having appeared in 1646.

DANETT, Thomas.

The Historie of Philip de Commines.... 1596 *See* Commines, Philippe de.

DANIEL, Samuel.

The Whole Workes of Samuel Daniel Esquire in Poetrie. *London, Printed by Nicholas Okes, for Simon Waterson, and are to be sold at his shoppe in Paules Church-yard, at the Signe of the Crowne.* 1623. 4°. ($6\frac{7}{8} \times 5\frac{3}{8}$). S. 25.

Collation: 2 leaves unsigned, $A–C^4 D–Q^8 R^4 2A–2S^8 2T^6$, $A–M^8 N^4$, paged. Wanting A 4 (? blank) and E 4 in the 'Civil Wars'. The two preliminary leaves (here misplaced after signature A) contain the general titlepage and an epistle dedicatory to Prince Charles signed by Iohn Daniel, brother of the author, who superintended the edition. Then follows the edition of the 'Civil Wars' which had previously appeared as a separate publication in 1609. It has an engraved titlepage containing portrait, signed T. Cockson and dated 1609; also epistle dedicatory to Mary Countess Dowager of Pembroke, signed. In the rest of the volume 'Philotas', 'Hymens Triumph', 'The Queens Arcadia', 'The Vision of the Twelve Goddesses', 'Cleopatra', 'The Letter of Octavia' etc., and 'The Panegyrike' etc. have separate titlepages with the same imprint; 'Musophilus' and 'Rosamond' half-titles, after which follow 'Delia' and the miscellaneous verses and epistles. The 'Defence of Rime' mentioned on the titlepage to the 'Panegyrick' does not appear in the volume. This was the first complete edition of Daniel's poetical works. Some copies are said to have a titlepage: 'Drammaticke Poems...... 1635', which was probably designed for issue with the remaining sheets after the stock of the 1609 'Civil Wars' was exhausted.

BM 445.

DAVIES, *Sir* JOHN.

A Discouerie of the true Causes why Ireland was neuer entirely Subdued, nor brought vnder Obedience of the Crowne of England, vntill the Beginning of his Maiesties happie Raigne. *Printed for Iohn Iaggard, dwelling within Temple Bar, at the Signe of the Hand and Star.* 1612.

4°. ($6\frac{3}{4} \times 5$). U. 1.

Collation: A–2N⁴2O², paged. Wanting A 1 (? blank). Dedication to King James 'By his Maiesties Atturney Generall, of Ireland', (*i.e.* Sir John Davies). Errata at the end. Republished the following year under the title of 'A Discoverie of the State of Ireland'.

BM 453.

Nosce teipsum. This Oracle expounded in two Elegies. 1. Of Humane knowledge. 2. Of the Soule of Man, and the immortalitie thereof. *London, Printed by Richard Field for Iohn Standish.* 1599. 4°. ($7\frac{3}{4} \times 5\frac{3}{4}$). Q. 9. 1.

Collation: A²B–L⁴M², paged. Wanting M 2 (? blank). Dedicatory verses to Queen Elizabeth signed by the author, Iohn Davies.

BM 453.

[Another copy.] 4°. ($7\frac{3}{4} \times 5\frac{7}{8}$). Q. 9. 3.

Also wanting M 2.

[Another copy.] 4°. ($7\frac{1}{8} \times 5$). S. 36. 4.

This copy wants, besides the blank, the titlepage and the last leaf of text. These have been supplied in MS. by Capell. The copy contains a large number of analytical notes in an early hand. It has also been carefully collated throughout by Capell with the subsequent edition of 1602 and the results entered in red ink. The edition of 1602 is also in quarto, but somewhat more closely printed so as to get the whole into eleven sheets, and has the following titlepage: 'Nosce teipsum. This Oracle expounded in two Elegies. 1. Of Humane knowledge. 2. Of the Soule of Man, and the immortalitie thereof. Newly corrected and amended. London, Printed by Richard Field for Iohn Standish. 1602'. (BM 453.)

Nosce Teipsum. This Oracle expounded in two Elegies. 1. Of Humane Knowledge. 2. Of the Soule of Man, and the immortalitie thereof. Hymnes of Astræa in Acrosticke Verse. Orchestra, or, A Poeme of Dauncing. In a Dialogue betweene Penelope, and one of her Wooers. Not finished. *London, Printed by Augustine Mathewes for Richard Hawkins, and are to be sold at his Shop in Chancery Lane, neere Serieants Inne.* 1622. 8°. ($6\frac{3}{8} \times 4\frac{1}{4}$). X. 1.

Collation: A–L^4, unpaged. Wanting A 1 and L 4 (? blank). Dedicatory verses 'To my most gracious dread Soveraigne' (*i.e.* Queen Elizabeth) signed by the author Iohn Davies. 'Astrea' and 'Orchestra' have each a separate titlepage bearing the same date. Fifth edition. 'Astræa' was added in the fourth edition, 1619; the 'Orchestra' first appeared in the present edition, which was the last issued during the life of the author.

BM 453.

DAVIES, JOHN, *of Hereford.*

Microcosmos. The Discouery of the Little World, with the government thereof.

Manilius.

An mirum est habitare Deum sub pectore nostro?
Exemplumq; Dei quisq; est sub imagine paruâ.

By Iohn Davies. *At Oxford, Printed by Ioseph Barnes, and*

are to bee solde in Fleetestreete at the signe of the Turkes head by Iohn Barnes. 1603. 4°. ($7\frac{1}{4} \times 5\frac{3}{8}$). R. 12. 1.

Collation: A–2O⁴2P², paged. Dedicatory verses to King James and to the Queen, both signed. Five copies of verses by Davies. Commendatory verses signed: Io. Sanfordus (Lat.), Robertus Burhillus (Lat.), N. Debillus (Lat.), Iohn Iames (Lat. and Eng.), T. R. (Lat.), Douglas Castilion (one copy unsigned), Charles Fitz-Ieffry (one copy unsigned), Nicholas Deeble, Nathanael Tomkins (Lat.), and the author's brother Richard Davies. Verse Preface to the King, signed. Verses to the Prince of Wales, signed. 'Microcosmus' is followed by 'An Extasy'; both are in verse. Sonnets and poems by Davies. Commendatory verses from N. Deeble and Ed. Lapworth (Lat.).

BM 452.

DEKKER, Thomas.

English Villanies seven severall Times Prest to Death by the Printers; But (still reviving againe) are now the eighth time, (as at the first) discovered by Lanthorne and Candle-Light; And the helpe of a New Cryer, called O-Per-Se-O: Whose loud voyce proclaimes to all that will heare him; Another Conspiracy of Abuses lately plotting together, to hurt the Peace of this Kingdome; which the Bell-man (because he then went stumbling i'th darke) could never see, till Now. And because a Company of Rogues, cunning Canting Gypsies, and all the Scumme of our Nation fight here under their Tattered Colours, At the end is a Canting Dictionary, to teach their Language: with Canting Songs. A Booke to make Gentlemen Merry. Citizens Warie. Countrimen Carefull. Fit for all Iustices to reade over, because it is a Pilot, by whom they may make Strange Discoveries. *London, Printed by M. Parsons, and are to be sold by Iames Becket, at the Inner-Temple Gate in Fleet-street.* 1638. B. L. 4°. ($7\frac{1}{4} \times 5\frac{1}{2}$). S. 28. 4.

Collation: A–O⁴, unpaged. Woodcut of the Bellman with verses below on verso of titlepage. Epistle dedicatory to the Middlesex Justices of the Peace, signed T. Dekker. Address to the reader. Table of contents. This work was constantly reprinted under different titles. The earliest edition appeared in 1608 as 'Lanthorne and Candle-light. Or The Bell-mans second Nights walke' (Haz. II. 688), being a sequel to 'The Belman of London' which was likewise first printed in 1608. Apparently the eighth edition, but it is not possible to trace all previous ones.

BM 461.

DES PERIERS, BONAVENTURE.

The Mirrour of Mirth, and pleasant Conceits: containing, Many proper and pleasaunt inuentions, for the recreation and delight of many, and to the hurt and hinderance of none. Framed in French by that Worshipfull and learned Gentleman Bonaduentura de Periers, Groom to the right excellent and vertuous Princesse, the Queen of Nauara: And Englished by R. D. *At London, Printed by Roger Warde: dwelling a litle aboue Holburne Conduit, at the Signe of the Talbot.* 1583.

B. L. 4°. ($7 \times 5\frac{1}{4}$). S. 33. 4.

Collation: $A^2B\text{–}N^4O^2$, folios numbered. Address to the reader, signed T. D. (*sic*). Table of contents at end. Supposed unique.

Sinker 647.

DEVEREUX, ROBERT, *Earl of Essex*.

A Declaration of the Practises and Treasons attempted and committed by Robert late Earle of Essex.... 1601. *See* BACON, Francis.

DOBSON.

Dobsons Drie Bobbes: Sonne and Heire to Skoggin. *London Printed by Valentine Simmes* 1607.

B. L. 4°. ($7\frac{3}{4} \times 5\frac{7}{8}$). Q. 8. 2.

Collation: $A\text{–}O^4$, unpaged. Wanting A 1 and O 4 (? blank). Address to the reader. Table of contents. 'This Dobson, it appears from a note in Harl. MS. 5910, was the adopted son of Sir Thomas Pentley, a priest in Queen Mary's days.' (Haz. H. 300.)

DONDI DALL' OROLOGIO, GIUSEPPE.

L'Inganno dialogo di M. Gioseppe Horologgi. Con priuilegio. *In Vinegia appresso Gabriele Giolito de' Ferrari.* M D LXII. 8°. ($5\frac{1}{2} \times 3\frac{3}{4}$). Z. 7. 5.

Collation: $*^8$A–N^8, paged. Epistle dedicatory from the author to the 'Academici Olimpici di Vicenza', dated, Venice, Jan. 12, 1562. Alphabetical table. At the end, an epistle dated from Venice, headed 'Al Mag. S.N.'

DONNE, John.

Iuuenilia: or certain Paradoxes, and Problems, written by I. Donne. *London, Printed by E. P. for Henry Seyle, and are to be sold at the signe of the Tygers head, in Saint Pauls Church-yard, Anno Dom.* 1633.

4°. (7 × 5¼). S. 20. 2.

Collation: A–H^4, unpaged. A 1 blank. Table of Paradoxes on verso of Title. Eleven Paradoxes. License for Paradoxes signed by Henry Herbert and dated Oct. 25, 1632. Half-title to Problems, Table on verso. Ten Problems.

BM 490.

Poems, By J. D. With Elegies on the Authors Death. *London. Printed by M. F. for Iohn Marriot, and are to be sold at his shop in St Dunstans Church-yard in Fleet-street.* 1633.

4°. (7 × 5¼). S. 20. 1.

Collation: A^4; A^{2}B–3F^4, paged. 3F 4 blank. Wanting first leaf (? blank). Epistle. Printer's address to the reader. Verses signed Jo. Mar. (=John Marriot). Poems. Satires. Letters. Elegies upon the Author, Dr Donne. This is the first collected edition of his poems. The prose 'Iuvenilia' of the same year forms a supplement.

BM 490.

DOUGLAS, Gawin.

The .xiii. Bukes of Eneados.... 1553. *See* Vergilius Maro, Publius.

DRAYTON, Michael.

The Battaile of Agincourt. Fought by Henry the fift of that name, King of England, against the whole power of the French: vnder the Raigne of their Charles the sixt, Anno Dom. 1415. The Miseries of Queene Margarite, the infortunate Wife, of that most infortunate King Henry the sixt.

Nimphidia, the Court of Fayrie. The Quest of Cinthia. The Shepheards Sirena. The Moone-Calfe. Elegies vpon sundry occasions. By Michaell Drayton Esquire. *London, Printed for William Lee, at the Turkes Head in Flecte-Streete, next to the Miter and Phœnix.* 1627. F°. ($9\frac{3}{4} \times 5\frac{7}{8}$). I. 2.

Collation: portrait prefixed, $A^4a^2B^6C$–$2E^4$, paged. Wanting A^4 containing John Reynolds' verses, and 2E 4 (? blank). Engraved portrait signed Wil Hole, with Latin verses subscribed, facing title. The plate had already been used in the 'Poems' of 1619. Dedication to the Gentlemen of Great Britain, signed. Commendatory verses by J. Vaughan, J. Reynolds, and Ben Jonson. First edition.

BM 498.

Englan[ds] Heroic[all] Epistles. Newly Correcte[d.] With Idea. By Michaell Drayton. *At London, Printed by I. R. for N. L. and are to be sold at his shop in Fleetstreete, neere Saint Dunstones Church.* 1602. 8°. ($5\frac{7}{8} \times 4$). Z. 2.

Collation: A^4B–Q^8, unpaged. Address to the reader, signed M.D. Commendatory verses signed: E. Sc. Gent., Thomas Hassell, William Alexander. The 'Epistles' are divided into groups to which are prefixed dedicatory epistles to Lucy Countess of Bedford, Lady Anne Harington, Sir Walter Acton, Edward Earl of Bedford, Iames Huish, Elizabeth Tanfelde, Sir Thomas Munson, Sir Henry Goodere, Henry Lucas, and Lady Frauncis Goodere, each signed. 'Idea' begins on O 7^v. The first sonnet should belong to the 'Epistles', of which it contains a list, the second and third are prefatory, addressed to the reader. The first edition appeared in 1597; the present is the fifth. 'Idea' which had appeared separately was first added to the third edition, 1599.

BM 499.

Mortimeriados. The lamentable ciuell warres of Edward the second and the Barrons. *At London, Printed by I. R. for Mathew Lownes, and are to bee solde at his shop in S. Dunstons Churchyard.* 1596. 4°. ($7\frac{1}{4} \times 5\frac{1}{4}$). R. 18. 3.

Collation: A–S^4T^2, unpaged. Wanting A 4 (? blank as in BM copy). Dedicatory verses to Lucie Countess of Bedford, signed Michaell Drayton. Verses to the same, signed E. B. This is the original form of 'The Barons' Wars' (1603). There was another issue of this edition, differing in the titlepage alone, which has Humfry Lownes as bookseller and is without date.

Sinker 472. BM 498.

Poems: by Michael Drayton esquire, Newly Corrected by the Author. *London Printed by W. Stansby for Iohn Smethwicke, and are to bee sold at his Shop in Saint Dunstanes Church-yard, vnder the Diall.* 1613. 8°. ($6\frac{1}{2} \times 4$). Y. 2.

Collation: $A^4 B–2I^8$, paged in part. Wanting 2I 7 and 8 (? blank). 'The Arguments' (*i.e.* list of contents). Dedicatory verses to Sir Walter Aston, signed. Address to the reader. Commendatory verses signed John Beaumont and Thomas Greene. 'The Barons Warres', paged. 'Englands Heroical Epistles' with fresh pagination as in the separate edition of 1602, with addition of one epistle dedicatory to Sir John Swinerton. Catalogue sonnet to the 'Epistles'. Two sonnets to the reader, 'Idea' and other sonnets, and 'Legends', unpaged. Fourth edition (*vide infra*).

BM 498.

Poems: by Michael Drayton Esquire. Viz. The Barons Warres, Englands Heroicall Epistles, Idea, Odes, The Legends Of Robert, Duke of Normandie, Matilda, Pierce Gaveston, And, Great Cromwell, The Owle, Pastorals, Contayning Eglogues, With the Man in the Moone. *London, Printed by W. Stansby for Iohn Smethwicke, and are to be sold at his Shop in Saint Dunstanes Church-yard in Flect-streete vnder the Diall.* F°. ($10\frac{1}{4} \times 6\frac{3}{8}$). H. 2.

Collation: $A–3Q^4$, paged. Engraved portrait signed Wil. Hole on verso of printed title. Engraved titlepage (unsigned) 'Poems by Michael Drayton Esquyer. Collected into one Volume. With sondry Peeces inserted neuer before Imprinted London printed for Iohn Smethwick.' Epistle dedicatory to Sir Walter Aston, signed. Address to the reader. Commendatory verses signed: Thomas Greene, Iohn Beaumont, E. Heyward, I. Selden. 'The Barons' Wars' with head-title. 'England's Heroical Epistles', 'Idea', 'Odes', 'Legends', 'The Owle', and 'Pastorals' have each a separate titlepage with imprint 'London, Printed for Iohn Smethwicke. 1619.' There are apparently no less than five collections entitled 'Poems' previous to the present, the earliest being that of 1605, all of which are substantially the same, while the present one is enlarged by the addition of the poems which originally appeared in the 'Poemes Lyrick and pastorall' of about 1606. Some copies of the present edition (BM, G. 11573) differ from the above in reading in the imprint to the general titlepage 'Fleetstreete. 1620.'. The separate titlepages however are dated 1619.

BM 498.

Poly-olbion. or A Chorographicall Description of Traicts, Riuers, Mountaines, Forests, and other Parts of this renowned Isle of Great Britaine, With intermixture of the most Remarquable Stories, Antiquities, Wonders, Rarityes, Pleasures, and Commodities of the same: Digested in a Poem By Michael Drayton. With a Table added, for direction to those occurrences of Story and Antiquitie, whereunto the Course of the Volume easily leades not. Esq. [*sic*] *London. Printed by H. L. for Mathew Lownes: I. Browne: I. Helme, and I. Busbie.* 1613. F°. ($11\frac{3}{8} \times 7\frac{1}{8}$). E. 5.

Collation: 4 leaves unsigned, 2 leaves unsigned, A^4 ❧^{4} $B–2C^6 2D^2$, paged, with eighteen double-page engraved maps inserted. Wanting first leaf (? blank) and sig. A. Printed title misplaced after the two unsigned leaves. First leaf blank (wanting), second leaf verses 'Vpon the Frontispice' on verso, third leaf engraved titlepage signed W. Hole, fourth leaf printed titlepage. The verses and engraved titlepage certainly form one sheet and the printed titlepage probably occupies the second leaf of an outer sheet. The two unsigned leaves which follow, and which certainly form one sheet, contain Epistle dedicatory to Prince Henry, signed, verses on the prince, and a very fine engraved portrait of him at pike exercise, signed William Hole. The quire A (wanting) contains address to the reader and 'To my Friends, the Cambro-Britans', also 'From the Author of the Illustrations' (*i.e.* J. Seldon). Then follow an alphabetical Table, and the eighteen songs, each with engraved map and Seldon's notes. This is the first edition but there was an earlier undated issue without printed titlepage or sigs. A and ❧, and with the portrait of the prince in an earlier state, *i.e.* without the 'Henricus Princeps' on the plate. The volume was re-issued with a second part in 1622.

BM 499.

DRUMMOND, William.

Poems: By William Drummond, of Hawthorne-denne. The second Impression. *Edinburgh, Printed by Andro Hart.* 1616. 4°. (8 × 6). P. 2. 2.

Title within woodcut border. Collation: $A–Q^4$, unpaged. Wanting Q 4 (? blank). Commendatory verses signed 'Parthenius' (A 2), 'Sr. W. Alexander' (K 1^v), 'D. Murray' (M 3). No earlier edition is known, but there is another issue of this one with a different titlepage (same imprint) on which only the author's initials appear.

BM 500.

The most elegant, and elabourate Poems Of that Great Court-wit, M[r] William Drummond. Whose Labours, both in Verse and Prose, being heretofore so precious to Prince Henry, and to K. Charles, Shall live and flourish in all Ages whiles there are men to read them, or Art & Judgment to approve them.

Horat. Carm. Lib. 1.
—Multaq; pars mei
Vitabit Libitinam—

London, Printed for William Rands Bookseller, at his House over against the Beare Taverne in Fleetstreet, 1659.

8°. ($6\frac{3}{8} \times 4\frac{1}{8}$). X. 3.

Collation: A–O^4, paged. Engraved portrait by R. Gaywood. The titlepage is a cancel pasted over the original one printed by W. H. for the Company of Stationers in 1656. Address to the reader signed E. P. Commendatory verses signed: Edw : Phillips, D. F. (Lat.), (one copy in Lat. unsigned), Iohn Spotswood, Mary Oxlie of Morpet. 'Tears on the Death of Moeliades', 'The Wandering Muses' and 'Speeches to the high and excellent Prince, Charles,...Delivered from the Pageants the 15th of June, 1633', have each a separate titlepage with the imprint 'London, Printed in the Yeare, 1656.' The 'Poems' were first published in 1616 and the present edition appears to be the third; both the former ones however had several issues.

DU BARTAS, Guillaume de Saluste.

Du Bartas his Deuine Weekes and Workes: With A Complete Collection of all the other most delightfull Workes, Translated and Written by that famous Philomusus Josuah Syluester, Gent. With Additions. *London, Printed by Robert Young, and are to bee sold by William Hope, at the signe of the Unicorne in Cornehill,* 1641.

F°. ($13\frac{1}{4} \times 9\frac{1}{8}$). A. 1.

Collation: 3 leaves unsigned, A^6 B^8 C–3M^6, paged. Engraved portrait of Sylvester signed Corn: v. Dalen facing engraved titlepage signed R. Elstracke, the inscription on which is altered from the previous edition of 1633. The printed titlepage follows. Anagram on James Stuart. French and Italian verses to James signed Josua Sylvester and J. S. respectively. 'Corona Dedicatoria'. Table of contents. Woodcut portrait of Du Bartas with verses in French and English. Verses on Sylvester signed John Vicars. Printer's address to the reader. Memorial to Sidney. Verses 'Indignis' and 'Optimis'. Commendatory verses in Latin signed: Jo. Bo. Miles, Car. Fitz-Geofridus Lati-Portensis, (2 copies unsigned), E. L. Oxon., G. B. Cantabrig.; in English signed: Ben Jonson, John Davies of Hereford, Jos. Hall, Samuel Daniel, G. Gay-wood; also Jo. Mauldeus Germanus (Lat.), Si. Ca. Gen. (Lat.), E. G., R. H., R. R., R. N. Gent., and R. N. Various parts have separate titlepages, and more dedicatory verses, etc. At sig. 2G 1 begins 'A Briefe Index, explaining most of the hardest words', preceding the 'History of Judith'. On I 4^v is a woodcut of Eden, and after 3H 1 is inserted a folding plate facing the titlepage of the 'Posthumi'. Mr Hazlitt (H. 171) supposes that the first edition appeared in 1593, but only separate portions are known of this, or of the 1598–99 edition. The earliest of which complete copies survive is that of 1605–7. The present is the last and most complete edition and contains some of Sylvester's original poems.

EDWARD III, *King of England.*

The Raigne of King Edward the third: As it hath bin sundrie times plaied about the Citie of London. *London, Printed for Cuthbert Burby.* 1596.

4°. ($6\frac{1}{2} \times 4\frac{5}{8}$). W. 5. 1.

Collation: A–I^4K^2, unpaged. Wanting A 1 (? blank). First edition.

Sinker 794. BM 518.

The Raigne of King Edward the third. As it hath bene sundry times played about the Citie of London. *Imprinted at London by Simon Stafford, for Cuthbert Burby: And are to be sold at his shop neere the Royall Exchange.* 1599. 4°. ($6\frac{7}{8} \times 4\frac{3}{4}$). T. 7. 2.

Collation: A–I^4, unpaged. Second edition.

Sinker 816. BM 518.

EDWARDS, Richard.

The Paradice of Dainty Deuises. Containing sundry pithie precepts, learned Counsailes and excellent Inuentions: right pleasant and profitable for all estates Deuised and written for the most parte by M. Edwardes, sometime of her Maiesties Chappell: the rest by sundry learned Gentlemen both of Honor and Worship, whose names heer-after followe. Whereunto is added sundry new Inuentions, very pleasant and delightfull. *At London Printed by Edward Allde for Edward White dwelling at the little North doore of Saint Paules Church, at the signe of the Gunne. Anno.* 1596.

B. L. 4°. ($7\frac{1}{4} \times 4\frac{3}{4}$). S. 8. 1.

Collation: A–L⁴, unpaged. Wanting L 4 containing end of text and colophon. On the verso of the titlepage are 'The names of those who wrote these devices': Saint Bernard, E[dward Vere, Earl of] O[xford], Lord Vaux the Elder, W. Hunnis, Iasper Haywood, F. Kindlemarshe, D. Sande, M. Ylope. The collection went through many editions; this is apparently the seventh, the first having appeared in 1576.

Sinker 660. BM 519.

EDWARDS, THOMAS.

The Canons of Criticism, and Glossary; The Trial of the Letter Υ, alias Y, and Sonnets. By Thomas Edwards, Esq; *London: Printed for C. Bathurst, opposite St. Dunstan's Church in Fleet-street.* M.DCC.LVIII. 8°. ($8 \times 5\frac{1}{4}$). P. 7.

Titlepage and advertisement on two leaves prefixed after the author's death in 1757. The original titlepage 'By the other Gentleman of Lincoln's-Inn....The Sixth Edition, with Additions' follows, with the same date and imprint. First published as 'A Supplement to Mr. Warburton's Edition of Shakspeare' in 1747.

ELDER, JOHN.

Historia Maioris Britanniæ, tam Angliȩ q̃ Scotiȩ, per Ioannẽ Maiorem, nomine quidem Scotum, professione autem Theologum, e veterum monumentis concinnata. *Vȩnundatur Iodoco Badio Ascensio.* [Colophon] *Ex officina Ascensiana ad Idus Aprilis* . MDXXI. 4°. ($7\frac{1}{2} \times 5\frac{3}{8}$). Q. 5. 2.

Collation: $A^2a\text{–}p^8q\text{–}s^6t^8 2A^4$ (2A 1–2 misprinted AA iii–iiii, 3–4 unsigned) A^6 (A 1–4 misprinted A iii–vi, 5–6 unsigned) 2 leaves unsigned; folios numbered. Woodcut of the arms of Scotland and dedicatory verses from the printer to James V on verso of title. Epistle dedicatory to James from the author, subscribed 'E Gymnasio Montisacuti apud Parrhisios frugi & non ignobili'. Alphabetical tables at end, after colophon. The sheets containing the irregular signatures at the end are wanting in all three copies at the BM. Ruled throughout in red. This work is said to contain the earliest printed notice of Robin Hood.

ELYOT, *Sir* THOMAS.

The Castle of Health, Corrected, and in some places Augmented by the first Authour thereof, Sir Thomas Elyot Knight. Now newlie pervsed, amended, and corrected, this present yeare, 1610. *London, Printed for the Company of Stationers,* 1610. 4°. (7 × 5¼). S. 32. 3.

Collation: ¶[4]A–S[4], paged. 'The Proheme of Sir Thomas Eliot Knight, into his Booke.' Alphabetical table. The first edition appeared in 1539; this appears to be the seventh.

The Image of Gouernance compiled of the Actes and Sentences notable, of the moste noble Emperour Alexander Seuerus, late translated out of Greke into Englyshe, by syr Thomas Eliot knight, in the fauour of Nobylitie. *Anno* .M.D.XLI. [Colophon] *Londini in Officina Thomæ Bertheleti typis impress. Cum priuilegio ad imprimendum solum. Anno* .M.D.XL. B. L. 4°. (7 × 5⅛). S. 7. 2.

Title within woodcut border. Collation: a–b[4]A–2C[4], folios numbered. Preface. Table of contents. Fine woodcut of the arms of Sir Thomas Elyot on verso of title, and one of Berthelet's 'Lucrece' device on b 4[v]. The work purports to be translated out of the Greek of one Eucolpius, presumably a fictitious authority. First edition.

Sinker 65. BM 600.

ERASMUS, DESIDERIUS.

The praise of Folie. Moriæ Encomium a booke made in latyne by that great clerke Erasmus Roterodame. Englisshed by sir Thomas Chaloner knight. *Anno* .M.D.XLIX. [Colophon] *Imprinted at London in Fletestrete in the House of*

Thomas Berthelet. Cum priuilegio ad imprimendum solum. Anno . M . D . LXIX . **B. L.** 4°. ($7\frac{1}{4} \times 5\frac{1}{4}$). R. 16.

Title within ornamental border, at the foot of which are printed the initials 'T. P.' (misprint for T. B. *i.e.* Thomas Berthelet, see 'A necessary doctrine' etc. by T. Berthelet, 1543, T. C. C. VI[d]. 3. 7.). The date in the colophon is likewise a misprint for 1549 as in title. Collation: A^4; A–T^4, unpaged. Translator's address to the reader. At the beginning is inserted a leaf of MS. in a 17th century hand containing biographical notes concerning Sir Thomas Chaloner. There is also some writing in an early hand on the verso of A 4 (preliminary sheet), but it has been pasted over and one blank leaf inserted before the next sheet.

Sinker 69. BM 596.

Prouerbes or Adagies, gathered oute of the Chiliades of Erasmus by Rycharde Tauerner. With newe addicions as well of La- of ue rbes [*sic*] as Englyshe. *An.* M . D . LII. *Cum priuilegio ad imprimendum solum.* [Colophon] *Imprinted at London by Rycharde Kele, dwellynge in Lombarde strete nere vnto the stockes market at the sygne of the Egle. Anno.* M . D . LII. **B. L.** 8°. ($5\frac{1}{4} \times 3\frac{3}{8}$). *. 5.

Title within woodcut border with the initials N. H. printed in a compartment at the foot. Collation: A–K^8, folios numbered. 'The Prologue of the Author'. A collection of Latin quotations with translations and explanations in English. At the end an alphabetical table. The first edition appeared in 1539, the present is the second.

Sinker 110. BM 593.

⌜Seuen Dialogues both pithie and profitable.

The
1 Is of the right vse of things indifferent.
2 Sheweth what comfort Poperie affordeth in time of daunger.
3 Is betweene a good Woman and a Shrew.
4 Is of the conversion of a Harlot.
5 Is of putting forth Children to Nurse.
6 Is of a Popish Pilgrimage.
7 Is of a Popish Funerall.

By W. B. *London. Printed for Nicholas Ling, and are to bee sold at his shop in Saint Dunstans Church-yard in Fleet-streete.* 1606.⌟ **B. L.** 4°. ($6\frac{7}{8} \times 5\frac{1}{8}$). T. 4. 2.

Collation. $A^4a^2B–V^4$, unpaged. Wanting A 1 (title) and V 4 (?blank). Epistle dedicatory to the 'Maior, Sheriffes and Aldermen' of Norwich, signed by the translator, William Burton, and dated 'Reading, in Barkeshire, 1606.' Address to the reader, signed by the same. Printer's note to the reader. The seven dialogues translated from the Latin 'Colloquia' of Erasmus.

BM 594.

EUNAPIUS.

The Lyues, Of Philosophers and Oratours: Written in Greeke, by Eunapius, of the Cittie of Sardeis in Lydia. Brought into light, Translated into Latine, and Dedicated to the Queenes most excellent Maiestie, our moste gracious Princesse and Soueraigne, Queene Elizabeth. By the great learned man, Hadrianus Iunius Hornanus. 1568. And now set foorth in English, at his request: and Dedicated to the right Honourable, the Lord Chauncellour of England. 1579. Wherein may be seene, The deepe knowledge of Philosophie. The wonderfull workes of secrete Artes. The maruelous effects of perfight eloquence. The singuler giftes of naturall qualities. The enuie of the ambitious, against the learned. The daingerous dayes that then befell for faythe. The one of Christians, the other of Infidels. *Imprinted at London by Richard Iohnes, and are to be solde at his shop ouer against S. Sepulchres Church without Newgate. The* .xx. *daye of May.*

B. L. 4°. ($7 \times 5\frac{1}{4}$). T. I. 2.

Collation: *A*^{4} A–N^4, folios numbered. Epistle dedicatory to Sir Thomas Bromley, signed by the translator: H. I. H. Epistle to Queen Elizabeth, signed: Hadrianus Iunius Hornanus, the original editor and Latin translator, and dated Harlem, March 1, 1568. Acrostic verses to the Queen. Hadrianus' address to the reader. Verses by 'Gerarde Phalcepurgie of Nimega'. Life of Eunapius. At the end another address to the reader by Hadrianus, followed by alphabetical table and list of errata.

Sinker 467. BM 601.

FABYAN, Robert.

The Chronicle of Fabyan, whiche he hym selfe nameth the concordaunce of historyes, nowe newely printed, & in many places corrected, as to the dylygent reader it may apere. 1542. *Cum priuilegio ad imprimendum solum. Printed by Iohn Reynes, dwellynge at the sygne of saynte George in Pauls churcheyarde.* B. L. F°. ($10\frac{7}{8} \times 7\frac{3}{8}$). F. 16.

Title within woodcut border, with initials W. R. (*i.e.* William Rastel). Collation: $A^6 B^4 a$–$x^6 y^8 z^6 A$–$E^6 *^6 2a$–$2z^6 3A$–$3S^6$, paged. Title mounted. * 1 is inserted the wrong way round. Table of contents. Parts I–VII. 'Lenuoye' in verse. At sig. E 6 occurs a separate titlepage 'The secōde volume of Fabyans cronycle, conteynynge the cronycles of England & of Fraunce from the begynnyng of the reygne of Kynge Richarde the fyrste, vntyll the xxxii. yere of the reygne of oure moste redoubted soueraygne lorde kyng Henry the viii.', without imprint, within the same border. Table of contents. 'Prologue'. Lists of the Wards of London and the parish churches within and without the city. The whole of vol. ii, which has fresh pagination, is headed 'The seuenth part'. The collation given above follows that in Dr Sinker's catalogue, but there is strong reason to suppose that we should assume that E 6 was blank and that vol. ii began with a single sheet, unsigned, the first leaf being blank and the second containing the titlepage to that volume. The first edition appeared anonymously in 1516. In some copies of the present edition, the third, William Bonham is given as the printer's name.

Sinker 97. BM 608 (Bonham).

FAIRE EM.

A Pleasant Comedie Of Faire Em, The Millers Daughter of Manchester: With the loue of William the Conqueror. As it was sundty [*sic*] times publiquely acted in the Honourable Citie of London, by the right Honourable the Lord Strange his Seruants. *London, Printed for Iohn Wright, and are to be sold at his shop at the signe of the Bible in Guilt-spur street without New-gate.* 1631. 4°. ($7\frac{1}{8} \times 5\frac{3}{8}$). R. 20. 3.

Collation: A–F⁴, unpaged. Wanting F 4 (? blank). Second edition, the first having appeared undated a good many years earlier.

BM 527.

FAIRFAX, Edward.

Godfrey of Bulloigne, or The Recouerie of Ierusalem.... 1600. *See* TASSO, Torquato.

FENTON, Geoffrey.

Certain Tragicall Discourses.... 1567. *See* Bandello, Matteo.

FLETCHER, John.

See Beaumont, Francis, and Fletcher, John.

FLETCHER, Phineas.

⌜Locustæ, vel Pietas Iesuitica. Per Phineam Fletcher Collegii Regalis Cantabrigiæ. *Apud Thomam & Ioannem Bucke, celeberrimæ Academiæ Typographos. Ann. Dom.* MDCXXVII.⌟ 4°. ($7\frac{1}{8} \times 5\frac{1}{4}$). R. 11. 2.

Collation: ¶[4]A–M[4]N[2], paged. Wanting sheet ¶ of which the first leaf is blank, the second contains the titlepage and the rest the preliminary matter. Epistle dedicatory in Latin to Sir Roger Townshend, signed. Commendatory Latin verses signed S. Collins. 'Locustæ' in Latin hexameters. English version with separate titlepage at sig. D 2. 'The Locusts, or Apollyonists. By Phineas Fletcher of Kings Colledge in Cambridge. Printed by Thomas Bucke and Iohn Bucke, Printers to the Vniversitie of Cambridge. 1627.' Epistle dedicatory to Lady Townshend, signed P. F. Commendatory verses signed H. M. In 1902 Mr B. Dobell had a MS. of the Latin portion containing an unpublished dedication to Prince Henry. This version, which presented variations from the printed text, must therefore have been written before Nov. 1612.

BM 636.

FLORIO, John.

The Essayes...of Lord Michael De Montaigne.... 1632. *See* Montaigne, Michel de.

A Worlde of Wordes, Or Most copious, and exact Dictionarie in Italian and English, collected by Iohn Florio. *Printed at London, by Arnold Hatfield for Edw. Blount.* 1598. [Colophon] *Imprinted at London by Arnold Hatfield, for Edward Blunt: and are to be sold at his shop ouer against the great North dore of Paules Church.* 1598.

F°. ($10 \times 7\frac{3}{8}$). H. 3.

Title within ornamental border with initials C T. Collation: a[6]b[4]A–2P[6]2Q[4], paged. Wanting a 1 (blank save for sig.) and 2Q 4

(? blank). The original leaf S 2 has been cut out and another, presumably a cancel, placed in loose. Three columns on a page. Epistle dedicatory to Roger Earl of Rutland, Henry Earl of Southampton, and Lucy Countess of Bedford, signed. Address to the reader, signed. Dedicatory sonnets to the same persons as the epistle, each subscribed 'Il Candido'. Commendatory verses in English and Latin signed B. B. List of texts read for the compilation of the work. 'Il Candido' has been identified, on the authority of an old MS. note, with Matthew Gwinne, 'gwin' being the Welsh for white. 'B. B.' is supposed to have been Barnabe Barnes. First edition.

Sinker 665. BM 637.

FULWELL, Ulpian.

The first part of the eight liberall science: Entituled, Ars adulandi, the art of Flattery, with the confutation thereof, both very pleasant and profitable, deuised and compiled by Vlpian Fulwell.

His diebus non peractis,
Nulla fides est in pactis.
Videto.

Mel in ore, verba lactis
Fel in corde fraus in factis
Caveto.

Who reads a booke rashly,
at randome doth runne,
He goes on his arant,
yet leaues it vndone.

Imprinted at London, by William Hoskins, and are to be solde at his shop ioyning to the midle Temple gate, within Temple Barre. 1576. B. L. 4°. ($7 \times 5\frac{1}{8}$). S. 6. 2.

Collation: ¶^{4}A^{2}B–M^{4}N^2, folios numbered. 'A dialogue betwene the Author and his Muse, as touching the dedication of this booke', giving in anagram the name 'Mildred Burgley'. Epistle dedicatory to Lady Burleigh (wife of the Lord Treasurer), signed. Address to the reader. The printer to the reader, in verse. 'A description of the seuen liberall sciences, into whose company the eight hath intruded her selfe' in verse. Text in eight dialogues. This is the first edition and is supposed to be unique. Another edition, 1579, is in the Bodleian, and a third (1580?) in the British Museum.

Sinker 539.

GARLAND.

The Golden Garland of Princely Delight; Wherein is contained the History of many of the Kings, Queens, Princes, Lords, Ladies, Knights, and Gentlewomen of this Kingdom. Being most pleasant Songs and Sonnets, to sundry New Tunes much in request. In Two Parts. The Thirteenth Edition, with Additions, Corrected and Amended. Licensed according to Order. *Printed for J. Deacon at the Angel in Giltspur-street without Newgate,* 1690.

B. L. 8°. ($6\frac{1}{4} \times 3\frac{3}{4}$). Y. 3. 1.

Title partly within woodcut border. Collation: A–G^8, unpaged. Table to the two parts. The volume is a collection of ballads etc., Part 1 purporting to be of an historical nature, Part 2 containing songs and imaginary subjects. At the end is a publisher's advertisement of books, headed 'Books Printed for, and sold by J. Deacon at the Angel in Gilt-spur-street, without Newgate; where Country Chapmen may be furnished with all sorts of Histories, &c. small Books and Ballads.'

GASCOIGNE, George.

The Whole woorkes of George Gascoigne Esquyre: Newlye compyled into one Volume, That is to say: His Flowers, Hearbes, Weedes, the Fruites of warre, the Comedie called Supposes, the Tragedie of Iocasta, the Steele glasse, the Complaint of Phylomene, the storie of Fernando Ieronimi, and the pleasure at Kenelworth Castle. *London Imprinted by Abell Ieffes, dwelling in the Fore Streete, without Creeplegate, neere vnto Grubstreete.* 1587.

B. L. in part. 4°. ($7\frac{1}{8} \times 5\frac{1}{8}$). S. 2.

Collation: ¶–4¶^{4} 5¶^{2} a–k^4 B^4 C–P^8 Q^4 S–Y^8 ❡^{4}; S^4 V–Y^8; A–B^8; A–C^8(D)^{2}D^2, paged in part, folios numbered in part. Wanting 2¶ 4 and 5¶ 2 (? blank). Addresses, 'To the reverende Deuines', 'To all young Gentlemen' dated, 'Waltamstowe in the Forest' Feb. 2, 1575, and 'To the Readers generally'. Commendatory verses from T. B., E. C., M. C., R. S., T. Ch., G. W., P. B., A. W., I. B., I. D., Richard Smith, M. A. Perugino (Italian prose), A. de B. (Fr.), and in Latin from H. M., B. C., K. D. (2 copies), W. P., G. H., E. H. The order of the works is as follows: 'Flowers' including 'Dan Bartholomew of Barth' and 'The Fruits of war';

'Herbes' including the plays 'Supposes' and 'Jocasta'; 'Weeds' including 'Ferdinando Jeronimi'; 'The Steel Glass' including 'The Complaint of Philomene'; 'The Princely Pleasures at Kenelworth Castle', and 'Certain notes of Instruction concerning the making of verse or rime in English'. Of these the only one that has a regular titlepage is 'The Steel Glass', 'Imprinted Ano. 1587.' The 'Complaint' which follows bears the date 1576 without imprint. This is the third edition, the first being undated and the second having appeared in 1575. Some copies have a different titlepage reading 'The pleasauntest workes' etc.

Sinker 670. BM 678.

GELLI, GIOVANNI BATTISTA.

The Fearefull Fansies of the Florentine Cooper. Written in Tuscane, By Iohn Baptista Gelli, one of the free Studie of Florence. And for recreation translated into English by W. Barker. Pensoso d' altrui. Seene & allowed according to the order appointed. *At London Printed by Tho. Purfoot, for the Companie of Stacioners.* 1599.

B. L. 8°. ($5\frac{1}{4} \times 3\frac{5}{8}$). *. 8. 1.

Collation: A–R[8], folios numbered. Address to the reader. The head-title runs 'The Reasoning of Iust the Florentine Cooper and his Soule. Gathered by his Nephew Sir Byndo.' The first edition appeared in 1568, the present appears to be the second.

Sinker 375. BM 683.

GEOFFREY *of Monmouth.*

Britannię vtriusq; Regũ Et Principium Origo & gesta insignia ab Galfrido Monemutensi ex antiquissimis Britannici sermonis monumentis in latinum traducta: *& ab Ascensio rursus maiore accuratione impressa. Vęnundantur in eiusdem ædibus.* [Colophon] *Ex ædibus nostris iterũ Ad Idus Septẽb. Anni* .MDXVII. 4°. ($7\frac{1}{2} \times 5\frac{5}{8}$). Q. 5. 1.

Collation: 2A[4] A–M[8] N[6]; folios numbered. N 6 (? blank). Epistle dedicatory from the editor Ivo Cavellatus to Hervius Kaerquiffinennus dated, 'Ex collegio nostro Corisopitensi ad Idus Iulias anni salutiferi. M.D.VIII.' Commendatory verses, etc. Armorial woodcut on 2A 4[v]. A note to the reader at the end is headed 'Io. Badius Ascensius Lectori Sa.' Ruled in red throughout. The first edition appeared in 1508.

GEORGE, *Saint.*

The Life and Death of the Famous Champion of England, St. George. [Woodcut.] *Printed for F. Coles, T. Vere, J. Wright, and J. Clarke.* B. L. 8°. ($5\frac{3}{8} \times 3\frac{3}{8}$). Y. 3. 2.

Collation: A[8] B[4], unpaged. Half-title 'St. George', with woodcut of St. George and the Dragon as on title. 'The Life and Death' in prose. 'The Worthy Deeds of St. George of England, and how he married the Kings Daughter of Ægypt, whom he delivered from death. The Tune is, Queen Dido,' in verse, with woodcut of the princess and the dragon and also the woodcut of the titlepage repeated. The recto and verso of the last leaf are also occupied by woodcuts, which however do not belong to the story. Hazlitt dates the volume *circa* 1670 (H. 225).

GILPIN, George.

⌜The Bee Hiue of the Romish Church.... 1623.⌝ *See* MARNIX, Philip van.

GIRALDI, Giovanni Battista, (*Cintio*).

De gli Hecatommithi di M. Giouanbattista Gyraldi Cinthio nobile ferrarese. Parte prima. [La seconda Parte de gli Hecatommithi di M. Giouanbattista Giraldi Cinthio nobile ferarese Nella quale ei contengono tre Dialoghi della uita ciuile.] *Nel Monte Regale Appresso Lionardo Torrentino* M D LXV. 2 vols. 8°. ($6\frac{3}{8} \times 4\frac{1}{8}$). U. 6–7.

For the elaborate collation see Brunet (1861), vol. II, col. 1607 etc. The present copy is perfect except for blanks. The 'Capitolo' in vol. II. (sig. 3H) is of the long form and runs to 11 leaves (Brunet only mentions 10). First edition.

GOFFE, Thomas.

The Careles Shepherdess. A Trigi-Comedy Acted before the King & Queen, And at Salisbury-Court, with great Applause. Written by T. G. Mr. of Arts. Pastorum Tittere pingues Pascere oportet oves, deductum ducere Carmen. With an Alphabeticall Catologue of all such Plays that ever were Printed. *London, Printed for Richard Rogers and William Ley, and are to be sould at Pauls Chaine nere Doctors commons*, 1656. 4°. ($7\frac{3}{4} \times 5\frac{1}{2}$). Q. 10. 3.

Collation: titlepage unsigned, B–K[4] L[2], 3 leaves unsigned, paged. Argument. Præludium in Salisbury Court. Prologue. Prologue at Whitehall. Personae. Epilogue at end. The Catalogue of plays occupies the three unsigned leaves at the end. First ascribed to Goffe by Kirkman in 1661. The Præludium must have been written after the opening of Salisbury Court in 1629 and before the author's death on July 27, of that year.

GOLDING, ARTHUR.

The excellent and pleasant worke of Iulius Solinus Polyhistor.... 1587. *See* SOLINUS, Julius.

The worke of Pomponius Mela.... 1585. *See* MELA, Pomponius.

GOOGE, BARNABE.

The Zodiake of Life.... 1565. *See* MANZOLLI, Pietro Angelo.

Eglogs Epytaphes, and Sonettes. Newly written by Barnabe Googe: 1563. 15. *March. Imprynted at London, by Thomas Colwell, for Raffe Newbery, dwelyng in Fleetstrete a litle aboue the Conduit in the late shop of Thomas Bartelet.* [Colophon] [*Imprinted at London in S. Brydes Churchyarde, by Thomas Colwell, for Raufe Newbery. And are to be sold at his shop in Fleetestrete, a lytle aboue the Conduit.* 1563. 15. *Die Mensis March.*] B. L. 8°. ($4\frac{7}{8} \times 3\frac{1}{2}$). *. 19. 2.

Collation: A[8] B[4]; A–C[8] D[4] E–K[8], unpaged. Wanting B 4 in preliminary sheets (? blank), K 7 containing errata and colophon, and K 8 (? blank). Commendatory verses headed (probably by) 'Alexander Nevyll'. Woodcut of a coat of arms subscribed 'B. Googe'. Epistle dedicatory to William Lovelace, signed. Woodcut of Daphnes and Amintas. Address to the reader by L. Blundeston, dated May 27, 1562. Verse 'Preface' by the same. Errata at the end, below colophon. A new edition appears to have been in preparation in 1587 (Haz. I. 187), but is not known. For variations between the present copy and that in the possession of Mr Huth, see Prof. Arber's reprint.

Sinker 358.

GOULART, SIMON.

Admirable and memorable Histories containing the wonders of our time. Collected into French out of the best Authors. By I. Goulart. And out of French into English. By Ed. Grimeston. The Contents of this booke followe the Authors aduertisement to the reader. *Imprinted at London by George Eld* 1607. 4°. (7 × $5\frac{1}{8}$). S. 22.

Collation: $A^4b^2B–2S^8{}_2T^4$, paged. 2T 4 blank. Wanting A 1 (? blank), A 4, containing the author's and printer's addresses, Q 3 and 6. Epistle dedicatory to Sir Walter Cope, signed Edw. Grimeston. Author's 'adwertisement' to the reader and printer's address to the same. Table of contents. On 2T 3^v is the note 'The end of the first Volume'. Nothing further however was published. The original was the work of Simon not of Jean Goulart.

BM 714.

GOWER, JOHN.

Io. Gower de confessione Amantis. *Imprinted at London in Fletestrete by Thomas Berthelette the* .XII. *daie of Marche. An.* M.D.LIIII. *Cum priuilegio.* F°. ($10\frac{1}{4}$ × $7\frac{3}{8}$). H. 1.

Title within ornamental border. Collation: $*^6A–2I^6$, folios numbered. 2I 6 blank. 'Epigramma autoris' in Latin. Epistle dedicatory to Henry VIII. Address to the reader. Table of contents. The first edition appeared in 1483, printed by Caxton; the second in 1532 by Berthelet; this is the third.

Sinker 71. BM 714.

GRAFTON, RICHARD.

Graftons Abridgement of the Chronicles of Englande. Newly and diligently corrected, and finished the last of October. 1570. The Contents whereof apeareth in the next Page of this lefe. Seene and allowed, according to an order taken. *In ædibus Richardi Tottyll. Cum Priuilegio.*

B. L. 8°. ($5\frac{3}{4}$ × 4). Z. 4.

Collation: 8 leaves unsigned, $¶^8 2C–3C^8 4C^4 A–2B^8 2C^4$, folios numbered. Wanting 2C 4 (? blank). Table of contents. Calendar. Almanack for 24 years. Rules for terms, signs of the Zodiac, dog-days, divisions of the year, Vigils, number of days in the months. Epistle dedicatory to Robert Dudley, Earl of Leicester. Grafton's address to the reader. Alphabetical table of contents. At the end: list of Colleges at Oxford and Cambridge, Shires, Cities, and Boroughs of England, Wards of the City of London, Parish Churches in London, Out parishes adjoining to London, Principal Fairs, Highways to London. The first edition of the 'Abridgement' appeared in 1562–3. This is the third and is quite distinct from that of 1570–1 (Haz. II. 255). The present copy differs from that in the BM in having no colophon.

Sinker 251. BM 716.

GREENE, Robert.

The Pleasant History of Dorastus and Fawnia. [Woodcut.] Peasant [*sic*] for Age to avoid drowsy thoughts, profitable for Youth to avoyd other wanton pastimes: and bring to both a desired content. By Robert Green, Master of Arts in Cambridge. *London, Printed for Ed. Blackmore, and are to be sold at his shop at the sign of the Angell in Pauls Church-yard* 1655. **B. L.** 4°. (7 × 5¼). S. 33. 2.

Collation: A–G⁴, unpaged. Verses, facing title, on verso of A 1. The first edition appeared in 1588, under the title of 'Pandosto. The Triumph of Time.' The present title was first used in the edition of 1636. This is probably the eleventh edition.

The pleasant History of Dorastus and Fawnia. [Woodcut.] Pleasant for Age to shun drowsie Thoughts, profitable for Youth to avoid other wanton Pastimes, and bringing to both a desired content. By Robert Green, Master of Arts in Cambridge. *London, Printed by Robert Ibbitson, for John Wright, and are to be sold by W. Thackery at the Black-spead Eagle and Sun in the Old-Bailey.* 1664. **B. L.** 4°. (7⅛ × 5½). S. 28. 3.

Collation: A–G⁴, unpaged. Verses facing titlepage. With Licence at the end signed Roger L'estrange, and dated July 9, 1664. Twelfth edition (?).

Euphues his Censure to Philautus, Wherein is presented a Philosophical combat betweene Hector and Achilles, discovering in foure discourses, interlaced with divers delightfull Tragedies, The vertues necessary to be incident in every gentleman: had in question at the siege of Troy betwixt

sundrie Grecian and Trojan Lords: especially debated to discover the perfection of a Souldier. Containing mirth to purg melancholly, wholsome precepts to profit manners, neither unsavoury to youth for delight, nor offensive to age for scurrility. Ea habentur optima quæ & jucunda, honesta' & utilia. Robertus Greene, in Artibus Magister. *London, Printed by Eliz. All-de dwelling neere Christ-Church.* 1634.
B. L. 4°. (7 × 5). S. 36. 1.

Collation: A–K⁴, unpaged. Epistle dedicatory from Greene to Robert, Earl of Essex. Second edition, the first having appeared in 1587.

BM 726.

Greenes Groats Worth of Witte: bought with a million of Repentance: Describing the Folly of Youth, the falshood of Make-shift Flatterers, the miserie of the negligent, and mischiefes of deceyuing Curtezans. Published at his dying request: and, Newly corrected, and of many errors purged. Fœlicem, fuisle [*sic*] infaustum. *London, Printed by N. O. for Henry Bell, and are to be sold at his shop in Bethlem at the signe of the Sun.* 1621. **B. L.** 4°. (7 × 5). S. 36. 2.

Collation: A–F⁴, unpaged. Wanting F 3 (? blank). Address 'To Wittie Poets, or Poeticall Wittes' signed I. H. At the end is a letter purporting to have been written by Greene to his wife and 'found with this Booke after his death', signed. Also 'Greenes Epitaph' in verse, signed I. H. The first edition appeared in 1592; it does not contain the address and verses by I. H. The present is the sixth.

BM 727.

Greene's Groatsworth of Wit, bought with A Million of Repentence. Describing the folly of Youth, the falshood of make-shift Flatterers, the Misery of the Negligent, and Mischieves of deceiving Curtezans. Published at his dying request, and Newly corrected and of many errors purged. Felicem fuisse infaustum. *London, Printed for Henry and Moses Bell.* 1637. **B. L.** 4°. ($7\frac{5}{8} \times 5\frac{3}{4}$). Q. 14. 6.

Collation: A–F⁴, unpaged. Wanting F 4 (? blank). Contents as before. Eighth edition.

BM 727.

Greenes Ghost Haunting Cony-catchers: Wherin is set downe The Art of Humouring. The Art of carrying Stones. Will. St. Lift. Ja. Fost. Law. Ned Bro. Catch. and Black Robins Kindnesse. With the merry Conceits of Doctor Pinch-backe a notable Makeshift. Ten times more pleasant than any thing yet published of this matter. Non ad imitandum, sed ad euitandum. *London, Printed for Francis Williams.* 1626. 𝔅. 𝔏. 4°. ($7\frac{3}{4} \times 6$). Q. 9. 4.

Collation: A–G[4], unpaged. Wanting A 1 and G 4 (? blank). Epistle 'To all Gentlemen' etc. signed S. R. Verses to the reader. 'The Notable, Slie, and Deceitfull Prankes of Doctor Pinchback', begins with head-title on sig. F 4. The first edition appeared after Greene's death, namely in 1602, edited and possibly written by S. R., probably Samuel Rowlands. The present is the second edition.

BM 727.

Greenes Neuer too Late. Both Partes. Sent to all youthfull Gentlemen, deciphering in a true English Historie, those particular vanities, that with their Frostie vapours, nip the blossomes of euery braine, from attaining to his intended perfection. As pleasant as profitable, being a right Pumice stone, apt to race out idlenesse with delight, and folly with admonition. By Robert Greene, In artibus Magister. Omne tulit punctum. *London, Printed by William Stansby for Iohn Smithwicke, and are to bee sold at his Shop in Saint Dunstanes Churchyard in Fleete-streete vnder the Diall.* [1621.] 𝔅. 𝔏. 4°. ($7\frac{1}{8} \times 4\frac{7}{8}$). R. 17. 2.

Collation: A–Q[4], unpaged. Epistle dedicatory to Thomas Barnaby, signed. Address to the readers, signed. Verses by Ralph Sidney and Rich. Hake. The first edition of Part I appeared in 1590; Part II the same year under the title of 'Francescos Fortunes'; the two parts together for the first time in 1600. The date, which is shorn, appears to be either 1621 or 1631. It is not the same edition as any of the BM copies, but the titlepage corresponds almost exactly with that of the 1616 edition.

A Quip for an vpstart Courtier: or, A quaint Dispute betweene Velvet-breeches and Cloth-breeches. Wherein is plainely set downe the disorders in all Estates and Trades.

By Robert Greene. [Woodcut.] *London, printed by E. Purslow, dwelling at the East end* [*of Christs-Church.* 1635.]

𝕭. 𝕷. 4°. ($6\frac{1}{2} \times 4\frac{3}{4}$). W. 5. 4.

Collation: A–G⁴, unpaged. Wanting A 1 (? blank). Epistle dedicatory to Thomas Burnaby, signed. Address to the readers. The fourth extant edition, the first having appeared in 1592. There were however probably two issues in 1592 previous to the one extant, which were suppressed.

BM 730.

GRIMESTON, Edward.

Admirable and memorable Histories.... 1607. *See* Goulart, Simon.

GUEVARA, Antonio de.

The Dial of Princes Compiled by the reuerend father in God, Don Antony of Gueuara, Byshop of Guadix, Preacher, & Chronicler to Charles the fift, late of that name Emperour. Englished out of the French by Thomas North, sonne of Sir Edward North Knight L. North of Kirtheling. And nowe newly reuised and corrected by hym, refourmed of faultes escaped in the first edition: with an amplification also of a fourth booke annexed to the same, Entituled The fauoured Courtier, neuer heretofore imprinted in our vulgare tongue. Right necessarie and pleasaunt to all noble and vertuous persons. *Nowe newly imprinted by Richarde Tottill. An. Domini.* 1582. *Cum priuilegio.*

𝕭. 𝕷. 4°. ($7\frac{3}{4} \times 5\frac{1}{2}$). Q. 1.

Title within woodcut border. Collation: A–C⁸D⁶; A–3N⁸3O⁴, folios numbered. Epistle dedicatory to Queen Mary, signed by the translator and dated Lincolnes Inn, December 20 [1557]. Guevara's two Prologues. Argument. Table of contents. The third edition, the first having appeared in 1557.

Sinker 283. BM 739.

HAKLUYT, Richard.

The principal Nauigations, Voiages, Traffiques and Discoueries of the English Nation, made by Sea or ouer-land, to the remote and farthest distant quarters of the Earth, at any time within the compasse of these 1500. yeeres: Deuided into three seuerall Volumes, according to the positions of the Regions, whereunto they were directed. This first Volume containing the woorthy Discoueries, &c. of the English toward the North and Northeast by sea, as of Lapland, Scrikfinia, Corelia, the Baie of S. Nicolas, the Isles of Colgoieue, Vaigatz, and Noua Zembla, towards the great riuer Ob, with the mighty Empire of Russia, the Caspian sea, Georgia, Armenia, Media, Persia, Boghar in Bactria, and diuers kingdoms of Tartaria: Together with many notable monuments and testimonies of the ancient forren trades, and of the warrelike and other shipping of this realme of England in former ages. Whereunto is annexed also a briefe Commentarie of the true state of Island, and of the Northern Seas and lands situate that way. And lastly, the memorable defeate of the Spanish huge Armada, Anno 1588. and the famous victorie atchieued at the citie of Cadiz, 1596. are described. By Richard Hakluyt Master of Artes, and sometime Student of Christ-Church in Oxford. *Imprinted at London by George Bishop, Ralph Newberie and Robert Barker.* 1598. 𝔅. 𝔏. F°. ($11\frac{1}{2} \times 7\frac{1}{2}$). E. I. I.

Collation: ✱–2✱[6]A–3E[6]3F[4], paged. Wanting all after 3E 3, containing the account of the victory at Cadiz, also the hydrographical map. Epistle dedicatory to Charles Howard, Earl of Nottingham, signed. Preface with postscript containing errata. Commendatory verses from Hugo Broghton (Greek), Rich. Mulcaster (2 copies, Lat.), Gulielmus Camdenus (Lat.), and Marc' Antonio Pigafeta (It.). Table of contents. The portion wanting at the end was suppressed, but is found in BM, 683. h. 5. In some copies (*e.g.* Grylls 31, 148) a cancel with sigs. a–d[2] (last leaf blank) has been substituted. The map to this volume, which is wanting in the present copy, was the first English map on Mercator's projection. There is another title-page to the present volume (found in the Grylls copy) which is dated 1599 and has various differences from that given above.

Sinker 419 (1). BM 760.

The second Volume of the principal Nauigations, Voyages, Traffiques and Discoueries of the English Nation, made by Sea or ouer-land, to the South and South-east parts of the World, at any time within the compasse of these 1600. yeares:

Diuided into two seuerall parts: Whereof the first containeth the personall trauels, &c. of the English, through and within the Streight of Gibraltar, to Alger, Tunis, and Tripolis in Barbary, to Alexandria and Cairo in AEgypt, to the Isles of Sicilia, Zante, Candia, Rhodus, Cyprus, and Chio, to the Citie of Constantinople, to diuers parts of Asia minor, to Syria and Armenia, to Ierusalem, and other places in Iudæa; As also to Arabia, downe the Riuer of Euphrates, to Babylon and Balsara, and so through the Persian gulph to Ormuz, Chaul, Goa, and to many Islands adioyning vpon the South parts of Asia; And likewise from Goa to Cambaia, and to all the dominions of Zelabdim Echebar the great Mogor, to the mighty Riuer of Ganges, to Bengala, Aracan, Bacola, and Chonderi, to Pegu, to Iamahai in the kingdome of Siam, and almost to the very frontiers of China. The second comprehendeth the Voyages, Trafficks, &c. of the English Nation, made without the Streight of Gibraltar, to the Islands of the Açores, of Porto Santo, Madera, and the Canaries, to the kingdomes of Barbary, to the Isles of Capo Verde, to the Riuers of Senega, Gambra, Madrabumba, and Sierra Leona, to the coast of Guinea and Benin, to the Isles of S. Thomé and Santa Helena, to the parts about the Cape of Buona Esperanza, to Quitangone neere Mozambique, to the Isles of Comoro and Zanzibar, to the citie of Goa, beyond Cape Comori, to the Isles of Nicubar, Gomes Polo, and Pulo Pinaom, to the maine land of Malacca, and to the kingdome of Iunsalaon. By Richard Hackluyt Preacher, and sometime Student of Christ-Church in Oxford. *Imprinted at London by George Bishop, Ralph Newbery, and Robert Barker. Anno* 1599. **B. L.** F°. ($11\frac{1}{2} \times 7\frac{1}{2}$). E. 1. 2.

Collation: $*^8$A–2C^{6}3A–3R^6, paged. Epistle dedicatory to Sir Robert Cecil, signed. Table of contents. Part ii begins with fresh pagination and head-title at sig. 3A 1.

Sinker 419 (2). BM 760.

The third and last Volume of the Voyages, Navigations, Traffiques, and Discoueries of the English Nation, and in some few places, where they have not been, of strangers, performed within and before the time of these hundred yeeres, to all of the Newfound world of America, or the

West Indies, from 73. degrees of Northerly to 57. of Southerly latitude: As namely to Engronland, Meta Incognita, Estotiland, Tierra de Labrador, Newfoundland, vp The grand bay, the gulfe of S. Laurence, and the Riuer of Canada to Hochelaga and Saguenay, along the coast of Arambec, to the shores and maines of Virginia and Florida, and on the West or backside of them both, to the rich and pleasant countries of Nueua Biscaya, Cibola, Tiguex, Cicuic, Quiuira, to the 15. prouinces of the kingdome of New Mexico, to the bottome of the gulfe of California, and vp the Riuer of Buena Guia: And likewise to all the yles both small and great lying before the cape of Florida, The bay of Mexico, and Tierra firma, to the coasts and Inlands of Newe Spaine, Tierra firma, and Guiana, vp the mighty Riuers of Orenoque, Dessekebe, and Marannon, to euery part of the coast of Brasil, to the Riuer of Plate, through the Streights of Magellan forward and backward, and to the South of the said Streights as far as 57. degrees: And from thence on the backside of America, along the coastes, harbours, and capes of Chili, Peru, Nicaragua, Nueua Espanna, Nueua Galicia, Culiacan, California, Noua Albion, and more Northerly as farre as 43. degrees: Together with the two renowmed, and prosperous voyages of Sir Francis Drake and M. Thomas Candish round about the circumference of the whole earth, and diuers other voyages intended and set forth for that course. Collected by Richard Hakluyt Preacher, and sometimes student of Christ-Church in Oxford. *Imprinted in London by George Bishop, Ralfe Newberie, and Robert Barker. Anno Dom.* 1600.

B. L. F°. ($11\frac{1}{2} \times 7\frac{1}{2}$). E. 2.

Collation: (A)^{8}A–I^{6}K^{8}L–4C^6, paged. Epistle dedicatory to Sir Robert Cecil, signed. Table of contents.

Sinker 419 (3). BM 760.

HALL, JOSEPH.

Virgidemiarum, Sixe Bookes. First three Bookes, Of Tooth-lesse Satyrs. 1. Poeticall. 2. Academicall. 3. Morall. *London Printed by Thomas Creede, for Robert Dexter.* 1597.

8°. ($5 \times 3\frac{3}{8}$). *. 17. 1.

Collation: A–E^{8}F^4, paged. Ornament at head and foot of each page. F 4 blank. Wanting A 1 (? blank). Verses headed 'His Defiance to Envy'. Latin verses 'De suis Satyris'. Three books of satires. Verse 'Conclusion'. Two editions are supposed to have been issued this year.

Sinker 653. BM 1543.

Virgidemiarum. The three last Bookes. Of byting Satyres. Corrected and amended with some Additions. by I. H. *Imprinted at London for Robert Dexter, at the signe of the Brasen Serpent in Paules Church yard.* 1599.

8°. (5 × 3$\frac{3}{8}$). *. 17. 2.

Collation: A^{2}B–H^8, paged. Wanting H 6–8 (? blank), H 5 defective. (In Dr Sinker's catalogue last sheet is given as H^6, wrongly.) Ornament at head and foot of each page. Verses headed 'The Authors charge to his Satyres'. At the end, 'A Post-script to the Reader' in prose, followed by errata. Each book has a half-title with border. Books iv–vi first appeared in 1598; it is possible that there may have been two editions that year.

Sinker 758. BM 750.

HALLE, EDWARD.

[The Vnion of the two noble and illustre famelies of Lancastre & Yorke, beyng long in continuall discension for the croune of this noble realme, with al the actes done in both the tymes of the Princes, both of the one linage & of the other, beginnyng at the tyme of kyng Henry the fowerth, the first aucthor of this deuision, and so successiuely proceadīg to ye reigne of the high and prudent Prince kyng Henry the eyght, the indubitate flower and very heire of both the saied linages. Whereunto is added to euery kyng a seuerall table. 1550.] [Colophon] *Imprynted at London by Rychard Grafton, Prynter to the Kynges Maiestye.* 1550. *Cum priuilegio ad Imprimendum solum.*

B. L. F°. (10$\frac{7}{8}$ × 7$\frac{5}{8}$). F. 14.

Title within elaborate genealogical woodcut border of the houses of York and Lancaster (wanting). Collation: ☞^{4}; (Part i, Henry IV) A^{8}B–E^{6}F^2; (Part ii, Henry V) a^{6}b^{4}c–g^{6}h^{8}I^2; (Part iii, Henry VI) a–q^{6}r^{8}s^4; (Part iv, Edward .IV) A–I^{6}K^{8}L^4; (Part v, Edward V) 2A–2D^6; (Part vi, Table to Edward V followed by Richard III)

2a–2e[6]2f[8]; (Part vii, Henry VII) 3a–3i[6]3k[8]3l[4]; (Part viii, Henry VIII) a–z[6]A–Z[6]; paged afresh in each part. Wanting: Part iii. s 4, Pt. iv. L 4, Pt. vi. 2f 8, Pt. vii. 3k 8, 3l 4, Pt. viii. Z 6, (? blank in each case); also all before Part ii. d 2 (supplied from a different edition) and Part viii. Z 1 (this last and title supplied in MS.). Epistle dedicatory to Edward VI from Edward Halle. Printer's address to the reader. List of authorities with Table of contents on verso. There is an alphabetical Table at the end of each reign. This is the second edition but there appear to have been no less than four issues of the first, portions being in each case reprinted, the bibliography of which has never yet been fully worked out. The defect at the beginning is supplied from the edition of 1548.

HARINGTON, *Sir* JOHN.

Orlando Furioso.... 1591. [And subsequent editions.] *See* ARIOSTO, Lodovico.

HARSNETT, SAMUEL, *Archbishop of York.*

Á Declaration of egregious Popish Impostures, to withdraw the harts of her Maiesties Subiects from their allegeance, and from the truth of Christian Religion professed in England, vnder the pretence of casting out deuils. Practised by Edmunds, alias Weston a Iesuit, and diuers Romish Priests his wicked associates. Where-vnto are annexed the Copies of the Confessions, and Examinations of the parties themselues, which were pretended to be possessed, and dispossessed, taken vpon oath before her Maiesties Commissioners, for causes Ecclesiasticall. *At London Printed by Iames Roberts, dwelling in Barbican.* 1603. 4°. (7 × 4¾). S. 24.

Collation: A–2N[4]2O[2], paged. Table of contents. Epistle 'To the seduced Catholiques of England', signed S. H. (*i.e.* the author, Samuel Harsnett). Errata at the end. First edition.

BM 753.

HEATH, BENJAMIN.

A Revisal of Shakespear's Text, wherein The Alterations introduced into it by the more modern Editors and Critics, are particularly considered.... *London: Printed for W. Johnston, in Ludgate-Street.* MDCCLXV. 8°. (8 × 5¼). P. 6.

Dedicated to Lord Kaimes. The author was Benjamin Heath.

HEATH, John.

Two Centuries of Epigrammes. Written by Iohn Heath, Bachelour of Arts, and fellow of New Colledge in Oxford.

Quicquid agunt homines, votum, timor, ira, voluptas,
Gaudia discursus, nostri farrago libelli est.

London, Printed by Iohn Windet. 1610.

8°. ($5\frac{5}{8} \times 3\frac{3}{4}$). *. I. 2.

Collation: A–F[8], unpaged. Wanting A 1 and F 8 (? blank). Epistle dedicatory to Thomas Bilson, son of the Bishop of Winchester, signed. Commendatory verses, all in Latin, signed Tho. Watkins, Tho. Tucker, Franciscus Souch, Iohannes Heath, Hugo Robinson, (two copies unsigned), Io. Rogers, Io. Harris, (one copy unsigned), Rich. Zouch, (one copy unsigned), Eduardus Pit, Io. Richards, Io. South. Author's verses to the reader in English. 'Epigrammata Centuria secunda' begins with head-title on D 4.

BM 785.

HELIODORUS.

An Æthiopian Historie, written in Greeke by Heliodorus, no lesse wittie then pleasaunt: Englished by Thomas Vnderdowne, & newly corrected and augmented with diuers and sundry newe additions by the said Authour. Whereunto is also annexed the argument of euery booke in the beginning of the same, for the better vnderstanding of the storie. *Imprinted at London, for Frauncis Coldocke, and are to be sold at his shop in Paules church yeard, at the signe of the greene Dragon. Anno.* 1587. B. L. 4°. ($7\frac{1}{8} \times 5\frac{1}{4}$). R. 11. 1.

Collation: ¶[2]A–S[8]T[6], folios numbered. Epistle dedicatory to Edward Deviere, Earl of Oxford, signed. The first edition appeared about 1567 and there appears to have been a second in 1577. The present edition represents the final text.

Sinker 357. BM 787.

HENRY V, *King of England.*

The famous Victories of Henry The fifth. Containing the Honourable Battell of Agin-Court. As it was Acted by the Kinges Maiesties Seruants. *London Imprinted by Barnard Alsop, dwelling in Garter place in Barbican.* 1617.

4°. ($6\frac{3}{4} \times 5$). T. 9. 3.

Collation: A–F⁴G², unpaged. Second edition, the first having appeared in 1598. There was another issue of this edition the same year, with a different titlepage on which it is said to be "sold by Tymothie Barlow".

BM 790.

HERODOTUS.

The Famous Hystory of Herodotus. Conteyning the Discourse of dyuers Countreys, the succession of theyr Kyngs: the actes and exploytes atchieued by them: the Lawes and customes of euery Nation: with the true Description and Antiquitie of the same. Deuided into nine Bookes, entituled with the names of the nine Muses. *At London Printed by Thomas Marshe.* 1584.

B. L. 4°. $(7 \times 5\frac{1}{4})$. T. I. I.

Title within woodcut border. Collation: A⁴B–Q⁸, folios numbered. Last leaf blank. Epistle dedicatory to Robert Dormer, son to Sir William Dormer, signed by the translator, B. R. Address to the readers also signed B. R. (*i.e.* possibly Barnaby Rich). The translation only contains two books.

Sinker 325. BM 800.

HEYWOOD, JOHN.

Iohn Heywoodes woorkes. A dialogue conteyning the number of the effectuall prouerbes in the English tonge, compact in a matter concernynge two maner of Mariages. With one hundred of Epigrammes: and three hundred of Epigrammes upō three hundred prouerbes: and a fifth hundred of Epigrams. Whereunto are now newly added a sixte hundred of Epigrams by the sayde Iohn Heywood. *Londini* 1566. [Colophon] *Imprinted at London in Fleetestrete by Henry Wykes. Cum priuilegio.*

B. L. 4°. $(6\frac{1}{2} \times 4\frac{7}{8})$. W. 2.

Collation: A–2D⁴2E², unpaged. Wanting 2D 2 and 3, containing epigrams 62–89 of the sixth hundred, and 2E 2 (? blank). Preface in verse. Two parts of the 'Dialogue', 'The first hundred of Epigrammes' with title, verses to the reader, and table of contents. 'Three hundred Epigrammes' with title, preceded by woodcut portrait of the author, and table of contents. 'The fifth hundred of Epygrammes' with title, verses to the reader and table of contents. 'A sixt hundred of Epigrammes', with title, verses to the reader and table of contents. This is the second edition of the so-called 'Works', the first having appeared in 1562. The 'Dialogue' first appeared separately in 1546.

Sinker 238. BM 806.

HEYWOOD, Thomas.

An Apology For Actors. Containing three briefe Treatises. 1 Their Antiquity. 2 Their ancient Dignity. 3 The true vse of their quality. Written by Thomas Heywood. Et prodesse solent & delectare— *London, Printed by Nicholas Okes.* 1612. 4°. ($7 \times 5\frac{1}{4}$). S. 32. 2.

Title within woodcut border. Collation: A^4a^4B–G^4, unpaged. Epistle dedicatory to Edward, Earl of Worcester, signed. Address 'To my good Friends and Fellowes, the Citty-Actors', signed T. H. Address to the reader, signed. Commendatory verses, signed: Aλ. Πρ. (Greek), 'Pessimus omnium Poëta', (Lat.), Ar: Hopton, Iohn Webster, Rich. Perkins, Christopher Beeston, Robert Pallant, Iohn Taylor. 'The Author to his Booke', signed. At the end, author's Epistle to Nicholas Okes (the printer), signed.

BM 807.

The Actors Vindication, containing, Three brief Treatises, viz. I. Their Antiquity. II. Their antient Dignity. III. The true Use of their Quality. Written by Thomas Heywood. Et prodesse solent & delectare—— *London, Printed by G. E. for W. C.* 4°. ($7\frac{1}{4} \times 5\frac{3}{8}$). R. 18. 5.

Collation: A^4a^4B–G^4, paged. Wanting G 4 (? blank). Epistle dedicatory to Henry, Marquis of Dorchester, signed W. C. (i.e. Cartwright, the bookseller.) Epistle 'To my good Friends and Fellows, the Actors of this City', signed T. H. Address to the reader signed T. Heywood. Commendatory verses signed: Aλ Πρ́ (Greek), 'Pessimus omnium Poëta' (Latin), A. H., J. W., R. P., C. B., R. P., J. T. (For names represented by these initials see the ed. of 1612.) 'The Author to his Booke', verses signed. This edition was probably printed about 1655.

Pleasant Dialogues and Dramma's, selected out of Lucian, Erasmus, Textor, Ovid, &c. With sundry Emblems extracted from the most elegant Iacobus Catsius. As also certaine Elegies, Epitaphs, and Epithalamions or Nuptiall Songs; Anagrams and Acrosticks; With divers Speeches (upon severall occasions) spoken to their most Excellent Majesties, King Charles, and Queene Mary. With other Fancies translated from Beza, Bucanan, and sundry Italian Poets. By Tho. Heywood. Aut prodesse solent, aut delectare—— *London, Printed by R. O. for R. H. and are to be sold by Thomas Slater at the Swan in Duck-lane* 1637.

8°. ($5\frac{5}{8} \times 3\frac{1}{2}$). *. 2.

Collation: A–V[8], paged. Wanting A 1 (? blank.) Epistle dedicatory to Henry Cary, Baron of Hunsdon, Earle of Dover, signed. Epistle to the reader, signed. Table of contents. Commendatory verses, signed: Sh. Marmion, D. E., S. N. The volume contains, eighteen 'Dialogues', three 'Dramas', 'An Emblematicall Dialogue', 'Prologues and Epilogues', 'Elegies and Epitaphs', 'Epithalamions', 'Epigrams', 'Sundry other Fancies', 'Annotations' on the dialogues &c., and some verses translated from Perisaulus Faustinus. Much that appeared in this volume must have been written at least forty years before.

BM 809.

HOBBES, Thomas.

De Mirabilibus Pecci: being the Wonders of the Peak in Darby-shire, Commonly called The Devil's Arse of Peak. In English and Latine. The Latine Written by Thomas Hobbes of Malmsbury. The English by a Person of Quality. *London, Printed for William Crook at the Green Dragon without Temple-Bar*, 1678. 8°. ($6\frac{1}{2} \times 4\frac{1}{4}$). W. 3. 2.

Collation: A–E[8] F[4], paged. Wanting F 4 (? blank). Licence, signed Rog. L'estrange, and dated Sept. 3, 1677. The poem is addressed to William, Earl of Devonshire. Advertisement at the end. The first edition containing the Latin only appeared in 1636. The present is the third.

HOLINSHED, Raphael.

1577. The Firste volume of the Chronicles of England, Scotlande, and Irelande. Conteyning, The description and

Chronicles of England, from the first inhabiting vnto the conquest The description and Chronicles of Scotland, from the first originall of the Scottes nation, till the yeare of our Lorde . 1571 The description and Chronicles of Yrelande, likewise from the firste originall of that Nation, vntill the yeare . 1547 . Faithfully gathered and set forth, by Raphaell Holinshed. *At London, Imprinted for Iohn Harrison. God saue the Queene.* **B. L.** F°. ($11\frac{1}{4} \times 7\frac{3}{4}$). F. I.

Title within woodcut border with Bynneman's mermaid device. Collation: ¶^{6} ∗^{2}A–P^{8}Q^6, one leaf signed r 1 inserted; a–s^8, one leaf signed t (see vol. ii.); A^2 (*b*)^2 *a*–*b*^{6}; A–2I^8 2K^4 2L–2M^6; ☛^{2} A–C^8 D^4; A–G^8 H^6, with one unsigned leaf inserted after H 5, I^2. Paged in part, folios numbered in part. *b*6 blank. Double columns. Woodcuts. In the last alphabet E 6–8 have been cancelled completely, and leaves F 2 and 7 are cancels (inserted separately) substituted for the original leaves. (Another copy in the Library, VI^b. 4. 7, contains E 6–8 and also the original leaves F 2 and 7.) The leaf signed r 1 which should follow Q 6 of first alphabet is misplaced in the middle of sheet ∗. On the verso of titlepage is a cut of the Holinshed arms quartered with those of the Goddistons of Essex, the whole charged with a crescent of difference. This reappears on the verso of both the separate titlepages. Epistle dedicatory to William Cecill, Lord Burleigh, signed. Preface. List of authorities. Head-title to the description of Britain with table of chapters to the first book. Epistle dedicatory to William Brook, Lord Cobham, signed W. H. Three books of the description, folios numbered. One leaf of errata inserted. History of England to the Conquest, paged. Separate titlepage '1577. The Historie of Scotlande, conteyning the beginning, increase, proceedings, continuance, Actes and Gouernemente of the Scottish nation, from the originall thereof vnto the yeare . 1571 . Gathered and written in the English tongue by R. H. At London, Imprinted for Iohn Harrison. God saue the Queene', within border as before. List of authorities. Epistle dedicatory to Robert Dudley, Earl of Leicester, signed. Head-title to 'The Description of Scotlande, written at the first by Hector Boethus in Latin, and afterwarde translated into the Scottish speech by Iohn Bellendon Archdeacon of Murrey, and now finally into English, for the benefite of such as are studious in the Histories, by W. H.', and list of chapters. Epistle dedicatory by the translator, William Harison, to Thomas Secford 'Maister of the Requestes.' The description, with fresh pagination. The History of Scotland, with fresh pagination, and with alphabetical table at end. Separate titlepage '1577. The Historie of Irelande from the first inhabitation thereof, vnto the yeare 1509. Collected by Raphaell Holinshed, and continued till the yeare 1547. by Richarde Stanyhurst. At London, Imprinted for Iohn Harison. God saue the Queene', within border as before. List of authorities. Epistle dedicatory to Sir Henry Sidney, signed. The description of Ireland by Stanyhurst, addressed to Sidney, with fresh pagination. The History of Ireland, with fresh pagination, having serpent device at end, followed by a table of the governors &c. of Ireland from 1174—1541. One leaf containing errata for Scotland and Ireland inserted. Alphabetical table. Copies differ in the titlepages (see below).

Sinker 463 (1). BM 823.

1577. The Laste volume of the Chronicles of England, Scotlande, and Irelande, with their descriptions. Conteyning, The Chronicles of Englande from William Conquerour vntill this present tyme. Faithfully gathered and compiled by Raphaell Holinshed. *At London, Imprinted for Lucas Harison. God saue the Queene.*

F°. B. L. ($11\frac{1}{4} \times 7\frac{5}{8}$). F. 2.

Collation: ¶[2] t 2–8 (continuing sig. t from vol. i. 2nd alphabet) v–z[8] A–4E[8] with one leaf, signed 4E 5, inserted after 4E 4, 4F–4Y[8] with two unsigned leaves inserted after 4Y 6, 4Z[2]; ()[2] A–M[4] N[2], paged continuously with the History of England in vol. i. Double columns. Woodcuts. In the present copy the sheet containing the two-page woodcut of Edinburgh, which should appear after 4Y 6 is inserted after 4Z 2. L 7 is a cancel printed on different paper in different type. Arms on verso of titlepage as before. Preface. History. At the end, sig. () contains errata to History of England in both volumes. This is followed by Alphabetical Table. With the exception of the cancelled leaves in vol. i. the present copy appears to be absolutely complete. In different copies various publishers' names appear on the titlepages which are otherwise printed from one setting up of the type. The book was entered in the Stationers' Register to John Harison and George Bishop, and a certain number of copies were printed for each. But copies also occur bearing the names of Lucas Harison and John Hunne. Copies are very frequently made up of the separate parts printed for different stationers. The printer was no doubt Bynneman.

Sinker 463 (2). BM 823.

HOLLAND, HENRY.

Herωologia Anglica: hoc est, clarissimorum et doctissimorum aliqout [*sic*] Anglorum qui floruerunt ab anno Cristi .M.D. usq' ad presentem annum M.D.C.XX. Viuæ Effigies, Vitæ et elogia: Duobus tomis. Authore. H. H. Anglo-Britanno: *Impensis Crispini Passæi Calcographus* [sic] *et Jansonij Bibliopolæ Arnhemiensis.* F°. ($11\frac{5}{8} \times 7\frac{5}{8}$). E. 3.

Titlepage engraved. ('Calcographus' altered to 'Calcographi,' in ink.) Collation:)(^{10}A–V^{6}, one leaf unsigned; paged. Wanting)(5 and 6 containing Post-præfatio and first copy of verses. Most of the engravings are included in the collation and have printing on the back, the following only are inserted: tomb of Queen Elizabeth, after D 2; Martin Frobisher, after H 6; John, Lord Harington of Exton (second portrait), after M 1; John Bale, after O 4. Dedication to King James. Præfatio. Post-Præfatio. Commendatory verses by T. D. (two copies), S. R. V. M. Eccl: Belg: Lond:, I. D. Scoto-Britannus (2 copies), A. B. (2 copies). Verses by A. G. Xylandrus. 'Tomus Secundus' begins with half-title at sig. M 5. On D 6^{v} is a portrait of Prince Henry which is a smaller copy with verses subscribed of the Hole engraving in Drayton's 'Poly-olbion' of 1613. The unsigned leaf at the end is occupied by a table of contents.

BM 824.

HOLLAND, PHILEMON.

The Philosophie...written by...Plutarch of Chæronea.... 1603. *See* PLUTARCH.

HOMER.

The Whole Works of Homer; Prince of Poetts. In his Iliads, and Odysses. Translated according to the Greeke, By Geo: Chapman. De Ili: et Odiss:

Omnia ab his; et in his sunt omnia: siue beati
Te decor eloquij, seu rerũ pondera tangunt. Angel: Pol:

At London Printed for Nathaniell Butter.

F°. ($11\frac{3}{8} \times 7\frac{1}{4}$). F. 4.

Engraved titlepage signed William Hole. Collation: 2 leaves unsigned, replacing original engraved titlepage. ✱ 2–6, with two leaves inserted after ✱ 5 (✱ 4 misprinted A 4), A–2F^{6}2G^8; A3–6 B–Q^{6}R^8 S–2H^{6}2I^8; paged. R 8 and 2I 8 in second alphabet blank. Wanting the two leaves inserted in sig. ✱, and ✱6, also 2G 8 (? blank). This edition is made up of earlier editions of both parts; the 'Odessey' is also inserted between the new title-sheet and the 'Iliad' instead of following the latter. The title-sheet contains, engraved titlepage, with engraved portrait of the translator on the verso; engraved memorial to Prince Henry on second leaf. (In some copies the engraved titlepage is found without the portrait on verso, and these seem to be the earlier impressions.) This sheet takes the place of the original titlepage (*c.* 1612–13) and the dedicatory verses to Sir Edward Philips found in some copies of the original issue. Dedicatory verses to Prince Henry, signed by the translator. Anagram on Prince Henry. Verses to Queen Anne, signed. Verses to Viscounts Cranborne and Rochester and Sir Edward Philips, occupying the two inserted leaves (wanting in the present copy). Verses to the reader (first leaf wanting). Preface. Errata. Twenty-four books of the 'Iliad'. Verses to the Duke of Lenox, the Lord Chancellor, Earl of Salisbury, Earl of Suffolk, Earl of Northampton, Earl of Arundell, Earl of Pembroke, Earl of Montgomerie, Lord Lisle, Countess of Montgomerie, Lady Wrothe, Countess of Bedford, Earl of Southampton, Earl of Sussex, the Lord Warden, and Sir Thomas Howard, signed at the end. The edition of the 'Odessey' had appeared in 1614, with an engraved title 'Homer's Odysses. Translated according to ye Greeke. By Geo : Chapman. Imprinted at London by Rich: Field, for Nathaniell Butter'. This and the blank leaf preceding it have been cancelled in the present as in most other copies of the collected edition. In some copies, *e.g.* in that in the Cambridge University Library, is found a printed title-page: 'Homers Odesses. Translated According to the Greeke. By George Chapman. [Motto.] London, Printed for Nathaniel Butter'. Epistle dedicatory in verse and prose to Robert, Earl of Somerset. Translations of Greek epigrams. Twenty-four books of the 'Odessey' with a few verses at the end. The present which was the first collected edition appeared about 1616. It seems to be generally assumed that the collected edition of 1616 contained, not the 1612–13 'Iliad', but a reprint. Copies in this state are found in the Cambridge University Library and the British Museum (G. 8837). The reprint, however, which appears in these copies must be of considerably later date, as is evident from the constant use of 'v' medially. It was probably printed about 1640. Two of the woodcut figures used as head-pieces were so used (with the same break in the St Francis) in a book printed, probably by T. Harper, in 1641 (namely the reprint of 'The Devil is an Ass' found in some copies of the second volume of Ben Jonson's works, *q.v.*). Evidently the stock of the 'Iliad' gave out before the 'Odessey' and the first part of the volume had in consequence to be reprinted. Probably therefore the majority of copies of Chapman's 'Homer' described as being of the edition of 1616 were not in reality issued till some twenty years later.

BM 828.

HORMANUS, HADRIANUS JULIUS.

The Lyues, Of Philosophers and Oratours.... [1579.] *See* EUNAPIUS.

HOWARD, HENRY, *Earl of Surrey.*

Songes and Sonettes written by the right honorable Lorde Henry Haward late Earle of Surrey, and other. *Apud Richardum Tottell. Cum priuilegio ad imprimendum solum.* 1557. [Colophon] *Imprinted at London in fletestrete within Temple barre, at the signe of the hand and starre, by Richard Tottill, the* .xxxi. *day of Iuly. Anno.* 1557. *Cum priuilegio ad imprimendum solum.* B. L. 4°. ($6\frac{3}{8} \times 4\frac{5}{8}$). W. 1.

Collation: A–2G[4], folios numbered. Prose address to the reader. Alphabetical table at the end. At the foot of f. 18[v] is the subscription 'Surrey', applying to the foregoing poems. So again at the foot of f. 49[v] is the subscription 'T. Wyate the elder', while f. 50 is headed 'Songes and Sonettes of vncertain auctours'. Again on f. 113 occurs the heading 'Songes written by N. G.' (*i.e.* Nicholas Grimald, the probable editor), while at the end of the poems the initials N. G. are also found. The 'Songs of uncertain Authors' are supposed to include poems by Thomas Lord Vaux, Sir Francis Bryan, John Heywood, Thomas Churchyard, and Edward Somerset. This is the second edition, the first, of which only one copy is known, having appeared on June 5 of the same year. In the second edition thirty poems by Grimald which appeared in the first are replaced by an additional thirty-nine poems by uncertain authors; some of the other matter is also rearranged. The present copy differs throughout from that in the BM, though the date in both is identical, the type having apparently been set up in duplicate. On the verso of the last leaf are some verses in an English hand of the sixteenth or early seventeenth century.

Sinker 222. BM 839.

Songes and Sonnets, written by the Right honourable Lord Henry Haward late Earle of Surrey, and others, *Imprinted at London by Iohn Windet.* 1585.

𝔅. 𝔏. 8°. ($6\frac{5}{8} \times 4\frac{1}{8}$). Y. I.

Collation: A–P[8], folios numbered. Address to the reader. Alphabetical table at end. The subscription 'Surrey' and 'S. T. Wyat the elder' occur respectively on fols. 19 and 49[v], the headings 'Vncertaine Auctours' and 'Songs written by N. G.' on fols. 50 and 113[v] respectively. Seventh edition.

Sinker 625. BM 839.

HOWELL, Thomas.

Newe Sonets, and pretie Pamphlets. Written by Thomas Howell Gentleman. Newly augmented, corrected and amended. [Woodcut.] *Imprinted at London in Fletestreete, at the signe of the S. Iohn Euangelist, by Thomas Colwell.*

𝔅. 𝔏. 4°. ($7\frac{1}{4} \times 4\frac{3}{4}$). S. 8. 2.

Collation: A–G[4], paged (B–E only). Wanting D 3 and 4. Epistle dedicatory to Henry Lassels, signed. Verses to the same, also signed. Commendatory verses from John Keper (English and Latin), and the author's brother William Howell. Several poems by J. Keeper occur in the course of the work. The present is the only known copy. It was licensed to Colwell in 1567/8, but of what is presumably the original issue (*c.* 1568) three leaves only are extant, in the Huth collection. The present reprint must date between the years 1568 and 1575 when Colwell ceased printing. On A 4[v] occurs a device formerly used by Robert Wyer (device 2, but without name).

Sinker 359.

HUSBAND.

The Husband. A Poeme expressed In a Compleat Man. Loripedem rectus derideat, Æthiopem albus: Iuv: sat: pri: *London Printed for Lawrence L'isle, dwelling at the Tygres head in Pauls Church-yard.* 1614. 8°. ($5\frac{3}{4} \times 3\frac{5}{8}$). Z. 3. 3.

Title within arabesque border, at the foot of which are the initials T C, probably those of Thomas Creede the printer. Ornament at head and foot of each page. Collation: A–F^8, unpaged. A 1 blank but for signature, and F 8 blank. Epistle dedicatory to Anth. Croftes, dated, Iune 29, 1614. Epistle to the reader. Commendatory verses from Ben: Jonson, I. C., Ra: Wym:, Io: Calue: Ex inter: Temp:, A: H: Ex Temp: Med:, Philomus: Ex Graij: Hospi:, Robertus Vescius (Lat.), R. V. (Lat.), M: Freeman. Verses from 'The Author to his præfix'd Approuers'. Argument in prose. The only other copy that can be traced was in Bibl. Anglo Poet. and Heber sale. The volume was reprinted in 1710. The author is not known. Two years later John Davies of Hereford published a similar work entitled 'A select second Husband for Sir Thomas Overburies Wife, now a matchless Widow.'

JAMES VI *of Scotland.*

The Essayes of a Prentise, in the deuine Art of Poesie. *Imprinted at Edinbrugh, by Thomas Vautroullier.* 1584. *Cum Priuilegio Regali.* 4°. (7 × 5⅛). S. 6. 1.

Collation: ✻^{4}A–P^4, unpaged. A 2, O 1 and O 3 are blank. Catalogue of contents on verso of titlepage. Sonnets, signed: T. H., R. H., M. W., M. W. F., A. M. 'De huius Libri Auctore, Herculis Rolloci coniectura' (Lat.). 'Acrosticon' reading 'Iacobus Sextus' signed 'Pa. Ad. Ep. Sanct.' in Latin with Latin epigram by the same. Twelve sonnets with 'Ane Quadrain of Alexandrin Verse' prefixed. 'The Vranie translated.' (half-title with cuts of zodiacal signs, C 2). Address to the reader. Text, French and English on opposite pages. 'Ane metaphoricall Inuention of a Tragedie called Phoenix' (half-title, G 2). 'A Paraphrasticall Translation out of the Poete Lucane' (half-title, I 3). 'Ane schort Treatise, conteining some reulis and cautelis to be obseruit and eschewit in Scottis Poesie' (half-title, K 1). 'A Quadrain of Alexandrin Verse, declaring to quhome the Authour hes directit his labour' ('to the docile bairns of knawledge'). Preface. 'Sonnet of the Author to the Reader.' 'Sonnet decifring the perfyte Poete' followed by the 'Treatise' in eight chapters. 'The CIIII. Psalme, translated out of Tremellius' (half-title, N 2). 'Ane schort Poeme of Tyme.' (O 2). 'A Table of some obscure Wordis with their Significations, efter the ordour of the Alphabet.' 'Sonnet of the Author.' 'I haue insert for the filling out of thir vacand pageis, the verie wordis of Plinius vpon the Phœnix, as followis.' This last is not found in all copies. Some copies are dated the following year. None of the contents were included in the collected works of 1616.

Sinker 849. BM 862.

JOHN, *King of England.*

The Troublesome Raigne of Iohn King of England, with the discouerie of King Richard Cordelions Base sonne (vulgarly named, The Bastard Fawconbridge): also the death of King Iohn at Swinstead Abbey. As it was (sundry times) publikely acted by the Queenes Maiesties Players, in the honourable Citie of London. *Imprinted at London for Sampson Clarke, and are to solde at his shop, on the backe-side of the Royall Exchange.* 1591. 𝔅. 𝔏. 4°. ($6\frac{3}{8} \times 4\frac{1}{2}$). W. 5. 2.

Collation: A–G[4], unpaged. With verse address to the readers. First edition. The only perfect copy of this and the following item known. An imperfect one, the only other known at all, was sold at Sotheby's, Apr. 25, 1899.

Sinker 725.

The Second part of the troublesome Raigne of King Iohn, conteining the death of Arthur Plantaginet, the landing of Lewes, and the poysning of King Iohn at Swinstead Abbey. As it was (sundry times) publikely acted by the Queenes Maiesties Players, in the honourable Citie of London. *Imprinted at London for Samson Clarke, and are to be solde at his shop, on the backe-side of the Royall Exchange.* 1591. 𝔅. 𝔏. 4°. ($6\frac{3}{8} \times 4\frac{1}{2}$). W. 5. 2.

Collation: A–E[4], unpaged. Verse address to the readers. First edition.

Sinker 726.

The First and second Part of the troublesome Raigne of Iohn King of England. With the discouerie of King Richard Cordelions Base sonne (vulgarly named, The Bastard Fawconbridge:) Also, the death of King Iohn at Swinstead Abbey. As they were (sundry times) lately acted by the Queenes Maiesties Players. Written by W. Sh. *Imprinted at London by Valentine Simmes for Iohn Helme, and are to be sold at his shop in Saint Dunstons Churchyard in Fleetestreet.* 1611. 4°. ($6\frac{7}{8} \times 4\frac{7}{8}$). T. 8. 4.

Collation: A–L[4] M[2], unpaged. M 2 blank. Part II begins with head-title at sig. H 4, with verse address to the readers prefixed. Second edition.

BM 1385.

The First and second Part of the troublesome Raigne of Iohn King of England. With the discouerie of King Richard Cordelions Base sonne (vulgarly named, the Bastard Fauconbridge:) Also the death of King Iohn at Swinstead Abbey. As they were (sundry times) lately acted. Written by W. Shakespeare. *London, Printed by Aug. Mathewes for Thomas Dewe, and are to be sold at his shop in St. Dunstones Church-yard in Fleet-street,* 1622. 4°. ($7\frac{1}{4} \times 5\frac{1}{4}$). R. 22. 3.

Collation: A–L^4M^2, unpaged. Part II begins with separate titlepage bearing the same imprint, at sig. G 4. On the verso is the verse address to the readers. Third edition.

BM 1393.

JONSON, Benjamin.

The Workes of Beniamin Ionson

—neque, me vt miretur turba, laboro:
Contentus paucis lectoribus.

Imprinted at London by Will Stansby An° D. 1616.

F°. ($10\frac{3}{8} \times 7\frac{1}{8}$). G. 1.

Engraved titlepage signed Guliel. Hole. Collation: $¶^6$A–$4P^6 4Q^4$, paged. Wanting ¶ 1 (? blank) and all after P 4. Catalogue of contents. Commendatory verses from I. Selden, Ed. Heyward, Geor. Chapman, H. Holland, I. D. (Lat.), E. Bolton (Lat.), Franc. Beaumont (3 copies). Each play, the 'Epigrammes' etc., 'Part of the King's Entertainment', 'A Panegyre', 'A Particular Entertainment' and the 'Masques' have separate titlepages. Copies present various points of difference. In the present copy 'Every man out of his Humour' and 'Cynthias Revels' have woodcut borders to their respective titlepages. G 2 is not paged and has 'your true Honorer' in the subscription. The stage direction is omitted on G 5^v. The titlepage to 'Poetaster' bears the stationer's as well as printer's name. This is the first edition of the first volume of the collected works, and the only one published during the author's life. It was reprinted when the second volume was collected in 1640. The present copy has an elaborate heraldic bookplate of Thomas Cokayne.

BM 893.

The Workes of Benjamin Jonson. The second Volume. Containing these Playes, Viz. 1 Bartholomew Fayre. 2 The Staple of Newes. 3 The Divell is an Asse. *London, Printed for Richard Meighen*, 1640. F°. ($11\frac{1}{4} \times 7\frac{1}{8}$). F. 8.

Collation: $A^6B–Y^4 2A–2H^4 2I^6$; $A–P^4Q^2R–V^4$; $B–Q^4R^2S–X^4Y^2 Z–2O^4 2P^2 2Q^4$; $A–K^4L^2M–R^4$; paged. Sigs. Z–2Q of third alphabet misplaced at end of second. The first three plays, those mentioned on the general titlepage, but in the order 1, 3, 2, each have a separate titlepage with imprint 'London, Printed by I. B. for Robert Allot, and are to be sold at the signe of the Beare, in Pauls Church-yard. 1631.' (2 also has fresh pagination.) These constitute the first alphabet of sigs., the first leaf of A (? originally blank) being replaced by the general titlepage. The second alphabet, with fresh pagination, contains three plays, 'The Magnetic Lady', 'A Tale of a Tub', 'The Sad Shepherd', each with a separate titlepage without printer's or stationer's name but dated, the first two 1640, the third 1641. The third alphabet, with fresh pagination, contains 'Masques' without separate titlepage, 'Underwoods' and the fragment of 'Mortimer' each with separate titlepage dated 1640. The last alphabet, again with fresh pagination, contains 'Horace his Art of Poetry', 'The English Grammar' and 'Timber or Discoveries', each with separate titlepage, the first two dated 1640, the last 1641. This is the first edition of the second volume and is for the most part composed of matter which had not previously appeared. It was later re-issued without the general titlepage and with the three 1631 plays replaced by a reprint dated 1641 of 'The Devil is an Ass' only.

BM 893.

Ben: Ionson's Execration against Vulcan. With divers Epigrams by the same Author to severall Noble Personages in this Kingdome. Never Published before. *London: Printed by J. O. for John Benson, and are to be sold at his shop at St. Dunstans Church-yard in Fleet-streete.* 1640.

4°. ($7 \times 5\frac{1}{4}$). S. 33. 5.

Collation: $A–G^4$, unpaged. Engraved portrait signed Ro. Vaughan, with verses below. Epistle dedicatory to Thomas, Lord Windsor, signed by the publisher. Imprimatur, signed Matth. Clay, and dated Dec. 14, 1639. Verses at end to Jonson signed Zouch Tounley, followed by list of errata.

BM 894.

KENDALL, TIMOTHY.

[Flowres of Epigrammes, out of sundrie the moste singular authours selected, as well auncient as late writers. Pleasant and profitable to the expert readers of quicke capacitie: By Timothe Kendall, late of the Vniuersitie of Oxford: now student of Staple Inne in London.

Horatius.

Aut prodesse volunt, aut delectare poetæ,
Aut simul & iucunda, aut idonea dicere vitæ.

Imprinted at London in Poules Churche-yarde, at the signe of the Brasen Serpent, by Ihon Shepperd. 1577.]

B. L. 8°. ($5\frac{1}{4} \times 3\frac{3}{8}$). *. 7.

Collation: a[8] A–S[8], folios numbered. Wanting all before A 1, also P 1, containing title to Part ii. The first sheet (wanting) contains titlepage with list of sources on verso; epistle dedicatory to Robert Dudley, Earl of Leicester, signed; address to the reader; commendatory verses from W. Seymour, George Whetstones, E. G., Abraham Fleminge, A. W., G. L. (2 copies, Latin). The Epigrams begin with head-title on A 1. 'Trifles by Timothie Kendall' with separate title and fresh foliation. At the end, below the colophon, appears a woodcut emblem with a couplet from Martial (Epig. XIII. 77).

Sinker 544. BM 908.

KIT, *of Kingstone* (*pseud.*).

Westward for Smelts. Or, The Water-mans Fare of mad-merry Western wenches, whose tongues albeit like Bell-clappers, they neuer leaue Ringing, yet their Tales are sweet, and will much content you. Written by Kinde Kit of Kingstone. [Woodcut.] *London, Printed for Iohn Trundle, and are to be sold at his shop in Barbican, at the Signe of the No-body.* 1620. B. L. 4°. ($7\frac{3}{4} \times 5\frac{3}{8}$). Q. 8. 4.

Collation: A–E[4] F[2], unpaged. Address to the reader, signed. Halliwell, who reprinted the collection for the Percy Society in 1848, from the present copy, supposed it to be unique. Another, however, formerly in the Roxburgh, is now in the Huth collection.

KNOLLES, Richard.

The generall Historie of the Turkes, from The first beginning of that Nation to the rising of the Othoman Familie: with all the notable expeditions of the Christian Princes against them. Together with the Lives and Conquests of the Othoman Kings and Emperours Faithfullie collected out of the best Histories, both auntient and moderne, and digested into one continuat Historie vntill this present yeare 1603: By Richard Knolles *London: Printed by Adam Islip.* 1603. F°. ($12\frac{7}{8} \times 8\frac{5}{8}$). B. 4.

Engraved titlepage signed Laurence Iohnson. Collation: A–$5G^6$ $5H^8$, paged. A 1 blank. Epistle dedicatory to King James, signed. Address to the reader, signed and dated, Sandwich, Sept. 30, 1603. List of authorities. The history, with engraved portraits in the text, signed L. I. and dated 1603. At the end 'A brief discourse of the greatnesse of the Turkish empire' (unpaged) with head-title on sig. 5F 1, after which is the alphabetical index and list of errata. First edition.

BM 915.

The generall Historie of the Turkes, from The first beginning of that Nation to the rising of the Othoman Familie: with all the notable expeditions of the Christian Princes against them. Together with the Lives and Conquests of the Othoman Kings and Emperours, vnto the yeare 1610 Written by Richard Knolles somtyme fellowe of Lincoln College in Oxford. The second edition. *Printed by Adam Islip.* 1610. F°. ($12\frac{1}{4} \times 8\frac{3}{8}$). C. 1.

Engraved titlepage as above, partly re-engraved. Collation: A–$5S^4$$6A$–$6B^6$$6C^8$, paged. Wanting A 1 and 6C 8 (? blank). Epistle dedicatory to King James, signed. Address to the reader, signed and dated, 'Sandwich the last of March, 1610'. In the text re-appear the engravings of 1603. At the end of the history is a note to the reader. 'A briefe discourse of the greatnesse of the Turkish Empire', unpaged, begins with head-title on 6A 1, followed by alphabetical table. At the end of this copy are inserted two leaves containing notes in an old handwriting. Second edition.

BM 915.

LANGLAND, William.

The vision of Pierce Plowman, nowe the seconde time imprinted by Roberte Crowley dwellynge in Elye rentes in Holburne. Whereunto is added certayne notes and cotations in the mergyne, geuynge light to the Reader. And in the begynning is set a briefe summe of all the principall matters spoken of in the boke. And as the boke is deuided into twenty partes called Passus: so is the Summary diuided, for euery parte hys summarie, rehearsynge the matters spoken of in euery parte, euen in suche order as they stande there. *Imprinted at London by Roberte Crowley, dwellyng in Elye rentes in Holburne. The yere of our Lord* .M.D.L. *Cum priuiligio ad imprimendum solum.*

B. L. 4°. (7 × 5¼). T. 5.

Collation: ✳⁴ ℭ⁴ A–2F⁴ 2G², folios numbered. Wanting 2G 2 (? blank). Printer's address to the reader. Arguments. This is the true second edition, the third equally bearing the words 'nowe the seconde time imprinted'. See Prof. Skeat's edition (1886), vol. II, p. lxxv.

Sinker 211. BM 1235.

LA RAMÉE, Pierre.

Petri Rami Basilea ad Senatum Populumque Basiliensem. *Anno* .M.D.LXXI. 4°. (8⅝ × 6¼). M. 2. 3.

Collation: a–d⁴ e², paged. Supposed to have been printed at Lausanne by Joannes Probus, who printed the author's 'Defensio pro Aristotele' the same year.

LATHAM, Simon.

Lathams Falconry or The Faulcons Lure, and Cure: in two bookes. The First, concerning the ordering and training vp of all Hawkes in generall; especially the Haggard Faulcon Gentle. The second, teaching approued medicines for the cure of all Diseases in them. Gathered by long practice and experience, and published for the delight of noble mindes, and instruction of young Faulconers in things pertaining to this Princely Art. By Simon Latham. Gent. [Woodcut.] *Printed at London by I. B. for R. Iackson, and are to be sold at his shop neere Fleet-street Conduit.* 1615.

4°. (7 × 5¼). S. 23. 2.

Collation: $A^4 ¶^4 a^4 B–T^4 V^2$, paged. Wanting A 1 (? blank). Epistle dedicatory to Sir Thomas Munson, signed. Address to the reader. Commendatory verses signed T. A. Glossary. Errata. Acrostic on the author's name. Table of contents. Introduction. First edition.

BM 930.

Lathams new and second Booke of Falconry; concerning the ordering and training vp of all such Hawkes as was omitted or left vnmentioned in his printed Booke of the Haggard Falcon and Gerfalcon, namely the Goshawke and Tassell, with the Sparhawke, the Lanner and Lanueret, as they are diuided in their generation: the Hobby and Marlyn in their kindes: Teaching approued Medicines for all such infirmities and diseases as are incident to them. Published for the delight of Noble mindes, and instruction of yong Falconers in all things pertaining to this Art. [Woodcut.] *At London Printed by I. B. for Roger Iackson, and are to bee sold at his shop neere Fleet Conduit.* 1618.

4°. (7 × 5¼). S. 23. 1.

With another titlepage preceding, ornamented with various cuts and bearing the author's name in full 'By Symon Latham, Gent.'. Collation: four leaves unsigned, $A^4 a^4 B–V^4$, paged. Wanting first and last leaves (? blank). Epistle dedicatory to Sir Patrick Hume, master falconer to King James, signed: S. L. Author's address to the reader, and acknowledgment to 'the right worshipfull maister Henrie Sadler of Euerly, who was my first and louing maister'. Commendatory verses, signed T. A. Table of contents. Text with woodcuts. Epilogue, by 'a worthy Devine, S. I.' First edition. The two parts were reprinted together in 1633.

BM 930.

LAZARILLO DE TORMES.

The plesant Historie of Lazarillo de Tormes a Spaniarde, wherein is conteined his marueilous deeds and life. With the Strange aduentures happened to him in the seruice of sundry maisters. Drawne out of Spanish by Dauid Rouland of Anglesey. Accuerdo, Oluid. *London Printed by Abell Ieffes, dwelling in the Blacke Fryers neere Puddle Wharfe.* 1596. 𝔅. 𝔏. 4°. (7⅝ × 5¾). Q. 14. 5.

The device on the titlepage is that of Roger Ward, his initials being however omitted. Collation: A–H[4], unpaged. Epistle dedicatory to Sir Thomas Gressam [*sic*], signed. On the last leaf are some verses 'To the Reader' signed G. Turbervile Gent. The first edition is supposed to have appeared in 1576 but of this no copy is now known. A second was published in 1586. The present is the third.

Sinker 676. BM 1501.

LE FÈVRE, RAOUL.

The ancient Historie of the destruction of Troy. Conteining the Founders and foundation of the sayde Citie, with the causes and manner of the first and second spoyles and sacking thereof by Hercules and his followers: and the third and last vtter desolation and ruine, effected by Menelaus, and all the notable Worthies of Greece. Here also are mentioned the rising and flourishing of sundry Kings with their Realmes, as also the decay and ouerthrow of diuers others. Besides many admirable, and most rare exploites of Chiualrie, and Martiall Prowesse, effected by valourous Knights, with incredible euents, compassed for, and through the Loue of Ladies. Translated out of French into English, by W. Caxton. Newly corrected, and the English much amended. The fifth Edition. *London, Printed by Barnard Alsop*, 1617.

𝔅. 𝔏. 4°. (7 × 5). S. 9.

Collation: A[4] 𝔄–2ℭ[8], paged. A 1 blank. Printer's address to the reader. Three books, each with Table of contents at the end, and the second and third having separate titlepages with same imprint. A copy of Latin verses before Table of Bk. III. Translated by Caxton from the French of Raoul le Fèvre. The first edition under the title of the 'recuyell of the historyes of Troye' was printed by Caxton at Bruges *c.* 1475.

BM 1512.

LESINA, Compagnia della.

La Lesina Dialogo, Capitoli, & Ragionamenti. Della celeberrima Compagnia de' Lesinanti. Con alcune piaceuoli Dicerie in lode di detta Compagnia, & altre Compositioni nel medesimo genere. *Stampata per Ordine de gli otto Operaij di detta Compagnia.* 1601. 8°. ($5\frac{1}{2} \times 3\frac{3}{4}$). Z. 7. 6.

Collation: A–D⁸, paged. List of 'Vfficiali della Compagnia delle Lesine'. Epistle from M. Quancunque Spillaccheri to M. Vnguento da Cancheri 'In lode della Compagnia delle Lesine'. The 'Dialogo' is ascribed in the heading to M. Giuntino Fulignati. An edition had already appeared in 1590.

La Vera Regola per mantenersi magro, Con pochissima Spesa. Scritta da M. Spilorcion de' Stitichi, Correttor della nobilissima Compagnia delle Lesine. A messer Agocchion Spontato suo Compare. Opera vtilissima per tutti coloro, che patiscono strettezza di borsa. Di Giulio Cesare della Croce. *In Ferrara. Per Vittorio Baldini,* MDCI. *Con licenza de' Superiuri* [sic]. [Colophon] *In Pavia, & ristampata in Torino, Appresso Gio. Michele Caualleri*j . 1598 . *Con licenza de Superiori.* 8°. ($5\frac{1}{2} \times 3\frac{3}{4}$). Z. 7. 7.

Collation: $D^4A^{16}B^{20}$, paged. 'Capitolo'. List of 'Vfficiali della compagnia della Bastina.' 'Commento di sodesco cavezza Nel prefato Soneto.' 'Capitoli da osservarsi Asinissimamente. Dalli Brigati della Bastina. Descritti da Messer Ragghiante Basticci Tesoriero delle Asinerie.' Followed by prose and verse by members of the society. The colophon is followed by two pages of woodcuts.

LINDSAY, *Sir* David.

A Dialogue between Experience and a Courtier, of the miserable state of the Worlde. Compiled in the Scottish tung by Syr Dauid Lindsey Knight, a man of great learning and science: First turned and made perfect Englishe: And now the seconde time corrected and amended according to the first Copie. A worke very pleasant and profitable for all Estates, but chiefly for Gentlemen, and such as are in aucthoritie. Herevnto also are annexed certain other workes inuented by the saide Knight, as may more at large appeare in a Table following. *Imprinted at London, in Newgate Market within the New Rentes, by Thomas Purfoote. An. Dom.* 1581. **B. L.** 4°. ($7\frac{1}{2} \times 5\frac{1}{2}$). R. 2.

Collation: four leaves, the second signed (ij.), A–S[8]T[4], folios numbered. Epistle to the reader. Verses to the buyer. Table of contents. Prologue and four books of the 'Monarch'. Really the third English edition, previous ones having appeared in 1566 and 1575. The original Scots version was published by John Skot at St Andrews, *c.* 1552.

Sinker 371. BM 957.

LODGE, THOMAS.

The Diuel coniured. *London Printed by Adam Islip for William Mats, dwelling in Fleetstreet at the sign of the Hand and Plough. Anno* 1596. **B. L.** 4°. ($7\frac{1}{4} \times 5\frac{1}{2}$). Q. 13. 5.

Collation: A–L[4]M[2], unpaged. Wanting A 1 (? blank). Epistle dedicatory to Sir Iohn Fortescue, signed T. L. (*i.e.* Thomas Lodge). Address to the reader, signed T. L.

Sinker 788. BM 920.

Euphues Golden Legacie. Found after his death in his Cell at Silexedra. Bequeathed to Philautus Sonnes, nursed vp with their Father in England. Fetcht from the Canaries, by T. L. Gent. *Imprinted at London for Iohn Smethwick, and are to be sold at his shop in Saint Dustanes* [sic] *Church-yard in Fleetstreet vnder the Dyall.* 1612.
B. L. 4°. ($7\frac{1}{4} \times 5\frac{1}{2}$). Q. 13. 2.

Collation: A–O[4], unpaged. Epistle dedicatory to Lord Hunsdon (*i.e.* George Carey, second lord, *ob.* 1603), signed by the author Thomas Lodge. Address to the readers, signed T. L. Euphues' testament. At the end postscript, signed. This edition, the sixth, bears the original title of 1590; several were published under the better known one of 'Rosalynde'.

BM 1011.

Euphues Golden Legacie. Found after his death in his Cell at Silexedra. Bequeathed to Philautus Sonnes, nursed vp with their Father in England. Fetcht from the Canaries, by T. L. Gent. *Imprinted at London for Iohn Smethwick, and are to be sold at his shop in Saint Dunstanes Church-yard in Fleetstreete, vnder the Dyall.* 1623.

B. L. 4°. ($7\frac{1}{4} \times 5\frac{7}{8}$). Q. 14. 1.

Collation etc. as above. Wanting O 4. Eighth edition.

Euphues Shadow, the Battaile of the Sences. Wherein youthfull folly is set downe in his right figure, and vaine fancies are prooued to produce many offences. Hereunto is annexed the Deafe mans Dialogue, contayning Philamis Athanatos: fit for all sortes to peruse, and the better sorte to practise. By T. L. Gent. *London Printed by Abell Ieffes, for Iohn Busbie, and are to be sould at his shop in Paules Churchyard, neere to the West doore of Paules.* 1592.

B. L. 4°. ($7\frac{3}{8} \times 5\frac{1}{2}$). Q. 13. 3.

Collation: A–N[4], unpaged. A 1 blank except for signature. Epistle dedicatory to Robert Ratcliffe, Viscount Fitzwaters, signed by Robert Greene, who purports to be seeing through the press the work of 'one M. Thomas Lodge, who nowe is gone to sea with Mayster Candish'. Address to the readers signed by the same. Philautus' address to his sons. The 'Dialogue' begins on L 3v.

Sinker 675. BM 1011.

⌜Phillis: Honoured with Pastorall Sonnets, Elegies, and amorous delights. Where-vnto is annexed, the tragicall complaynt of Elstred.

Iam Phœbus disiungit equos, iam Cinthia iungit.

At London, Printed for Iohn Busbie, and are to be sold at his shoppe, at the West-doore of Paules, 1593.⌟

4°. ($7\frac{1}{2} \times 5\frac{1}{2}$). Q. 13. 1.

Collation: A–L[4], unpaged. Wanting sig. A, A 1 blank (?), the rest containing titlepage, epistle dedicatory to the Countess of Shrewsbury signed by the author Tho: Lodge, and 'Induction' in verse; also B 1 (?blank, likewise wanting in BM copy). Ornament at foot of each page. 'The complaint of Elstred' begins at sig. H 4.

Sinker 756. BM 1011.

Wits Miserie, and the Worlds Madnesse: Discouering the Deuils Incarnat of this Age. *London, Printed by Adam Islip, and are to be sold by Cuthbert Burby, at his shop by the Roiall-Exchange.* 1596. **B. L.** 4°. (7¼ × 5½). Q. 13. 4.

Collation: A–P⁴, paged. Wanting A1 (? blank). Epistle dedicatory to Nicholas and John Hare from the author, Thomas Lodge, dated, Low-Laiton, Nov. 5, 1596. Address to the reader signed T. L.

Sinker 787. BM 1012.

LOMBARDI, Bernardino.

L'Alchimista Comedia di M. Bernardino Lombardi Comico Confidente. Nuouamente Ristampata. *In Venetia,* MDCII. *Appresso Lucio Spineda.* 12°. (5¼ × 2⅝). *. 14.

Collation: A–I¹², folios numbered. I 12 blank. Epistle dedicatory to Giulio Pallavicino, signed and dated, Ferrara, May 20, 1583. Personae. At the end, three sonnets to G. Pallavicino (or Pallavicini), one by Gio. Donato Cucchetti, one 'D'Incerto', and one by Lombardi. The present edition appears to be the third, the first having appeared in 1583.

LOVERS.

The Fortunate, the Deceiv'd, and the Unfortunate Lovers. Three Excellent New Novels, Containing Many Pleasant and Delightful Histories. The like never in any Language before. Printed in English and French, For the Satisfaction of the Ingenious. Written by the Wits of both Nations. *London, Printed for William Whitwood in Duck-Lane,* 1685.

8°. (6⅞ × 4¼). U. 3.

Collation: 2 leaves unsigned, 2 leaves signed A, B–M⁸; A–I⁸ K²; A–F⁸ G⁴, each part paged separately. Engraved titlepage with verses facing printed titlepage. Address 'Au Lecteur'. Same in English. Eight novels in each part.

LUCANUS, Marcus Annæus.

Lucans Pharsalia: or the civill Warres of Rome, betweene Pompey the great, and Iulius Cæsar. The whole tenne Bookes, Englished by Thomas May, Esquire. The second Edition, corrected, and the Annotations inlarged by the Author. *London, Printed by Aug. Mathewes, for Thomas Iones, and are to be sold at his shop in St. Dunstanes Church-yard.* 1631.

8°. ($5\frac{5}{8} \times 3\frac{1}{2}$). Z. 9. I.

Collation: a[8], with engraved titlepage inserted after a 1, A–S[8]T[2], unpaged. Engraved titlepage, signed Fridericus Hulsius, with explanatory verses opposite, followed by regular titlepage. Epistle dedicatory to William, Earl of Devonshire, signed by the translator. Life of Lucan. Commendatory verses from Ben. Ionson and I. Vaughan. Annotations at the end of each of the ten books. Books i–iii appeared in 1626; the complete work, of which the present is the second edition, in 1627. An earlier translation by Sir Arthur Gorges had appeared in 1614, and Marlowe's translation of Book i. as early as 1600.

BM 1026.

LYDGATE, John.

The auncient Historie and onely trewe and syncere Cronicle of the warres betwixte the Grecians and the Troyans, and subsequently of the fyrst euercyon of the auncient and famouse Cytye of Troye vnder Lamedon the king, and of the laste and fynall destruction of the same vnder Pryam, wrytten by Daretus a Troyan and Dictus a Grecian both souldiours and present in all the sayde warres and digested in Latyn by the lerned Guydo de Columpnis and sythes translated in to englyshe verse by Iohn Lydgate Moncke of Burye. *And newly imprinted. An* . M . D . L . V . [Colophon] *Imprinted at London, in Fletestrete at the sygne of the Princes armes, by Thomas Marshe. Anno. do.* M . D . L . V.

B. L. F°. ($11\frac{1}{8} \times 7\frac{3}{4}$). F. 15.

Title within elaborate woodcut border of the genealogies of the Houses of York and Lancaster (as in E. Halle's 'Union of York and Lancaster' *q.v.*). Collation: A[2] B–2C[6] 2D–E[4], unpaged. 'The pistle to the reader', signed by the editor, Robert Braham. The signature has been printed 'Quod Robert Braham' and an ornament has then been stamped over the 'Quod'. Translator's prologue in verse. Books i–v. Verses to Henry V. 'Lenvoye' and 'Verba translatoris ad librum suum' in verse. Table of contents. Lydgate's 'Troybook' is a verse rendering of the prose 'Historia Destructionis Troiæ' written in Latin by Guido delle Colonne. This is in its turn based on the French 'Roman de Troie' by Benoît de Sainte-More, the chief sources of which are the 'De Excidio Troiæ' the reputed work of Dares Phrygius, which may have been then extant in a fuller version than we now possess, and the 'Ephemeris Belli Trojani' which goes under the name of Dictys Cretensis. An earlier edition of Lydgate's work had appeared from R. Pynson's press in 1513.

Sinker 307. BM 448.

Here begynneth the boke of Iohan Bochas / discryuing the fall of prĩces / princesses / and other nobles: Translated in to Englysshe by Iohñ Lydgate monke of Bury / begynning at Adam and Eue / and endyng with kyng Iohan of Fraunce / taken prisoner at Poyters by prince Edwarde. [Woodcut.] [Colophon] *Imprinted at London in flete strete by Richarde Pynson / printer vnto the kynges moste noble grace / & fynisshed the* .xxi. *day of Februarye / the yere of our lorde god* .M.CCCCC.xxvii. B. L. F°. ($10\frac{1}{2} \times 7\frac{3}{4}$). G. 2.

Collation: $a^6 A–X^6 2A–2O^6 2P^8$, folios numbered. Table of contents. Translator's prologue in verse. Nine books, with woodcuts. Verses of the translator at the end. The work is a verse rendering of Boccaccio's 'De Casibus Virorum Illustrium' (prose). Pynson published an edition of the work as early as 1494; the present is the second.

Sinker 32. BM 239.

LYLY, John.

Euphues. The Anatomy of Wyt. Very pleasant for all Gentlemen to reade, and most necessary to remember: wherin are contained the delights that Wyt followeth in his youth by the pleasauntnesse of Loue, and the happynesse he reapeth in age, by the perfectnesse of Wisedome. By Iohn Lyllly Master of Arte. Oxon. *Imprinted at London for Gabriell Cawood, dwelling in Paules Church-yarde.*

B. L. 4°. ($7\frac{1}{8} \times 4\frac{7}{8}$). R. 17. 1.

Collation: $A^4 B–E^8 F–T^4$, folios numbered. Epistle dedicatory to William West, Lord Delaware, signed I. Lyly. Address to the readers. At the end is a device of a sable horse (as crest) charged with a crescent of difference encircled by the motto 'Mieulx vault mourir ẽ vertu que vivre en honcte'. This is the device of Th. East. The text of this edition presents peculiarities, which, as

Dr Sinker has shown, prove it to be the first. Having been entered to Cawood in the S. R. Dec. 2, 1578, it probably appeared about the close of the year. Two further editions appeared in 1579, *viz.* the second (undated) the only known copy of which is also in the library (VI^a^. 4. 14 (2) imperfect) and that (dated) represented by the Malone and Morley copies. For particulars see Bond's 'Lyly' (Oxford, 1902) vol. i. p. 85 etc.

Sinker 547. BM 953.

MALORY, *Sir* THOMAS.

The most ancient and famous History of the renowned Prince Arthur King of Britaine, Wherein is declared his Life and Death, with all his glorious Battailes against the Saxons, Saracens and Pagans, which (for the honour of his Country) he most worthily atchieued. As also, all the Noble Acts, and Heroicke Deeds of his Valiant Knights of the Round Table. Newly refined, and published for the delight, and profit of the Reader. *London, Printed by William Stansby, for Iacob Bloome,* 1634. B. L. 4°. ($7 \times 5\frac{3}{8}$). S. 1.

Three Parts, each with separate titlepage and signatures distinct. Collation: Part I, ¶^{4}§^{4}A–2I^4; Pt. II, 2 leaves unsigned, ¶^{4}A–2Q^{4}2R^2; Pt. III, ¶^{4}[2]¶^{4}A–2P^4; unpaged. Wanting 2R 2 in Pt. II (? blank). Each part has the same woodcut of the Round Table and list of knights facing the titlepage, and a Table of contents. Part I has also a Preface, and a Prologue, besides Caxton's address to the reader. The first edition was printed by Caxton in 1485.

BM 56.

MALESPINI, CELIO.

Ducento Nouelle Del Signor Celio Malespini, nelle quali si raccontano diuersi Auuenimenti così lieti, come mesti & strauaganti. Con tanta copia di sentenze graui, di scherzi, e motti, Che non meno sono profitteuoli nella prattica del viuere humano, che molto grati, e piaceuoli ad vdire. *Con Licenza de' Superiori, & Priuilegio. In Venetia,* MDCIX. *Al Segno dell' Italia.* 4°. ($7\frac{1}{2} \times 5\frac{1}{2}$). Q. 6–7.

Collation: Part I, ✻^{8}A–2L^{8}2M^{10}; Part II, a–2p^{8}2q^4; folios numbered in each part separately. 2M 10 blank. Part II has a separate head-title.

MANZOLLI, PIETRO ANGELO.

The Zodiake of Life Written by the Godly and zealous Poet Marcellus Pallingenius stellatus, wherein are conteyned twelue Bookes disclosing the haynous Crymes & wicked vices of our corrupt nature: And plainlye declaring the pleasaunt and perfit pathway vnto eternall lyfe, besides a numbre of digressions both pleasaunt & profitable, Newly translated into Englishe verse by Barnabæ Googe. Probitas laudatur & alget. *Imprinted at London by Henry Denham, for Rafe Newberye dwelling in Fleete streate. Anno .* 1565 . *Aprilis* . 18 .

B. L. 8°. ($5\frac{3}{8} \times 3\frac{3}{4}$). *. 4. 1.

Collation: *[8](‡)[4]A–Y[8]2A–2X[8]2Y[4], unpaged. Coat of arms with initials B. G. (*i.e.* Barnabe Googe). Commendatory verses, from Gilbertus Duke, Christoferus Carlilus, Iacobus Itzuertus, G. Chatertonus, David Bellus, Richardus Stephanus, all in Latin except the last, which is in Greek with Latin translation. Epistle dedicatory to Sir William Cecill, signed by the translator. Address to the reader. Errata. Palingenius was the pseudonym under which Manzolli wrote. Books i–iii of the translation appeared in 1560, books i–vi in 1561; the present is the first edition of the complete work.

Sinker 331. BM 1189.

MARLOWE, CHRISTOPHER.

Hero And Leander.... 1637. *See* MUSÆUS.

MARNIX, PHILIP VAN.

⌈The Bee Hiue of the Romish Church. A worke of all good Catholikes to be read, and most necessary to bee vnderstood. Wherein the Catholike Religion is substantially confirmed, and the Heretikes finely fetcht ouer the coales. Translated into English by George Gilpin the Elder. 1. Thes. 5. 21. Proue all things, and keepe that which is good. *London. Printed by Iohn Dawson.* 1623.⌋

B. L. 8°. ($5\frac{1}{4} \times 3\frac{1}{2}$). *. 11.

Collation: *–2*[8]¶–4¶[8]5¶[2]A–2X[8]2Y[2], folios numbered. Wanting all before 2¶ and after 2V 1. Epistle dedicatory to Philip Sidney Esquire, signed John Stell. Address to the reader signed by the same. 'Interpretation of the Epistle of Master Gentian Haruet,' signed Isaac Rabbotenu (*i.e.* Philip von Marnix van Sant Aldgonde.) Epistle dedicatory to Franciscus Sonnius signed Isaac Rabbotenu of Louen, and dated Jan. 5, 1569. Argument. One leaf blank (?). Table of authors quoted. Table of doctrines. At the end of the second Table is the note 'Gathered by Abraham Fleming.' Six books of the exposition of the 'Epistle of Gentian Haruet' followed by twelve chapters of additional exposition and a postscript to the reader headed 'The locke of this Booke' occupying the verso of the last leaf. The present copy begins in the middle of the first Table and ends in the 'conclusion' to the sixth book.

BM 1281.

MASSINGER, PHILIP.

The Excellent Comedy, called The Old Law: or A new way to please you. By Phil. Massinger. Tho. Middleton. William Rowley. Acted before the King and Queene at Salisbury House, and at severall other places, with great Applause. Together with an exact and perfect Catalogue of all the Playes, with the Authors Names, and what are Comedies, Tragedies, Histories, Pastoralls, Masks, Interludes, more exactly Printed then ever before. *London, Printed for Edward Archer, at the signe of the Adam and Eve, in Little Britaine.* 1656. 4°. ($7\frac{1}{4} \times 5\frac{3}{8}$). R. 18. 4.

Collation: $A^2B–K^4L^2a–b^4$, paged. Personae. At the end the catalogue of plays, occupying the last two sheets.

MASSUCCIO, *Salernitano.*

Le cinquanta Nouelle di Massuccio Salernitano intitolate il Nouellino nuouamente con somma diligentia reuiste corrette et stampate. Dissimilium infida societas.

8°. ($6\frac{5}{8} \times 4$). U. 4.

Collation; $A–V^8X^{10}$, paged. Table on last page. The titlepage bears the cat and mouse device of M. Sessa with his initials. Otherwise there is no indication of date, place or printer. The first edition appeared in 1476.

MAY, THOMAS.

Lucans Pharsalia.... 1631. *See* LUCANUS, Marcus Annæus.

A Continuation of Lucan's Historicall Poem till the death of Iulius Cæsar By T M *London Printed for James Boler at the Signe of the Marigold in Pauls Church-yard*, 1630.

8°. ($5\frac{5}{8} \times 3\frac{1}{2}$). Z. 9. 2.

Titlepage engraved by T. Cockson. Collation: A–K[8], unpaged. A 1 and 2 and K 8 blank. Epistle dedicatory to Charles I, signed Tho. May. Commendatory verses from Iohannes Sulpitius Verulanus. (Lat.) 'The Complaint of Calliope' in verse. Annotation at the end of each of the seven books. First edition. A later edition bears the date 1567 by misprint for 1657.

BM 1085.

MEAN TO DIE WELL.

[Running title] A Meane to dye wel. [Colophon] *Imprinted at London in Fletestrete at the sygne of the George nexte to saynt Dunstones churche by Wyllyam Myddleton.*

𝔅. 𝔏. 8°. ($5\frac{3}{8} \times 3\frac{5}{8}$). *. 4. 2.

Collation: A–B[8] (?), unpaged. A fragment consisting of B 1 (signed) and the corresponding leaf, presumably B 8. The text ends on the recto of the second leaf with the words '✳ By your louer ĩ almighty god for whome I beseche you to say, Iesu have mercy vpõ my soule. ¶ AMEN.' The verso is occupied by the colophon and the larger of Middleton's devices. The fragment which is unidentified, apparently formed part of the binding of the volume, which also contains a fragment of a musical MS on vellum.

Sinker 1077.

MELA, POMPONIUS.

The worke of Pomponius Mela, The Cosmographer, concerninge the Situation of the world, wherein euery parte, is deuided by it selfe in most perfect manner, as appeareth in the Table at the ende of the booke. A booke right plesant and profitable for all sortes of men: but speciallie for Gentlemen, Marchants, Mariners, and Trauellers, translated out of Latine By Arthur Golding Gentleman. *At London, Printed for Thomas Hacket, and are to be sold at his shop in Lumbert streete, vn-* [sic] *the signe of the Popes head.* 1585.

𝔅. 𝔏. 4°. ($7 \times 5\frac{1}{4}$). T. 1. 4.

Collation: A4 C–O4, paged. A 1 blank but for signature. Epistle dedicatory to William, Lord Burleigh, signed by the translator, and dated Febr. 6, 1584. Table of contents at end.

Sinker 346. BM 1088.

MERES, FRANCIS.

Palladis Tamia. Wits Treasury Being the Second part of Wits Common wealth. By Francis Meres Maister of Artes of both Vniuersities. Viuitur ingenio, cætera mortis erunt. *At London Printed by P. Short, for Cuthbert Burbie, and are to be solde at his shop at the Royall Exchange.* 1598.

8°. ($5 \times 3\frac{1}{8}$). *. 16.

Collation: A4 B–2V8, folios numbered. List of authors. At the end, alphabetical table of headings. In this copy the list of authors, occupying leaves A 2–4, is misplaced at the end of the volume. The famous 'comparatiue discourse of our English Poets, with the Greeke, Latine, and Italian Poets' occurs at sig. 2N 7. First edition. 'Wits Common wealth' of which the present work purports to be the continuation, was written by John Bodenham.

Sinker 775. BM 1093.

MERRY DEVIL OF EDMONTON.

The merry Deuill of Edmonton. As it hath beene sundry times Acted, by his Maiesties Seruants, at the Globe, on the banke-side. *London Printed by Henry Ballard for Arthur Johnson, dwelling at the signe of the white-horse in Paules Churchyard, ouer against the great North doore of Paules.* 1608. 4°. ($7\frac{1}{4} \times 5$). R. 23. 5.

Collation: A–F4, unpaged. Wanting A 1 (? blank). Prologue. First edition. No other copy recorded.

The Merry Diuel of Edmonton. As it hath beene sundry times Acted, by his Maiesties Seruants, at the Globe on the Banke-side. *At London. Printed by G. Eld, for Arthur Johnson, dwelling at the signe of the white-Horse in Paules Churchyard, ouer against the great North Doore of Paules.* 1617. 4°. ($6\frac{7}{8} \times 5$). T. 8. 1.

Collation: A–F⁴, unpaged. Wanting A 1 (? blank). Prologue. Third edition, the second having appeared in 1612.

BM 517.

The Merry Deuill of Edmonton. As it hath been sundry times Acted, by his Maiesties Seruants, at the Globe on the Banke-side. *London printed by A. M. for Francis Falkner, and are to be sold at his Shoppe neere vnto S. Margarites-hill in Southwarke.* 1626. 4°. ($6\frac{7}{8} \times 5\frac{1}{8}$). T. 7. 5.

Collation: A–F⁴, unpaged. Wanting A 1 (? blank). Prologue. Fourth edition.

BM 517.

The Merry Deuill of Edmonton. As it hath been sundry times Acted, by his Maiesties Seruants, at the Globe on the Banke-side. *London. Printed by T. P. for Francis Falkner, and are to be sold at his Shoppe neere vnto S. Margarites-hill in Southwarke.* 1631. 4°. ($7 \times 5\frac{1}{4}$). S. 30. 2.

Collation: A–F⁴, unpaged. Wanting A 1 (? blank). Prologue. Fifth edition.

BM 517.

The Merry Devil of Edmonton. As it hath been sundry times Acted, by His Majesties Servants at the Globe on Bank side. [Woodcut.] *London, Printed for William Gilbertson, and are to be sold at his Shop, at the Sign of the Bible in Giltspur-street without N*⌜*ewgate.* 1655.⌝ 4°. ($7 \times 4\frac{7}{8}$). S. 35. 5.

Collation: A–F⁴, unpaged. Wanting A 1 (? blank). Titlepage folded in. Prologue. Sixth edition.

MILTON, John.

A Maske presented At Ludlow Castle, 1634: On Michaelmasse night, before the Right Honorable, Iohn Earle of Bridgewater, Vicount Brackly, Lord Præsident of Wales, And one of His Maiesties most honorable Privie Counsell.

Eheu quid volui misero mihi! floribus austrum
Perditus—

London, Printed for Hvmphrey Robinson, at the signe of the Three Pidgeons in Pauls Church-yard. 1637.

4°. ($7\frac{3}{8} \times 5\frac{3}{4}$). Q. 14. 3.

Collation: A²B–E⁴F², paged. Epistle dedicatory to the young Viscount Bracly, signed H. Lawes. Personae at end. This, the only separate edition of 'Comus', was published with Milton's consent by his friend Lawes, the composer.

BM 1027.

Paradise lost. A Poem Written in ten Books By John Milton. Licensed and Entred according to Order. *London Printed, and are to be sold by Peter Parker under Creed Church neer Aldgate; And by Robert Boulter at the Turks Head in Bishopsgate-street; And Matthias Walker, under St. Dunstons Church in Fleet-street,* 1667. 4°. ($7 \times 5\frac{3}{8}$). S. 10.

Collation: titlepage unsigned, A–2T⁴2V², unpaged. The first edition, with Lowndes' first titlepage (Bohn). The poem begins on A 1. It was not divided into twelve books till the second edition. The second titlepage differs in having the author's name in smaller type.

Paradise lost. A Poem in ten Books. The Author J. M. Licensed and Entred according to Order. *London Printed, and are to be sold by Peter Parker under Creed Church neer Aldgate; And by Robert Boulter at the Turks Head in Bishopsgate-street; And Matthias Walker, under St. Dunstons Church in Fleet-street,* 1668. 4°. ($7\frac{1}{8} \times 5\frac{1}{4}$). S. 11.

[Another copy.] 4°. ($7 \times 5\frac{1}{4}$). S. 12.

Both copies of the first edition, having Lowndes' third titlepage. Except for the alterations observable in the transcript, the titlepage has been printed from the same setting up of the type as the first, the rules round the title are however new. A fourth titlepage also bearing the date 1668 was printed by S. Simmons and has four rows of fleurs-de-lis under the author's name. Of the fifth and sixth titlepages recorded in Bohn's Lowndes no copies are known. The second of the above copies has the heraldic bookplate of Rob. Hodges, Fellow of Pembroke (1703).

Paradise lost. A Poem in ten Books. The Author John Milton. *London, Printed by S. Simmons, and are to be sold by T. Helder at the Angel in Little Brittain.* 1669.
4°. (7 × 5¼). S. 14.

Collation: A^4a^4A etc. as before. Titlepage on *A* 1. Printer's address to the Reader, signed S. Simmons. (5 lines.) Arguments to the ten books. Note on the verse. Errata. Text as before. This is again the first edition with addition of preliminary matter, and has Lowndes' seventh titlepage.

Paradise lost. A Poem in ten Books. The Author John Milton. *London, Printed by S. Simmons, and are to be sold by T. Helder, at the Angel in Little Brittain,* 1669.
4°. (7 × 5⅛). S. 13.

Collation as above. No printer's address to the reader and preliminary matter reset. The first edition with Lowndes' eighth titlepage. This was printed from an entirely new setting of the type. It may be distinguished from the seventh by the commas after 'Helder' and 'Brittain' and by having 'Angel' in italic in place of roman type; also by having a reversed 'p' for the 'd' in 'Paradise'. On an inserted leaf at the beginning is the inscription: 'M^r. Hollis desires the favor of M^r. Payne to present this Copy, unless it should prove a duplicate, to M^r. Capel. Pall Mall mar. 18. 1761.'

Paradise Lost. A Poem in twelve Books. The Author John Milton. The Second Edition Revised and Augmented by the same Author. *London, Printed by S. Simmons next door to the Golden Lion in Aldersgate-street,* 1674.
8°. (6½ × 4¼). W. 4.

Collation: Portrait unsigned, A^4 B–Y^8, paged. Y 8 blank. Portrait engraved by W. Dolle. Commendatory verses, signed: S. B. *M. D.*, A. M. Note on the verse. The arguments are prefixed to the several books. This is the second edition, in which the poem first appeared divided into twelve books.

Paradise Regain'd. A Poem. In IV Books. To which is added Samson Agonistes. The Author John Milton. *London, Printed by J. M. for John Starkey at the Mitre in Fleetstreet, near Temple-Bar.* MDCLXXI. 8°. (7 × 4½). S. 15.

Collation: A^2B–O^8P^4, paged. Licence, dated July 2, 1670, on leaf preceding titlepage. 'Samson' has a separate titlepage with same imprint on I 1, and fresh pagination. Note on Tragedy. Argument. Personae. At the end is an omitted passage and errata. First edition.

Poems, &c. upon Several Occasions. By Mr. John Milton: Both English and Latin, &c. Composed at several times. With a small Tractate of Education To Mr. Hartlib. *London, Printed for Tho. Dring at the Blew Anchor next Mitre Court over against Fetter Lane in Fleet-street.* 1673.
8°. ($6\frac{1}{2} \times 4\frac{1}{4}$). W. 3. 1.

Collation: A^4A–S^8, paged. Wants S 7 and 8 containing part of the advertisement of books. Table of English Poems. Table of Latin Poems. Errata. English Poems. 'Joannis Miltoni Londinensis Poemata. Quorum pleraque intra Annum ætatis Vigesimum Conscripsit. Nunc primum Edita. Londini, Excudebat W. R. Anno 1673', *i.e.* the Latin Poems, with separate titlepage and fresh pagination but signatures continuous, and preceded by an address to the reader in Latin. Tractate of Education with pagination continuous with Latin Poems. Advertisement of books at end. This is the second edition of the 'Poems', of which there were two issues in the same year, the earlier bearing the White Lion as the sign of the stationer. The first edition of the poems both English and Latin appeared in 1645.

MINIATORE, Bartolomeo.

Formulario ottimo et elegante, ilquale insegna il modo del scriuere lettere messiue & respõsiue, cõ tutte le mansioni sue a li gradi de le persone conueneuoli. Et oltra di cio alcune nuoue & breuissime Orationi a diuersi Ambasciatori, de Prencipi attissime & necessarie, & di nuouo corrette. [Colophon] *Stampato in Vinegia per Giouanni Andrea detto Guadagnino, & Florio fratello de Vauassere. Nel anno del nostro Signore.* M D XLIIII. 8°. ($5\frac{1}{2} \times 3\frac{3}{4}$). Z. 7. 4.

Collation: A–F^8, unpaged. 'Litterà d'amore...ad vna tua amorosa.' 'Proemio' from 'Bartholomeo miniator' to Hercole Estense (Ercole d'Este) duke of Ferrara. The first edition of the collection appeared in 1506, an enlarged one in 1531.

MIRROR FOR MAGISTRATES.

A Mirrour for Magistrates. Wherein maye be seen by example of other, with howe greuous plages vices are punished: and howe frayle and vnstable worldly prosperity is founde, even of those whom Fortune seemeth most highly to fauour. Fælix quem faciunt aliena pericula cautum. *Anno.* 1563. *Imprinted at London in Fletestrete nere to Saynct Dunstans Churche by Thomas Marshe.*

B. L. 4°. ($7\frac{1}{4} \times 5\frac{1}{4}$). R. 13.

Title within woodcut border. Collation: ¶^{4}A^{4}B–N^{8}O–V^{4}X–Z^8 2A–2B^{8}2C^4, folios numbered. Epistle "To the Nobilitie" etc., signed William Baldwin. Prose address to the reader by the same. Part ii begins, with head-title, at sig. L 2, and another address to the reader by Baldwin. Table of contents and list of errata at the end. Part i had appeared in 1559; this second extant edition is the first containing Part ii. Part i contains nineteen legends; Part ii eight legends, besides Sackville's 'Induction' to his legend of Buckingham. The original edition of the 'Mirror' was printed by J. Wayland probably in 1554 or 1555 at the end of his edition of Lydgate's 'Falls of Princes'. The publication was stayed and the title only has survived. The first edition actually published was that of 1558, which contains Part i only. The contributors to the collection were William Baldwin (the editor), George Ferrers, Sir Thomas Chaloner, — Caryl, and John Skelton, in Part i; George Ferrers, Thomas Sackville Earl of Dorset, Thomas Churchyard, Francis Segars, and John Dolman, in Part ii; while nine legends are anonymous. For the authorship of the individual legends, see Mr W. F. Trench's dissertation on the 'Mirror' (1898): the ascriptions given in the British Museum catalogue are mostly erroneous. In the later editions initials were frequently placed at the end of the legends to indicate the authorship, but in many cases they are wrong and in all want authority.

Sinker 310. BM 91.

A Myrrour for Magistrates, Wherein may be seene by examples passed in this realme, with howe greueous plagues, vyces are punished in great princes and magistrates, and how frayle and vnstable worldly prosperity is founde, where Fortune seemeth moste highly to fauour. Newly corrected and augmented. Anno 1571. Fœlix quem faciunt aliena pericula cautum. *Jmprinted at London by Thomas Marshe dwellynge in Fleetstreete, neare vnto S. Dũstanes Churche.* [Colophon adds] 1571. **B. L.** 4°. ($7\frac{1}{2} \times 5\frac{1}{4}$). R. 3.

Title within woodcut border. Collation: $*^4A^4B–V^8X^4$, folios numbered. Epistle 'To al the Nobility' etc., signed W. B. Table of contents. Baldwin's address to the reader. This is a reprint of the 1563 edition; the order of the legends is altered, and in many cases the authors' names or initials appended. It is not divided into parts. In the Table appear legends of Duke Humphrey, and the Duchess of Gloucester, but they are not found in the book. One legend on these characters had similarly appeared in the Table in the 1559 edition. This is the third extant edition of the legends which originally formed Part i.

Sinker 318. BM 91.

The first parte of the Mirour for Magistrates, containing the falles of the first infortunate Princes of this lande: From the comming of Brute to the incarnation of our sauiour and redemer Iesu Christe. Ad Romanos. 13.2. Quisquis se opponit potestati, Dei ordinationi resistit. *Imprinted at London by Thomas Marshe. Anno.* 1574. *Cum Priuilegio.* **B. L.** 4°. ($7\frac{3}{4} \times 5\frac{1}{2}$). Q. 10. 1.

Title within woodcut border. Collation: $*^6A–I^8K^2$, folios numbered. Table of contents. Epistle 'To the nobilitie' etc., signed by the author, Iohn Higgins. Prose address to the reader by the same. This is an entirely new work, dealing with the early history and therefore entitled the 'First Part'. It contains seventeen legends, one being added at the end which is not among the sixteen mentioned in the Table. The former 'Mirror' was reprinted in this year, one legend enlarged, as 'The Last Part' etc. This 'First Part' was reprinted, slightly enlarged, the following year; also with 'The Last Part'.

Sinker 322. BM 813.

The Mirour for Magistrates, wherin may bee seene, by examples passed in this Realme, with how greeuous plagues vices are punished in great Princes and Magistrates, and how fraile and vnstable worldly prosperity is found, where Fortune seemeth most highly to fauour: Newly imprinted, and with the addition of diuers Tragedies enlarged. *At London in*

Fleetestreete, by Henry Marsh, being the assigne of Thomas Marsh. 1587. *Cum Priuilegio.* 𝔅. 𝔏. 4°. (7 × 5¼). S. 5.

Title within ornamental border. Collation: A–C^4 𝔄–2𝔐^8 (omitting ℨ), folios numbered. Wanting A 1 (? blank). Higgins' epistle 'To the Nobility' etc. as in 1574, but here dated, Winceham, December 7, 1586. Higgins' address to the reader, and table of contents. Commendatory verses by Thomas Newton, dated 1587. 'The Authors Induction.' Baldwin's address to the reader at sig. 𝔒 4^v. This edition consists of Higgins' and Baldwin's collections ('First' and 'Last Part') together. It is the first edition in which the two parts are really incorporated into one whole, with signatures continuous and a common Table of Contents. It is enlarged from the edition of 1575 by the addition of twenty-three legends to Higgins' part, and seven to Baldwin's, making a total of seventy-four, Sackville's 'Induction' being here for the first time counted as a separate legend.

Sinker 678. BM 814.

A Mirour for Magistrates: being a true chronicle Historie of the vntimely falles of such vnfortunate Princes and men of note, as haue happened since the first entrance of Brute into this Iland, vntill this our latter Age. Newly enlarged with a last part, called A Winter nights Vision, being an addition of such Tragedies, especially famous, as are exempted in the former Historie, with a Poem annexed, called Englands Eliza. *At London Imprinted by Felix Kyngston.* 1610. 4°. (7½ × 5½). R. 1.

Collation: A^8 B^2 C–3K^8 3L^6, paged. Higgins' epistle dated 1586. Address to the reader (by R. Niccols, the editor of this edition). Table of contents. Commendatory verses by Th. Newton. 'The Authors Induction'. Errata. At the end of Higgins' portion is added, at sig. O 5, but without any fresh title or heading, the legends by Thomas Blenerhasset originally published in 1578 as 'The Second Part of the Mirror for Magistrates'. These are signed with the author's name, and stand as legends 41—49 in the Table. The legends of Guidericus and Alured however have been omitted. The legend of Edricus is also omitted in the Table but appears in the text. Baldwin's portion begins at sig. S 6 with a separate titlepage 'The variable Fortunes and vnhappie Falles of such Princes as hath happened since the Conquest', bearing the same imprint except for the date 1609. For Baldwin's address is substituted a note to the reader signed with the editor's initials, R. N. Sackville's

'Induction' is for the first time placed at the beginning instead of immediately before the legend of Buckingham. Four legends (James I, Richard Duke of Gloucester, James IV, and Flodden) are omitted, while at the end is added Drayton's Legend of Cromwell, which had already appeared separately in 1607 and 1609. The editor also added two parts of his own. The first of these begins at sig. 2O 3 with a separate titlepage, 'A Winter Nights Vision....By Richard Niccols, Oxon. Mag. Hall', with the same imprint, dated 1610. This consists of an 'Induction' and ten legends, with a prose address to the reader, and is ornamented with woodcuts. The second begins at sig. 3E 2 with a separate title 'Englands Eliza: or the victorious and triumphant Reigne of that virgin Empresse of sacred memorie, Elizabeth, Queene of England, France and Ireland', &c., with woodcut portrait, again bearing the same imprint, dated 1610. This part contains dedicatory verses to Lady Elizabeth Clere, prose address to the reader, Induction, and the poem itself. This edition, the only one after 1587, was re-issued with a new titlepage 'The Falles of Vnfortunate Princes' in 1619 and again in 1620.

BM 814.

MONTAIGNE, MICHEL DE.

The Essayes or, morall, politike, and militarie Discourses of Lord Michael De Montaigne, Knight Of the noble Order of Saint Michael, and one of the Gentlemen in Ordinary of the French Kings Chamber. Thė Third Edition. Whereunto is now newly added an Index of the principall matters and personages mentioned in this Booke. *London, Printed by M. Flesher, for Rich: Royston, in Ivie-lane next the exchequer office.* MDCXXXII. F°. ($11\frac{1}{8} \times 7\frac{1}{8}$). F. 12.

Collation: A^6, with engraved titlepage inserted after A 1, B–$3G^6$ $3H^8 3I^2$, paged. Explanatory verses on verso of A 1. Engraved titlepage signed Martin Dr[oeshout]. Epistle dedicatory to Anne of Denmark signed by the translator, Iohn Florio (leaf signed A 2). Italian verses to the same signed 'Il Candido' (see Florio, 'World of Words'). Address to the reader signed by the translator. Commendatory verses to Florio signed Sam. Daniel. Verses 'Concerning the honour of bookes'. Table of contents. Author's address to the reader. Titlepage on A 6, *i.e.* the second half of the sheet containing the verses preceding engraved title. Books ii and iii have separate titlepages, the former with imprint 'London, Printed by Miles Flesher, 1631', the latter 'London, Printed in the yeare M DC XXXI.'. At the end, alphabetical table of contents. In the present copy sheet A is so arranged that the printed titlepage immediately follows the engraved, an arrangement which may be correct, but which necessitates binding the outer and two inner sheets of the quire separately. The arrangement proposed above is found in another copy in the Library (T. 11. 34).

BM 1108.

MONTEMAYOR, Jorge de.

Diana of George of Montemayor: Translated out of Spanish into English by Bartholomew Yong of the Middle Temple Gentleman. *At London, Printed by Edm. Bollifant, Impensis G. B.* 1598. F°. (11 × 7¼). F. 11.

Title within woodcut border. Collation: a^4A–$2R^6 2S^8$, paged. Epistle dedicatory to Lady Rich, signed by the translator and dated High Onger in Essex, Nov. 28, 1598. Preface signed B. Y. Author's epistle dedicatory to Iuan de Castella. Verses to the same. Commendatory verses to the author from Gaspar Romani and Hieronymo Sant-Perez. Argument and text of the first seven books. The second part begins on O 3 with head-title 'The first Booke of the second Part of Diana of George of Montemayor. Written by Alonso Perez.' Text of the eight books. The third part begins on 2I 2^v with head-title 'The first Part of Enamoured Diana made by Gaspar Gil Polo'. Epistle dedicatory from the author to 'Doña Maria de Austria y fuentes', dated, Valencia, Feb. 9, 1564. Text of the five books. At the end is the note 'All these three Partes were finished the first of May 1583. Boto el amor en Yugo', followed by errata.

Sinker 689. BM 1109.

MORE, Cresacre.

D.O.M.S. The Life and Death of Sir Thomas Moore Lord high Chancellour of England. Written by M.T.M. and dedicated to the Queens most gracious Maiestie.

4°. (7¾ × 5⅞). Q. 2.

Collation: ✠^{4}A–$3H^4$, paged. Wanting V 4, supplied in MS. The epistle dedicatory to Henrietta Maria is signed M.C.M.E. (*i.e.* Magister Cresacre More Eboracensis?). The initials on the titlepage refer to 'Mr. Thomas More', the great-grandson of Sir Thomas, but it is more probably the work of his younger brother Cresacre. The book was probably printed at Louvain in 1631. On the titlepage some biographical details concerning Thomas More are entered in an old hand.

BM 1042.

MORE, *Sir* THOMAS.

The Life and Death of Sir Thomas Moore. *See* MORE, Cresacre.

The workes of Sir Thomas More Knyght, sometyme Lorde Chauncellour of England, wrytten by him in the Englysh tonge. *Printed at London at the costes and charges of Iohn Cawod, Iohn Waly, and Richarde Tottell. Anno* . 1557 . [Colophon] *Imprinted at London in Fletestrete at the sygne of the hande and starre, at the coste and charge of Iohn Cawod, Iohn Walley, and Richarde Tottle. Finished in Apryll, the yere of our Lorde God* . 1557 . *Cum priuilegio ad imprimendum solum.* **B. L.** F°. ($11\frac{1}{4} \times 7\frac{3}{8}$). F. 3.

Title within woodcut border. Collation: ❡^{10}[2]❡^{8}a–f^{8} (f2–4 are signed f.g. ii–iiii) h–2z^{8} A–2C^{8}, with one leaf signed ☛ inserted after 2C 5, 2D–2Y^{8} 2Z^{6}, paged. Wanting ❡ 10 and 2Z^{6} (? blank). Double columns. Epistle dedicatory by the editor, 'Wyllyam Rastell, seriant at lawe' to Queen Mary. Table of contents. Alphabetical table collected by Thomas Paynell. The preliminary quire of eight leaves signed [2]❡ contains More's early poems, the remainder of the volume his prose works. The inserted leaf in sig. 2C contains an addition addressed to the reader printed on recto only.

Sinker 221. BM 1111.

A fruteful / and pleasaunt worke of the beste state of a publyque weale, and of the newe yle called Vtopia: written in Latine by Syr Thomas More knyght, and translated into Englyshe by Raphe Robynson Citizein and Goldsmythe of London, at the procurement, and earnest request of George Tadlowe Citezein & Haberdassher of the same Citie. *Imprinted at London by Abraham Vele, dwelling in Pauls churcheyarde at the sygne of the Lambe. Anno.* 1551.

B. L. 8°. ($5\frac{1}{2} \times 3\frac{5}{8}$). Z. 8.

Collation: +^{8}A^{4}B–R^{8}S^{4}, unpaged. Epistle dedicatory to William Cecylle from the translator. Another from Sir Thomas More to Peter Giles. First edition of Robinson's translation.

Sinker 289. BM 1112.

MUCEDORUS.

A Most pleasant Comedie of Mucedorus the Kings sonne of Valentia, and Amadine the Kings daughter of Aragon. With the merry conceits of Mouse. Amplified with new additions, as it was acted before the Kings Maiestie at White-hall on Shroue-sunday night. By his Highnes Seruantes vsually playing at the Globe. Very delectable, and full of conceited Mirth. *Imprinted at London for William Iones, dwelling neare Holborne Conduit at the signe of the Gunne.* 1610. 4°. (7 × 5). S. 30. 3.

Collation: A–F[4], unpaged. Wanting F 4 (? blank). Prologue. Personae. The first edition appeared in 1598 and it was frequently reprinted. Altogether there are sixteen known editions besides two doubtful (not included in the numbers given below). The second appeared in 1606. The present edition was the third and in it the additions first appeared (unless they were included in the doubtful edition of 1609).

BM 1121.

[Another edition.] 4°. (7¼ × 5½). R. 23. 7.

Collation: A–F[4], unpaged. Wanting A 1 containing titlepage and F 4 (? blank). Prologue. Personae. This does not agree with any other accessible edition. The fourth to tenth editions appeared in 1611, 1613, 1615, 1619, 1621, 1626, and 1631 respectively (with a doubtful edition in 1618). A comparison of the texts shows the present to be the eleventh edition, having appeared between those of 1631 and 1634. It is therefore probably that of 1629 mentioned in the 'Biographia Dramatica'.

A Most pleasant Comedy of Mucedorus the Kings Sonne of Valentia, and Amadine the Kings Daughter of Aragon. With the merry conceits of Mouse. Amplified with new Additions, as it was acted before the Kings Majestie at Whitehall, on Shrove-sunday night By his Highnesse servants usually playing at the Globe. Very delectable and full of conceited mirth. *London, Printed for John Wright, and are to be sold at his shop, at the signe of the Bible in Giltspurre-Street without Newgate.* 1639. 4°. (6⅞ × 5). T. 7. 4.

Collation: A–F[4], unpaged. Wanting F 4 (? blank). Prologue. Personae. Thirteenth edition, the twelfth having appeared in 1634.

A Most pleasant Comedy of Mucedorus the Kings Son of Valentia, and Amadine the Kings Daughter of Aragon. With the merry conceits of Mouse. Amplified with new Additions, as it was acted before the Kings Majestie at Whitehall, on Shrove-sunday night. By his Highness servants usually playing at the Globe. Very delectable and full of conceited mirth. *London, Printed for Francis Coles, and are to be sold at his shop, at the half Bowl in the Old Bayley.*

4°. ($6\frac{3}{4} \times 4\frac{7}{8}$). T. 8. 6.

Collation: A–F⁴, unpaged. Wanting F 4 (? blank). Prologue. Personae. Fourteenth edition, having appeared between those of 1639 and 1663.

A Most pleasant Comedy of Mucedorus The King's Son of Valentia, and Amadine the King's Daughter of Aragon. With the merry Conceits of Mouse. Amplifyed with new Additions, as it was Acted before the King's Majestie at White-hall on Shrove-sunday night. By His Highness's Servants usually playing at the Globe. Very delectable and full of conceited Mirth. *London, Printed by E. O. for Francis Coles, and are to be Sold at his Shop in Wine-street near Hatton-gardens.* 1668. 4°. ($6\frac{3}{4} \times 5$). T. 9. 5.

Collation: A–F⁴, unpaged. Prologue. Personae. Advertisement of books at the end. Sixteenth edition, the fifteenth having appeared in 1663.

MUSÆUS.

Hero And Leander: Begun by Christopher Marloe, and finished by George Chapman. Vt Nectar, Ingenium. *London: Printed by N. Okes for William Leake, and are to be sold at his shop in Chancery-lane neere the Roules.* 1637.

4°. (8×6). P. 2. 3.

Collation: A–K⁴, unpaged. Epistle dedicatory to Sir Thomas Walsingham signed E. B. (*i.e.* Edward Blount, the bookseller, who published the first edition in 1598).

BM 1062.

NORTH, *Sir* THOMAS.

The Dial of Princes.... 1582. *See* GUEVARA, Antonio de.

The Lives of the noble Grecians and Romanes.... 1579 [and subsequent editions]. *See* PLUTARCH.

OVERBURY, *Sir* THOMAS.

A Wife, now a Widowe. *London, Imprinted for Laurence L'isle dwelling at the Tygres head in Pauls Church-yard.* 1614. 8°. ($5\frac{3}{4} \times 3\frac{5}{8}$). Z. 3. 2.

Collation: A–D[8], unpaged. Ornament at head and foot of each page. Commendatory verses signed: I. F., D. T., C. R., W: Stra:, I. C., X. Z. 'The Authors Epitaph on the finishing of this his wife.' This is the first edition, and is anonymous.

A Wife. Now the Widdow of Sir Tho: Overburye. Being A most exquisite and singular Poem of the choise of a Wife. Whereunto are added many witty Characters, and conceited Newes, written by himselfe and other learned Gentlemen his friends:

Dignum laude virum musa vetat mori,
Cœlo musa beat. Hor: car: lib. 3.

The fourth Impression, enlarged with more Characters, than any of the former Editions. *London Printed by G. Eld, for Lawrence Lisle, and are to be sold in Paules Church-yard, at the Tygers head.* 1614. 4°. (7×5). S. 36. 6.

Collation: A–H[4], unpaged. Printer's address to the reader, dated May 16, 1614. Commendatory verses signed: I. S. Lincolniensis, G. R., T. B., X. Z. 'Of the choise of a Wife', verses, unsigned. 'A Wife' with 'The Authors Epitaph' at the end. 'Characters' in prose, with 'The Character of a happie life' in verse by H. W. (*i.e.* Sir Henry Wotton). 'Newes, from any whence' in prose, most of the items signed with initials: Sr. T. O., Sr. T. R., I. D., A. S., W. S., R. B., M[ris]. B., I. C., R. S. No less than five editions of the work were published in 1614, the present, as stated on the titlepage, being the fourth. It is doubtful whether the 'Characters', which first appeared in the second edition, are by Overbury.

Sir Thomas Ouerbury his Wife. With addition of many new Elegies vpon his vntimely and much lamented death. As Also New Newes, and diuers more Characters, (neuer before annexed) written by himselfe and other learned Gentlemen. The ninth impression augmented. *London, Printed by Edward Griffin for Laurence L'isle, and are to be sold at his shop at the Tigers head in Paules Churchyard.* 1616. 8°. ($5\frac{1}{4} \times 3\frac{3}{8}$). *. 6.

The author's name is within an ornament. Collation: ¶[8]2¶[8] A–R[8]S[4], unpaged. S4 blank. Wanting ¶1 (? blank). Sheet 2¶ is erroneously placed after sheet A. Address to the reader signed by the stationer. Commendatory and memorial verses, signed: D. T., C. B., W. S., W. B. Int: Temp., B. G. medij Temp., Cap: Tho: Gainsford, Io: Fo:, R. Ca., E. G., F. H., R. C., I. F. (two copies), D. T. (two copies), X. Z., (one copy unsigned), G. R., W: Stra:, 'Of the choyce of a Wife' (unsigned), P. B. medij Temp., (three copies unsigned), I. M. Elegy on William Howard, Baron Effingham. Elegy on Lady Rutland (usually ascribed to Francis Beaumont). 'A Wife' in verse, with ornaments at head and foot of page; followed by Characters in prose (including 'The Character of a happy life. By Sir H. W[otton]' in verse), 'Certaine Edicts from a Parliament in Eutopia; Written by the Lady Southwell', 'Newes from any whence', and more 'Characters'. There were two editions this year, both styled the ninth on the titlepage.

BM 1172.

OVIDIUS NASO, Publius.

The Heroycall Epistles of the Learned Poet Publius Ouidius Naso, In English Verse: set out and translated by George Turberuile Gent. with Aulus Sabinus Aunsweres to certaine of the same. *Anno Domini* 1567. *Imprinted at London, by Henry Denham.* 8°. ($5\frac{5}{8} \times 3\frac{3}{4}$). Z. 6.

Collation: *A*[8]A–V[8]X[4], folios numbered. Wanting *A* 1 and X4 (? blank). Epistle dedicatory to Thomas Howard, Viscount Byndon, signed by the translator. Verses, 'The Translator to his Muse'. Address to the reader, signed. 'Epistles', each preceded by a verse Argument. The answers are translated from Angelus, not Aulus, Sabinus. At the end are verses headed 'The Translator to the captious sort of Sycophants'. First edition.

Sinker 333. BM 1173.

Ouidius Naso his Remedie of Loue. Translated and Intituled to the Youth of England.

Plautus in Trinummo.
......Mille modis Amor
Ignorandu'st, procul adhibendus est, atq; abstinendus.
Nam qui in Amore precipitauit, peius perit, quam si saxo saliat.

London Printed by T. C. for Iohn Browne, and are to be sold at his shop in Fleetstreet, at the signe of the Bible. 1600.

4°. ($7\frac{3}{8} \times 5\frac{1}{4}$). Q. 14. 2.

Collation: A–H4, unpaged. Wanting H 4 (? blank). Epistle dedicatory to M. I., signed by the translator, F. L. The 'Remedy of Love' is followed by a translation of Ovid's epistle of Dido to Æneas and an answer from Æneas to Dido. An earlier edition had, according to Lowndes, appeared in 1599.

Sinker 658.

PAINTER, WILLIAM.

⌜The Palace of Pleasure Beautified, adorned and wel furnished with Pleasaunt Historyes and excellent Nouelles, selected out of diuers good and commendable Authours. By William Painter Clarke of the Ordinaunce and Armarie. 1569. *Imprinted at London in Fletestreate neare to S. Dunstones Church by Thomas Marshe.*⌟

B. L. 4°. ($7\frac{3}{8} \times 5\frac{1}{2}$). R. 5.

Title within woodcut border. Collation: ¶4[2]¶8A–2K8, folios numbered. Wanting all before B 2 and after 2I 6. This is the second edition of the first volume, the first having appeared in 1566.

Sinker 316.

The second Tome of the Palace of Pleasure contayning store of goodlye Histories, Tragical matters, & other Morall argumentes, very requisite for delight and profyte. Chosē and selected out of diuers good and commendable Authors, and now once agayn corrected and encreased. By Wiliam Painter, Clerke of the Ordinance and Armarie *Imprinted at London In Fleatstrete by Thomas. Marshe.*

B. L. 4°. ($6\frac{7}{8} \times 5\frac{1}{2}$). U. 2.

Title within woodcut border. Collation: A8A–2P82T4, folios numbered. Wanting A 1 (? blank), C 2–7, T 1 and 8. Epistle dedicatory to Sir George Howard, signed and dated 'From my pore house besides the Towre of London', Nov. 4, 1567. Address to the reader. List of sources. Table of contents at end. This is the second edition of the second volume, and was printed about 1580, the first having appeared in 1567.

Sinker 323. BM 1188.

PARABOSCO, Girolamo.

Del[le Lettere] Amoros[e di M. Giro]lamo Pa[rabosco] Libro se[condo con] alcune [sue nouel]le e[t rime.] Con priu[i]legio. *In Vinegia per Pauolo Gherardo* M.D.XLVIII. [Colophon] *In Vinegia per Comin da Trino di Monferrato.* M.D.XLVIII. 8°. ($5\frac{1}{2} \times 3\frac{3}{4}$). Z. 7. 2.

Collation: A^4B–G^8, folios numbered. Epistle dedicatory to Gianpaulo Rizzo, signed Girolamo Parabosco, and dated 'Di Vinegia alli XXII de Agosto del XXXVIII.'. This is the first edition of the second book. The original 'Lettere Amorose' appeared in 1545. Altogether four books appeared, which were first printed together in 1558.

PASQUIL, *pseud.*

Pasquils Iests: with the Merriments of Mother Bunch. Wittie, pleasant, and delightfull. *London: Printed by M. F. and are to be sold by Andrew Kembe, dwelling at Saint Margarets hill in Southwarke.* 1635.

B. L. 4°. ($7\frac{3}{4} \times 5\frac{7}{8}$). Q. 8. 1.

Collation: A–H^4, unpaged. Wanting H 4 (? blank). On verso of titlepage is the note 'Read the Epistle, or reade nothing' within small woodcut titlepage border. Address to the reader. Verses. The first edition appeared in 1604, the present being apparently the fifth.

PEELE, George.

The Araygnement of Paris A Pastorall. Presented before the Queenes Maiestie, by the Children of her Chappell. *Imprinted at London by Henrie Marsh. Anno.* 1584.

4°. ($6\frac{7}{8} \times 5\frac{1}{8}$). T. 7. 3.

Collation: A–E^4, unpaged. Prologue. Epilogue at end. The play is ascribed to Peele in Nash's preface to R. Green's 'Menaphon' of 1589.

BM 1194. Sinker 677.

Merrie Conceited Iests, of George Peel Gentleman, sometimes student in Oxford. Wherein is shewed the course of his life, how he lived: a man very well known in the City of London, and elsewhere.

Buy, read, and judge,
The price do not grudge:
It will do thee more pleasure,
Then twice so much treasnre [*sic*].

London, Printed for Wiliiam [sic] *Gilbertson, at the Bible in Giltspur-street without New-gate.* 1657.

B. L. 4°. ($7\frac{1}{8} \times 5\frac{1}{8}$). S. 29. 2.

Collation: A–C[4], paged. The first edition of these probably apocryphal jests appeared in 1607: the present appears to be the fourth.

PERCYVALL, Richard.

A Dictionarie in Spanish and English, first published into the English tongue by Ric. Perciuale Gent. Now enlarged and amplified With many thousand words,......... All done by Iohn Minsheu Professor of Languages in London. Hereunto for the further profite and pleasure of the learner or delighted in this tongue, is annexed an ample English Dictionarie, Alphabetically set downe with the Spanish words thereunto adioyned,......... *Imprinted at London, by Edm. Bollifant.* 1599 F°. ($11 \times 7\frac{1}{4}$). F. 10. 1.

Collation: A[6], with one sheet signed on first leaf A 2 inserted after A 1, B–2K[6], paged. (This, and not A[2]A[6], is the correct description of the preliminary matter.) Three columns on a page. Title on A 1. The inserted sheet contains, epistle dedicatory to Sir John Scot, Sir Henry Bromley, Sir Edward Grevel, and Master William Fortescue, signed Iohn Minsheu, and an address to the reader, signed by the same. On the original A 2 begins 'Directions for the understanding the vse of this Dictionary', signed Iohn Minshew. The Spanish-English part begins on A 3, the English-Spanish on Y 1 each with head-title. Percyvall's original work 'Bibliotheca Hispanica. Containing a Grammar with a Dictionarie in Spanish, English and Latine' appeared in 1591. The present work and the grammar that follows no doubt formed one publication, though they are bibliographically distinct. They are the first edition of Minsheu's revision.

Sinker 691. BM 1216.

A Spanish Grammar, first collected and published by Richard Perciuale Gent. Now augmented and increased with the declining of all the Irregular and hard verbes in that toong...... Done by Iohn Minsheu Professor of Languages in London. Hereunto for the yoong beginners learning and ease, are annexed Speeches, Phrases, and Prouerbes, expounded out of diuers Authors,...... Virescit vulnere Virtus. *Imprinted at London, by Edm. Bollifant.* 1599

F°. ($11 \times 7\frac{1}{4}$). F. 10. 2.

Collation: $a^4 b–h^6 i^2 k–o^6 p^2$, paged. (a 2 is misprinted i 2, and the quire is otherwise unsigned. Sheet i is also unsigned.) Epistle dedicatory to the students of Gray's Inn, signed Iohn Minsheu. Address to the reader signed by the same. Latin commendatory verses to Minsheu by Iohannes Keperus. 'Soneto de un capitan Español del Autór'. Proeme. The 'Pleasant and Delightfull Dialogues in Spanish and English' begin with special titlepage (with same imprint) and fresh pagination at sig. i 1. Epistle dedicatory in Spanish to 'Don Eduardo Hobby', signed Iohn Minsheu. Enlarged by Minsheu from the original work by Percyvall, as preceding entry.

Sinker 692. BM 1216.

PHAER, THOMAS.

The .xiii. Bookes of Æneidos... 1584. *See* VERGILIUS MARO, Publius.

PLUTARCH.

The Lives of the noble Grecians and Romanes, compared together by that graue learned Philosopher and Historiographer, Plutarke of Chæronea: Translated out of Greeke into French by Iames Amyot, Abbot of Bellozane, Bishop of Auxerre, one of the Kings priuy counsel, and great Amner of Fraunce, and out of French into Englishe, by Thomas North. *Imprinted at London by Thomas Vautroullier dwelling in the Blacke Friers by Ludgate.* 1579.

F°. ($12\frac{3}{8} \times 8\frac{1}{4}$). B. 9.

Collation: $*^8 A–5F^6$, paged. Wanting * 1 (? blank). (Sigs. * 3–5 are misprinted * ij–iiij.) Epistle dedicatory to Queen Elizabeth, signed Thomas North, and dated Jan. 16, 1579. Address to the reader, signed by the same and dated Jan. 24, 1579. Amyot's address to the reader. Table of contents. B 2v and B 5r have been left blank in the printing. First edition. Some copies have the imprint, 'Imprinted at London by Thomas Vautroullier and Iohn Wight'.

Sinker 481. BM 1243 (Wight).

The Lives of the noble Grecians and Romaines, compared together by that graue learned Philosopher and Historiographer Plutarke of Chæronea: Translated out of Greeke into French by Iames Amiot Abbot of Bellozane, Bishop of Auxerre, one of the Kings priuie Counsell, and great Almner of France: With the liues of Hannibal and Scipio African: translated out of Latine into French by Charles de l'Escluse, and out of French into English, By Sir Thomas North Knight. Hereunto are also added the liues of Epaminondas, of Philip of Macedon, of Dionysius the elder, tyrant of Sicilia, of Augustus Cæsar, of Plutarke, and of Seneca: with the liues of nine other excellent Chieftaines of warre: collected out of Æmylius Probus, by S. G. S. and Englished by the aforesaid Translator. *London, Printed by Richard Field.* 1612. F°. ($12\frac{3}{4} \times 8\frac{3}{8}$). B. 5.

Collation: A8 B–5O6 5P8, paged. Wanting A 1 (? blank). Epistle dedicatory to Queen Elizabeth, signed Thomas North. Address to the reader signed by the same. Amyot's address to the reader. Table of Lives. There is a medallion portrait to each life. The additional lives have a separate titlepage, dated 1610, at sig. 5B 1, followed by Epistle dedicatory to Queen Elizabeth, signed Thomas North. Alphabetical table at end. The additional lives first appeared in the third edition, in 1603. They were translated into French, not from Probus but from C. Nepos. The initials S. G. S. stand for Simon Goulart Senlisien. Fourth edition.

BM 1244.

The Philosophie, commonlie called, the Morals written by the learned Philosopher Plutarch of Chæronea. Translated out of Greeke into English, and conferred with the Latine translations and the French, by Philemon Holland of Coventrie, Doctor in Physicke. Whereunto are annexed the Summaries necessary to be read before every Treatise. *At London Printed by Arnold Hatfield.* 1603

F°. ($12\frac{5}{8} \times 8\frac{3}{8}$). B. 6.

Collation: ¶^{4}A–5Z^{6}6A–6E^{4}6F^6, paged. Epistle dedicatory to King James, signed Philémon Holland. Table of contents. At the end glossary of obscure terms, alphabetical index and list of errata. First edition.

BM 1243.

PORTO, Luigi da.

Historia nuouamente ritrouata, di due nobili amanti, Con la loro pietosa morte: Interuenuta già nella Città di Verona. Nel tempo del Signor Bartolomeo della Scala. Nuouamente stampata. *In Venetia Per Giouan. Griffio.* [Colophon adds date:] M. D. LIII. 8°. (6 × 4). X. 4. 1.

Collation: A–E^4, folios numbered. Epistle dedicatory to Lucina Savorgana. Introduction. 'Narratione della Historia.' The last leaf is blank except for the printer's device on the verso. Da Porta's 'historia' is supposed to have been the source of Bandello's 'novella' of Romeo and Juliet. It may in its turn have been founded on a tale of Massuccio. The earliest edition is undated, and there was another in 1536 before the present one.

PUTTENHAM, George.

The Arte of English Poesie. Contriued into three Bookes: The first of Poets and Poesie, the second of Proportion, the third of Ornament. *At London Printed by Richard Field, dwelling in the black-Friers, neere Ludgate.* 1589.
4°. (7¼ × 5⅛). R. 14.

Collation: AB^{4}C–H^{4}I^{2}K–2L^{4}2M^2, paged. Wanting AB 1 and 2M 2 (? blank). Epistle dedicatory to William Cecill, Lord of Burghley, signed R. F. (*i.e.* Richard Field) and dated May 28, 1589. Woodcut portrait of Q. Elizabeth with the legend 'A colei Che se stessa rassomiglia & non altrui'. The further legend 'Elizabetha D. G. Regina' is impressed in blind round the head. Table of contents at end. Attributed to George Puttenham. One copy in the BM differs from all others known in having an extra sheet signed i–iiii inserted between sheets N and O, the setting of the adjoining pages being rearranged to connect with the insertion.

Sinker 736. BM 581.

RALEIGH, *Sir* WALTER.

The Historie of the World. In five bookes. 1 Intreating of the Beginning and first Ages of the same, from the Creation unto Abraham. 2 Of the Times from the Birth of Abraham, to the destruction of the Temple of Salomon. 3 From the destruction of Jerusalem, to the time of Philip of Macedon. 4 From the Reigne of Philip of Macedon, to the establishing of that Kingdome, in the Race of Antigonus. 5 From the settled rule of Alexanders Successors in the East, untill the Romans (prevailing over all) made Conquest of Asia and Macedon. By Sir Walter Ralegh, Knight. [Portrait.] [Colophon] *London, Printed for G. Latham, and R. Young.* M.DC.XXXIV. F°. ($13\frac{1}{8} \times 8\frac{3}{4}$). B. 1.

Collation: 3 leaves unsigned, A–$B^6C^4a^6b^8$; A–$V^6$2A–2$V^6$3A–3V^6 4A–4$V^6$5A–5Z^6; $(a)^6(aa)^6(*)^6(**)^8$, paged. The three preliminary leaves contain verses headed 'The Mind of the Front,' engraved titlepage, signed Ren. Elstrack, with imprint 'At London Printed for Walter Burre. 1614', and printed titlepage with engraved portrait of the author signed Sim: Pass. Preface. Table of contents. Several two-page engraved maps and plans inserted. At the end, address to the reader, chronological tables, alphabetical table to Books i and ii, and to Books iii–v. The first edition appeared in 1614, and the engraved titlepage was used in several subsequent ones. There were at least two before the present.

BM 1284.

RETURN FROM PARNASSUS.

The Returne from Pernassus: Or The Scourge of Simony. Publiquely acted by the Students in Saint Iohns Colledge in Cambridge. *At London Printed by G. Eld, for Iohn Wri[ght,] and are to bee sold at his [shop at] Christ church [Gate.]* 1606. 4°. ($6\frac{7}{8} \times 5$). S. 33. 1.

Collation: A–H^4I^2, unpaged. Prologue. Personae. Wanting I 1, supplied in MS., and I 2 (? blank). Two editions appeared this year, having identical titlepages. The present is presumably the earlier.

The Returne From Pernassus :.... *At London Printed by G. Eld, for Iohn Wright, and are to bee sold at his shop at Christ church Gate.* [1606.] 4°. ($6\frac{3}{4} \times 5$). T. 9. 4.

Titlepage identical with the above, having been printed from the same setting up of the type. The date has been erased. Collation: A–H[4], unpaged. Prologue. Personae.

BM 1198.

ROBERTS, John.

An Answer to Mr. Pope's Preface To Shakespear. In a Letter to a Friend. Being a Vindication of the Old Actors who were the Publishers and Performers of that Author's Plays. Whereby The Errors of their Edition are further accounted for, and some Memoirs of Shakespear and Stage-History of His Time are inserted, which were never before collected and publish'd By a Stroling Player.

Say from what Cause (by all condemn'd and curst!)
Still Bays the Second rails like Bays the First!

Right Reading of the Dunciad Variorum from a Manuscript (revised and collated by this Author) which is interpolated by the last Editor.

London: Printed in the Year MDCCXXIX.

8°. ($7\frac{1}{4} \times 4\frac{3}{4}$). S. 28. 5.

The letter is signed Anti-Scriblerus Histrionicus. The Author was John Roberts.

ROBINSON, Ralph.

A fruteful / and pleasaunt worke...called Vtopia.... 1551. *See* More, *Sir* Thomas.

ROWLAND, David.

The plesant Historie of Lazarillo de Tormes.... 1596. *See* Lazarillo de Tormes.

ROWLANDS, Samuel.

A Fooles Bolt is soone shott. [Woodcut.] *Imprinted at London for George Loftus, and are to be sold at the signe of the White Horse at the Steps of the North doore of Paules.* 1614.

4°. (7 × 5). S. 33. 6.

Collation: A–E^4, unpaged. Ornament at foot of each page. Verse 'Epistle', signed S. R. (*i.e.* Samuel Rowlands).

ROWLEY, William.

The Birth of Merlin: or, The Childe hath found his Father. As it hath been several times Acted with great Applause. Written by William Shakespear, and William Rowley. Placere cupio. *London: Printed by Tho. Johnson for Francis Kirkman, and Henry Marsh, and are to be sold at the Princes Arms in Chancery-Lane.* 1662.

4°. (7⅛ × 5¼). R. 23. 6.

Collation: A–G^4, unpaged. Personae.

SACCHETTI, Franco.

Delle Novelle di Franco Sacchetti Cittadino Fiorentino Parte Prima. [Parte Seconda.] *In Firenze* .M.D.CC.XXIV.

2 vols. 8°. (8 × 5). P. 3–4.

The first and second editions both appeared in this year.

SALVIANUS, Massiliensis.

A second and third blast of retrait from plaies and Theaters: the one whereof was sounded by a reuerend Byshop dead long since; the other by a worshipful and zealous Gentleman now aliue: one showing the filthines of plaies in times past; the other the abhomination of Theaters in the time present: both expresly prouing that that Common-weale is nigh vnto the cursse of God, wherein either plaiers be made of, or Theaters maintained. Set forth by Anglo-phile Eutheo. Ephes . 5, verse . 15, 16. Take heede therefore that ye walke circumspectlie, not as vnwise, but as wise, redeeming the time, because the daies are euil. Allowed by auctoritie. 1580. [Colophon] 1580 *Imprinted at London* *by Henrie Denham, dwelling in Pater noster Row, at the signe of the Starre, being the assigne of William Seres. Cum priuilegio Regiæ Maiestatis.* 8°. ($5\frac{1}{8} \times 3\frac{3}{8}$). *. 15. 2.

Collation: A–I⁸, paged. Wanting A 2–7 (containing address to the reader and first leaf of text), and I 8 (? blank). The verso of title is occupied by the arms of the City of London. Address to the reader. The 'Third Blast' begins with head-title on sig. D 3. The 'Second Blast' is translated from the sixth book of the 'De Gubernatione Dei' of Salvianus, who wrote in the fifth century. The present work was intended as a continuation of Stephen Gosson's 'School of Abuse'.

Sinker 341. BM 1350.

SANDFORD, James.

The Garden of Pleasure: Contayninge most pleasante Tales, worthy deedes and witty sayings of noble Princes & learned Philosophers, Moralized. No lesse delectable, than profitable. Done out of Italian into English, by Iames Sanford, Gent. Wherein are also set forth diuers Verses and Sentences in Italian, with the Englishe to the same, for the benefit of students in both tongs. *Imprinted at London, by Henry Bynneman. Anno* . 1573. [Colophon] *Imprinted at London by Henry Bynneman, dwelling in Knight riders streate, at the signe of the Mermayde. Anno* . 1573. *And are to be sold at his shop at the Northwest dore of Poules Church.* B. L. 8°. ($5\frac{3}{8} \times 3\frac{5}{8}$). *. 13.

Collation: $A^4B–P^8$, folios numbered. Wanting B 6. The verso of the title is occupied by two heraldic woodcuts. The upper one, with the date 1573, is the Dudley crest charged with a crescent of difference within garter of the order, for Robert, Earl of Leicester. (The crescent has been added since the same block was used in Turberville's 'Epitaphs' etc. in 1570.) The lower with a Greek motto displays, according to Herbert (p. 973), the arms of the author. Verses to Leicester in Greek, Latin, Italian, French, and English. Epistle dedicatory to Leicester, signed. Address to the reader. At sig. O 5^v begins the collection of 'Certain Italian Prouerbes'. There was a later edition of the work in 1576 under the title of 'Hours of Recreation'. According to the author's statement the work is gathered out of a number of Italian writers.

Sinker 282. BM 1354.

SANDYS, George.

Sandys Travels, containing an History of the Original and present State of the Turkish Empire: Their Laws, Government, Policy, Military Force, Courts of Justice, and Commerce. The Mahometan Religion and Ceremonies: A Description of Constantinople, The Grand Signor's Seraglio, and his manner of living: Also, Of Greece, With the Religion and Customs of the Grecians. Of Ægypt; the Antiquity, Hieroglyphicks, Rites, Customs, Discipline, and Religion of the Ægyptians. A Voyage on the River Nylus: Of Armenia, Grand Cairo, Rhodes, the Pyramides, Colossus; The former flourishing and present State of Alexandria. A Description of the Holy-Land; of the Jews, and several Sects of Christians living there; of Jerusalem, Sepulchre of Christ, Temple of Solomon; and what else either of Antiquity, or worth observation. Lastly, Italy described, and the Islands adjoining; as Cyprus, Crete, Malta, Sicilia, the Æolian Islands; Of Rome, Venice, Naples, Syracusa, Mesena, Ætna, Scylla, and Charybdis; and other places of Note. Illustrated with Fifty Graven Maps and Figures. The Seventh Edition. *London, Printed for John Williams Junior, at the Crown in Little-Britain.* 1673. F°. ($12\frac{5}{8} \times 7\frac{7}{8}$). B. 7.

Collation: $A^4 B\text{-}X^6$, paged. Two-page engraved map inserted after sig. A, and a folding plate at sig. D 1. Engraved plates in the text. Wanting A 4 (? blank). Engraved title with imprint 'London, Printed for Philip Chetwin 1670' preceding printed title. Epistle dedicatory 'To the Prince' (afterwards Charles I), signed George Sandys. The text in four books. Originally published in 1615 under the title 'A Relation of a Iourney begun An: Dom: 1610'. The edition of 1652 is said on the titlepage to be the fifth, but it appears to be at least the sixth. The present is probably the eighth.

SANSOVINO, Francesco.

Cento Nouelle Scelte da piu nobili Scrittori della Lingua Volgare, di Francesco Sansovino, nelle quali piaceuoli & notabili auuenimenti si contingono: Di nuouo riformate, riuedute, & corrette, Con licentia de' Superiori, & aggiuntoui nouamente le Figure in principio d' ogni Nouella. Al Magnifico, & Eccellente Signore, & Padron Collendissimo Il Sig. Girolamo Rossetti. *Con Priuilegio. In Venetia,* M.D C III. *Appresso Alessandro de Vecchi.*

4°. (7½ × 5½). Q. 4.

Collation: †^{6}A–2E^{8}2F^{4}, paged. Printer's epistle to Rossetti, dated May 10, 1603. Table of contents. This is the only edition having the verses at the end of each novel. There are woodcuts to each novel (often repeated) and also to each 'Giornata'. The first edition of this collection appeared in 1561.

Del Secretario di M. Francesco Sansouino libri quattro. Ne quali con bell' ordine s' insegna altrui a scriuer lettere messiue & responsiue in tutti i generi, come nella Tauola contrascritta si comprende. Con gli essempi delle lettere formate et poste a lor luoghi in diuerse materie con le parti segnate. Et con uarie lettere di Principi a piu persone, scritte da diuersi Secretarii in piu occasioni, e in diuersi tempi. Con priuilegio. *In Venetia, Appresso Francesco Rampazetto.* 1565. 8°. (5½ × 3¾). Z. 7. 1.

Collation: *^{8}A–O^{8}, folios numbered. O 7 blank. Wanting O 8 (? blank). Epistle dedicatory by Sansovino to Ottaviano Valiero, 'Podestà & Capitano di Feltre', dated Venice, March 1, 1564. Table of contents. Classified table 'de generi delle lettere'. The first edition appeared the previous year.

SAVIOLO, VICENTIO.

Vincentio Sauiolo his Practise. In two Bookes. The first intreating of the vse of the Rapier and Dagger. The second, of Honor and honorable Quarrels. *London Printed by Iohn Wolfe.* 1595. 4°. (7½ × 5½). R. 1^{B}.

Collation: A–H^{4}❧–3❧^{4}I–2G^{4}¶^{2}2H–2M^{4}, unpaged. 2M 4 blank. Wanting A 1 (? blank). The first paragraph on ❧ 1 is repeated on I 1, the three sheets signed 1–3❧ having been inserted after printing off to repair the omission of 'The first dayes Discourse, concerning the Rapier and Dagger'; so also the catchword on 2G 4^{v} refers to

2H 1, the half-sheet signed ¶ being an insertion 'Of the Duello or Combat' at the head of which is the note to the binder 'This is to be placed before the first chapter of Satisfaction'. On K 3 and again on ¶ 2v occurs a fine device or emblem with motto '✠ O wormes meate: O froath: O vanitie: Why art thou so insolent'. Epistle dedicatory to Robert, Earl of Essex and Ewe, signed by the author. Address to the reader. The second book has a separate titlepage at sig. O 1, with same imprint but for date 1594. Preface. Woodcuts in the first part.

Sinker 609. BM 1358.

SCOT, REGINALD.

The discouerie of witchcraft, Wherein the lewde dealing of witches and witchmongers is notablie detected, the knauerie of coniurors, the impietie of inchantors, the follie of soothsaiers, the impudent falshood of cousenors, the infidelitie of atheists, the pestilent practises of Pythonists, the curiositie of figurecasters, the vanitie of dreamers, the beggerlie art of Alcumystrie, The abhomination of idolatrie, the horrible art of poisoning, the vertue and power of naturall magike, and all the conueiances of Legierdemaine and iuggling are deciphered: and many other things opened, which haue long lien hidden, howbeit verie necessarie to be knowne. Heerevnto is added a treatise vpon the nature and substance of spirits and diuels, &c: all latelie written by Reginald Scot Esquire. 1. Iohn . 4, 1. Beleeue not euerie spirit, but trie the spirits, whether they are of God; for manie false prophets are gone out into the world, &c. 1584 [Colophon] *Imprinted at London by William Brome.*

B. L. 4°. ($7\frac{1}{2} \times 5\frac{1}{2}$). Q. 3.

Collation: A^8B^6C–V^8 $2A$–$2C^8$ $*^2$ $2D$–$2S^8$, paged. Three epistles dedicatory: to Sir Roger Manwood; to Sir Thomas Scot; and to Dr. Coldwell, Dean of Rochester, and Dr. Readman, Archdeacon of Canterbury, each signed. Address to the readers. Errata. List of authorities. Table of contents at end. Woodcuts. Probably printed by Henry Denham, with Brome as bookseller.

Sinker 543. BM 1364.

8—2

SHAKESPEARE, William.

The Birth of Merlin.... 1662. 4°. *See* ROWLEY, William.

The Two Noble Kinsmen.... 1634. *See* BEAUMONT, Francis, and FLETCHER, John.

Mr. William Shakespeares Comedies, Histories, & Tragedies. Published according to the True Originall Copies. [Portrait.] *London Printed by Isaac Iaggard, and Ed. Blount.* 1623. [Colophon] *Printed at the Charges of W. Iaggard, Ed. Blount, I. Smithweeke and W. Aspley,* 1623.

F°. (13 × 8½). ✱. 1.

Engraved portrait on titlepage, signed Martin Droeshout. Collation: A^6, with titlepage inserted after *A* 1, 2 leaves unsigned, A–$2B^6 2C^2$a–$g^6 2g^8$h–x^4, 2 leaves unsigned, ¶–$2¶^6$, 1 leaf signed 3¶, 2a–$2f^6 2g^2 2G^6 2h^6$2k–$3b^6$, paged (irregularly and in three portions, beginning respectively on A 1, a 1 and 2a 1, in the last of which the numbering jumps from 156–257). Verses to the reader signed B. I. facing title. Titlepage with portrait. Epistle dedicatory to William Earl of Pembroke and Philip Earl of Montgomery, signed by Iohn Heminge and Henry Condell. Address to the readers, signed by the same. Commendatory verses signed Ben: Ionson and Hugh Holland. Table of contents (which omits 'Troilus and Cressida'). More commendatory verses signed L. Digges and I. M. List of the principal actors. The three parts, comedies, histories, and tragedies, have separate pagination and signatures. 'Troilus and Cressida' which is inserted at the head of the tragedies, is unpaged and occupies sigs. ¶–3¶ and the two unsigned leaves preceding them. The arrangement of the preliminary matter offers some difficulties. The only leaves signed are the third and fourth, *A* 2 and *A* 3, containing the epistle dedicatory and the address to the readers. The fifth leaf, containing Jonson's verses, certainly forms one sheet with *A* 3; and in the same way the sixth leaf, containing Holland's verses, certainly forms one sheet with *A* 2. It is further highly probable that the seventh leaf, containing the table of contents, forms one sheet with the verses signed B. I. (*A* 1), and that the titlepage is on a single leaf inserted; also that leaves eight and nine, containing the further commendatory verses and the list of actors, form one sheet together. As the present copy shows no trace of ever having been tampered with, the above arrangement is probably original. It should however be noted that in the Chatsworth copy the unsigned sheet here placed after quire *A* is there bound up in the middle. This may be the correct arrangement, but the copy is not in its original state. In the Grylls copy the preliminary matter has been rearranged. For the irregularities in the making up of the volume and the variations presented by different copies see Mr. Sidney Lee's Introduction to the Oxford Facsimile. The first collected edition of Shakespeare's plays, in which twenty appeared for the first time.

BM 1385.

Mr. William Shakespeares Comedies, Histories, and Tragedies. Published according to the true Originall Coppies. The second Impression. [Portrait.] *London, Printed by Tho. Cotes, for Robert Allot, and are to be sold at his shop at the signe of the blacke Beare in Pauls Church-yard.* 1632. [Colophon] *Printed at London by Thomas Cotes, for Iohn Smethwick, William Aspley, Richard Hawkins, Richard Meighen, and Robert Allot,* 1632.

F°. ($13\frac{3}{4} \times 9\frac{1}{8}$). ✳. 2.

Engraved portrait as before. Collation: A^6 (A 3 misprinted A 2) $*^4$; $A–2B^6 2C^2 a–y^6 2a–3c^6 3d^4$, paged (irregularly and in three parts, beginning respectively on A 1, a 1, and 2a 1, in the last of which the numbering jumps from 168 to 269). Verses to the reader, signed B. I., facing title. Epistle and address as before. Commendatory verses, two copies unsigned not in previous edition, copies signed L. Digges and I. M. List of principal actors. More commendatory verses signed Ben. Ionson, I. M. S. (not in previous edition), and Hugh Holland. Table of contents including 'Troilus and Cressida'. The three parts have separate pagination and signatures and 'Troilus and Cressida' begins those of the tragedies. The misprint in the signatures of the preliminary matter is accounted for by the fact of the compositor having reprinted that in the first folio, irrespective of the fact that the titlepage is here included in the quire. In the present copy sufficient room has not been allowed for the imposition of the portrait which consequently covers some of the printing of the titlepage. In some copies one of the other stationers' names replaces Allot's in the imprint. But beyond this there were two distinct settings up of the titlepage. Thus the Grylls copy differs from the present in reading 'Mr.' for 'Mr.', 'Copies' for 'Coppies', 'sold at the signe' for 'sold at his shop at the signe', and 'Blacke' for 'blacke'. There are also two settings of sig. A 5 in the preliminary matter, one having an ornamental initial 'S' at the beginning of the first copy of verses, the other a factotum. Second edition.

BM 1386.

Mr. William Shakespear's Comedies, Histories, and Tragedies. Published according to the true Original Copies. The third impression. And unto this Impression is added seven Playes, never before Printed in Folio. viz. Pericles Prince of Tyre. The London Prodigall. The History of Thomas Ld. Cromwell. Sir John Oldcastle Lord Cobham. The Puritan Widow. A York-shire Tragedy. The Tragedy of Locrine. *London, Printed for P. C.* 1664.

F°. ($13\frac{1}{8} \times 8\frac{3}{4}$). A. 2.

Collation: A⁴ (A 3 misprinted A 2) b⁶; A–2A⁶2B⁸2C–4D⁶4E⁴a⁶b⁴ *–4*⁴¶A–¶B⁶¶C–¶F⁴¶G⁶, paged (continuously in the original sheets and in two parts beginning at sigs. a 1 and * 1 in the additional; see below). Two leaves containing portrait with verses signed B. J. printed below and titlepage, replacing original A 1 and 2. The present copy has the original A 1 preserved after A 4. Epistle and address as before. Commendatory verses signed: L. Digges, (1 copy unsigned), J. M., Ben. Johnson, J. M. S., (1 copy unsigned), and Hugh Holland. List of principal actors. Table of contents. In the present copy the additional plays are misplaced immediately after the preliminary matter. There was an earlier issue of this edition with different titlepage and preliminary leaf, and without the additional plays. In that issue the leaf before the titlepage contains the verses only and the titlepage runs 'Mr. William Shakespeare's Comedies, Histories and Tragedies. Published according to the true Original Copies. The Third Impression. [Portrait.] London, Printed for Philip Chetwinde, 1663.' Third edition.

Mr. William Shakespear's Comedies, Histories, and Tragedies. Published according to the true Original Copies. Unto which is added, Seven Plays, Never before Printed in Folio: viz. Pericles Prince of Tyre. The London Prodigal. The History of Thomas Lord Cromwel. Sir John Oldcastle Lord Cobham. The Puritan Widow. A Yorkshire Tragedy. The Tragedy of Locrine. The Fourth Edition. *London, Printed for H. Herringman, E. Brewster, and R. Bentley, at the Anchor in the New Exchange, the Crane in St. Pauls Church-Yard, and in Russel-Street Covent-Garden.* 1685.

F°. ($14\frac{1}{4} \times 9\frac{1}{8}$). A. 3.

Collation: 2 leaves unsigned, A⁴; A–Y⁶Z⁴; 2B–3D⁶3E⁸; 3A–4B⁶ 4C², paged (in three parts beginning respectively at A 1, 2B 1, and 3A 1 in last set of signatures). Engraved portrait, as before, with verses printed below, and titlepage, unsigned. Epistle and address as before. Commendatory verses as before. List of principal actors. Table of contents. The fresh signatures and pagination begin with the comedies, histories, and 'Timon of Athens'.

The Works of Mr. William Shakespear; in six volumes. Adorn'd with Cuts. Revis'd and Corrected, with an Account of the Life and Writings of the Author. By N. Rowe, Esq; *London: Printed for Jacob Tonson, within Grays-Inn Gate, next Grays-Inn Lane.* MDCCIX.

6 vols. 8°. ($8\frac{1}{2} \times 5\frac{1}{2}$). N. 1–6.

The first edition after the four folios. Rowe published a second in 1714. The additional plays of 1664 are included.

The Works of Shakespear. In six Volumes. Collated and Corrected by the former Editions, By Mr. Pope....... *London: Printed for Jacob Tonson in the Strand.* MDCCXXV.

7 vols. 4°. ($11\frac{1}{4} \times 9$). E. 6–12.

With engraved portrait of Shakespeare by Vertue dated 1721. The 'Life' is by Rowe. Vols. ii–vi are dated 1723. The additional volume contains the Poems, with an essay on the stage and a glossary, 'The Whole Revis'd and Corrected, with a Preface, By Dr. Sewell,' and the imprint 'London; Printed by J. Darby, for A. Bettesworth, F. Fayram, W. Mears, J. Pemberton, J. Hooke, C. Rivington, F. Clay, J. Batley, E. Symon .M.DCC.XXV.' The 'Essay' in this volume is by C. Gildon. The texts of 'The Tempest' and 'A Midsummer Night's Dream' in vol. i, and of 'King Lear' in vol. iii, are corrected throughout in Capell's hand.

The Works of Shakespeare: in seven Volumes. Collated with the Oldest Copies, and Corrected; With Notes, Explanatory, and Critical: By Mr. Theobald. I, Decus, i, nostrum: melioribus utere Fatis. Virg. *London: Printed for A. Bettesworth and C. Hitch, J. Tonson, F. Clay, W. Feales, and R. Wellington.* MDCCXXXIII.

7 vols. 8°. ($9\frac{1}{8} \times 5\frac{1}{2}$). L. 1–7.

Facing the preface in the first volume (A 5^{v}) is the inscription: "This copy of M^{r}. Theobald's edition was once M^{r}. Warburton's; who has claim'd in it the Notes he gave to the former which that former depriv'd him of and made his own, and some Passages in the Preface, the Passages being put between hooks, and the notes sign'd with his name. E. C.".

The Works of Shakespear. In six Volumes. Carefully Revised and Corrected by the former Editions, and Adornd with Sculptures designed and executed by the best hands. —Nil ortum tale.—Hor. *Oxford: Printed at the Theatre,* MDCCXLIV. 6 vols. 4°. ($11\frac{3}{4} \times 9$). D. 1–6.

There is a MS. note by Capell on verso of titlepage to vol. i, dated Mar. 26, 1774, stating that the copy had been presented by the editor to the Rev. Arthur Kynnesman, headmaster of St. Edmond's Bury school, and by him bequeathed to Capell. Vols. ii–iv are dated 1743. There is a portrait of Shakespeare and an engraving by Gravelot to each play. Vol. vi contains a glossary but not the Poems. This is the first edition of the text prepared by Sir Thomas Hanmer. The engravings are after designs by Hayman.

The Works of Shakespear in eight Volumes. The Genuine Text (collated with all the former Editions, and then corrected and emended) is here settled: Being restored from the Blunders of the first Editors, and the Interpolations of the two Last: with A Comment and Notes, Critical and Explanatory. By Mr. Pope and Mr. Warburton.... *London: Printed for J. and P. Knapton, S. Birt, T. Longman and T. Shewell, H. Lintott, C. Hitch, J. Brindley, J. and R. Tonson and S. Draper, R. Wellington, E. New, and B. Dod.* MDCCXLVII.
8 vols. 8°. (8 × 5). P. 8–15.

Some copies of the first volume contain an engraved portrait of Shakespeare by Vertue.

Mr William Shakespeare his Comedies, Histories, and Tragedies, set out by himself in quarto, or by the Players his Fellows in folio, and now faithfully republish'd from those Editions in ten Volumes octavo: with an Introduction: Whereunto will be added, in some other Volumes, Notes, critical and explanatory, and a Body of Various Readings entire.

Qui genus humanum ingenio superavit, et omneis
Præstinxit, stellas exortus uti æthereus Sol.

Lucr. Lib. 3. l. 1056.

London: Printed by Dryden Leach, for J. and R. Tonson in the strand. 10 vols. 8°. ($7 \times 4\frac{1}{2}$). S. 40–49.

Epistle dedicatory to the Duke of Grafton, signed Edward Capell, and dated, Essex Court in the Temple. Nov. 9, 1767. The ten volumes appeared in 1767 and 1768. The additional volumes containing critical matter were not published till 1779–80, after the collection had been given to the College. In this copy the metre is marked throughout in the editor's hand.

Antony and Cleopatra: an historical Play, written by William Shakespeare: fitted for the Stage by abridging only; and now acted, at the Theatre-Royal in Drury-Lane, by his Majesty's Servants.

No grave upon the earth shall clip in it
A pair so famous. p. 99.

London: Printed for J. and R. Tonson in the Strand. MDCCLVIII. [Colophon] *From the Press of Dryden Leach, in Crane Court, Fleet-street. Oct.* 23, 1758.

8°. (7⅛ × 4⅛). S. 38.

Dedicatory verses to 'the Countess of * *', signed Ignoto, and dated Oct. 3, 1757. Addition to song in II. iii. Corrigenda. List of Personae with actors' names. List of Conjectural Readings at the end after the colophon. The version was prepared by Edward Capell and David Garrick.

The Tragicall Historie of Hamlet, Prince of Denmarke. By William Shakespeare. Newly imprinted and enlarged to almost as much againe as it was, according to the true and perfect Coppie. *At London, Printed by I. R for N. L. and are to be sold at his shoppe vnder Saint Dunstons Church in Fleetstreet.* 1605. 4°. (7⅞ × 5⅛). S. 31. 2.

Collation: titlepage unsigned, B–N⁴O², unpaged. The first edition appeared in 1603. The second, which first gave the full text, was printed in 1604. The present is a re-issue of the 1604 edition with the date altered.

BM 1386.

[The Tragedy of Hamlet Prince of Denmarke. By William Shakespeare. Newly imprinted and enlarged to almost as much againe as it was, according to the true and perfect Coppy. *At London, Printed for Iohn Smethwicke, and are to be sold at his shoppe in Saint Dunstons Church yeard in Fleetstreet. Vnder the Diall.* 1611.]

4°. ($7\frac{1}{4} \times 5\frac{1}{4}$). R. 19. 1.

Collation: titlepage unsigned, B–N⁴O², unpaged. Wanting titlepage. Third edition.

BM 1387.

The Tragedy of Hamlet Prince of Denmarke. Newly Imprinted and inlarged, according to the true and perfect Copy lastly Printed. By William Shakespeare. *London, Printed by W. S. for Iohn Smethwicke, and are to be sold at his Shop in Saint Dunstans Church-yard in Fleetstreet: Vnder the Diall.* 4°. ($7\frac{1}{8} \times 5\frac{3}{8}$). R. 20. 1.

Collation: A–N⁴, unpaged. N 4 blank. The fourth edition, printed between 1611 and 1637, not in 1607 as suggested in the BM Catalogue.

BM 1387.

The Tragedy of Hamlet Prince of Denmark. Newly imprinted and inlarged, according to the true and perfect Copy last Printed. By William Shakespeare. *London, Printed by R. Young for John Smethwicke, and are to be sold at his Shop in Saint Dunstans Church-yard in Fleet-street, under the Diall.* 1637. 4°. ($7\frac{1}{4} \times 5\frac{1}{4}$). R. 21. 1.

Collation: A–N⁴, unpaged. Fifth edition.

BM 1387.

The History of Henrie the fourth; With the battell at Shrewsburie, betweene the King and Lord Henry Percy, surnamed Henrie Hotspur of the North. With the humorous conceits of Sir Iohn Falstalffe. *At London, Printed by P. S. for Andrew Wise, dwelling in Paules Churchyard, at the signe of the Angell.* 1598. 4°. ($7\frac{1}{8} \times 5\frac{1}{4}$). R. 20. 4.

Collation: A–K⁴, unpaged. First edition.

Sinker 773. BM 790.

The History of Henrie the fourth; With the battell at Shrewsburie, betweene the King and Lord Henry Percy, surnamed Henry Hotspur of the North. With the humorous conceits of Sir Iohn Falstalffe. Newly corrected by W. Shakespeare. *At London, Printed by S. S. for Andrew Wise, dwelling in Paules Churchyard, at the signe of the Angell.* 1599. 4°. (7 × 5⅛). S. 37. 4.

Collation: A–K⁴, unpaged. Second edition.

BM 1387.

[The History of Henrie the fourth, With the battell at Shrewsburie, betweene the King, and Lord Henry Percy, surnamed Henry Hotspur of the North. With the humorous conceits of Sir Iohn Falstalffe. Newly corrected by W. Shakespeare. *London Printed by Valentine Simmes, for Mathew Law, and are to be solde at his shop in Paules Churchyard, at the signe of the Fox.* 1604.] 4°. (7¼ × 5¾). R. 23. 8.

Collation: A–K⁴, unpaged. Wanting A, B 1, D 2–3 and K. Third edition. The copy in the Bodleian, which appears to be the only other known, wants C 1.

The History of Henrie the fourth, With the Battell at Shrewseburie, betweene the King, and Lord Henrie Percy, surnamed Henrie Hotspur of the North. With the humorous conceites of Sir Iohn Falstaffe. Newly corrected by W. Shakespeare. *London, Printed by W. W. for Mathew Law, and are to be sold at his shop in Paules Church-yard, neere vnto S. Augustines Gate, at the signe of the Foxe.* 1613.

4°. (7¼ × 5¼). R. 21. 2.

Collation: A–K⁴, unpaged. Collated throughout in Capell's hand with the edition of 1608. Fifth edition, the fourth having appeared in 1608.

BM 1387.

The Historie of Henry the Fourth. With the Battell at Shrewseburie, betweene the King, and Lord Henry Percy, surnamed Henry Hotspur of the North. With the humorous conceits of Sir Iohn Falstaffe. Newly corrected. By William Shake-speare. *London, Printed by T. P. and are to be sold by Mathew Law, dwelling in Pauls Church-yard, at the Signe of the Foxe, neere S. Austines gate,* 1622.

4°. (7⅛ × 5½). S. 27. 4.

Collation: A–K⁴, unpaged. The sixth edition.

BM 1387.

The Historie of Henry the Fourth: With the battell at Shrewesbury, betweene the King, and Lord Henry Percy, surnamed Henry Hotspur of the North. With the humorous conceits of Sir Iohn Falstaffe. Newly corrected, By William Shake-speare. *London, Printed by Iohn Norton, and are to bee sold by William Sheares, at his shop at the great South doore of Saint Pauls-Church; and in Chancery-Lane, neere Serieants-Inne.* 1632. 4°. ($7\frac{1}{8} \times 5\frac{1}{4}$). S. 31. 1.

Collation: A–K[4], unpaged. Seventh edition.

BM 1387.

The Historie of Henry the Fourth: with the Battell at Shrewsbury, betweene the King, and Lord Henry Percy, surnamed Henry Hotspur of the North. With the humorous conceits of Sir Iohn Falstaffe. Newly corrected, By William Shake-speare. *London, Printed by John Norton, and are to be sold by Hugh Perry, at his shop next to Ivie-bridge in the Strand,* 1639. 4°. ($7\frac{1}{8} \times 5\frac{1}{8}$). S. 29. 4.

Collation: A–K[4], unpaged. Eighth edition.

BM 1387.

The Second part of Henrie the fourth, continuing to his death, and coronation of Henrie the fift. With the humours of sir Iohn Falstaffe, and swaggering Pistoll. As it hath been sundrie times publikely acted by the right honourable, the Lord Chamberlaine his seruants. Written by William Shakespeare. *London Printed by V. S. for Andrew Wise, and William Aspley.* 1600. 4°. ($7 \times 4\frac{3}{4}$). S. 35. 3.

Collation: A–K[4]L[2], unpaged. Prologue not distinguished from the text. Epilogue at the end. This is the original issue of the first edition. The second issue differs in having six leaves to sheet E, rectifying the omission of Act III. Sc. i.

Sinker 807. BM 1387 (second issue and sheet E of first).

The cronicle History of Henry the fift, With his battell fought at Agin Court in France. Togither with Auntient Pistoll. As it hath bene sundry times playd by the Right honorable the Lord Chamberlaine his seruants. *London Printed by Thomas Creede, for Tho. Millington, and Iohn*

Busby. And are to be sold at his house in Carter Lane, next the Powle head. 1600. 4°. (6½ × 4¾). W. 5. 5.

Collation: A–G[4], unpaged. Wanting G 4 (? blank). First edition. Sinker 657. BM 790.

The Chronicle History of Henry the fift, With his battell fought at Agin Court in France. Together with Auntient Pistoll. As it hath bene sundry times playd by the Right honorable the Lord Chamberlaine his seruants. *London Printed by Thomas Creede, for Thomas Pauier, and are to be sold at his shop in Cornhill, at the signe of the Cat and Parrets neare the Exchange.* 1602. 4°. (7 × 4¾). S. 35. 2.

Collation: A–F[4] G[2], unpaged. Second edition. Collated throughout in Capell's hand with the editions of 1600 and 1608.

The Chronicle History of Henry the fift, with his battell fought at Agin Court in France. Together with ancient Pistoll. As it hath bene sundry times playd by the Right Honourable the Lord Chamberlaine his Seruants. *Printed for T. P.* 1608. 4°. (7½ × 5⅝). Q. 12. 2.

Collation: A–G[4], unpaged. G 4 blank. Third edition. BM 790.

M. William Shak-speare: his True Chronicle Historie of the life and death of King Lear and his three Daughters. With the vnfortunate life of Edgar, sonne and heire to the Earle of Gloster, and his sullen and assumed humor of Tom of Bedlam: As it was played before the Kings Maiestie at Whitehall vpon S. Stephans night in Christmas Hollidayes. By his Maiesties seruants playing vsually at the Gloabe on the Bancke-side. *London, Printed for Nathaniel Butter, and are to be sold at his shop in Pauls Church-yard at the signe of the Pide Bull neere S*[t]*. Austins Gate.* 1608.

4°. (7 × 4⅞). S. 35. 1.

Collation: titlepage unsigned, B–L[4], unpaged. First edition (?). On the question of priority see preface to the eighth volume of the Cambridge Shakespeare, and Furness' edition of the play, p. 355. BM 1388.

M. William Shake-speare, His True Chronicle History of the life and death of King Lear, and his three Daughters. With the vnfortunate life of Edgar, sonne and heire to the Earle of Glocester, and his sullen and assumed humour of Tom of Bedlam. As it was plaid before the Kings Maiesty at White-Hall, vppon S. Stephens night, in Christmas Hollidaies. By his Maiesties Seruants, playing vsually at the Globe on the Banck-side. *Printed for Nathaniel Butter.* 1608. 4°. ($7\frac{1}{2} \times 5\frac{5}{8}$). Q. 11. 4.

Collation: A–L[4], unpaged. Second edition (?).
BM 1388.

M. William Shake-speare, his True Chronicle History of the life and death of King Lear, and his three Daughters. With the Vnfortunat life of Edgar, sonne and heire to the Earle of Glocester, and his sullen assumed humour of Tom of Bedlam. As it was plaid before the Kings Maiesty at Whit-Hall, vpon S. Stephens night, in Christmas Hollldaies [*sic*]. By his Maiesties Servants, playing vsually at the Globe on the Bank-side. *London. Printed by Jane Bell, and are to be sold at the East-end of Christ-Church.* 1655.
4°. ($7\frac{1}{8} \times 5\frac{1}{8}$). S. 31. 4.

Collation: A–L[4], unpaged. Third edition. Printer's advertisement of books on verso of titlepage.

A Pleasant Conceited Comedie called, Loues labors lost. As it was presented before her Highnes this last Christmas. Newly corrected and augmented By W. Shakespere. *Imprinted at London by W. W. for Cutbert Burby.* 1598.
4°. ($7 \times 5\frac{1}{8}$). S. 37. 3.

Collation: A–I[4] K[2], unpaged. First edition.
Sinker 713. BM 1389.

Loues Labours lost. A wittie and pleasant Comedie, As it was Acted by his Maiesties Seruants at the Blacke-Friers and the Globe. Written By William Shakespeare. *London, Printed by W. S. for Iohn Smethwicke, and are to be sold at his Shop in Saint Dunstones Church-yard vnder the Diall.* 1631. 4°. (7⅛ × 5¼). S. 31. 5.

Collation: A–I[4]K[2], unpaged. Second edition.
BM 1389.

The excellent History of the Merchant of Venice. With the extreme cruelty of Shylocke the Iew towards the saide Merchant, in cutting a iust pound of his flesh. And the obtaining of Portia, by the choyse of three Caskets. Written by W. Shakespeare. *Printed by I. Roberts,* 1600.
4°. (7½ × 5⅝). Q. 11. 5.

Collation: A–K[4], unpaged. First edition. On the question of priority between the two editions of this date see Furnival's introduction to the facsimile edition (1881), and the preface to the second volume of the Cambridge Shakespeare.
Sinker 475. BM 1389.

The most excellent Historie of the Merchant of Venice. With the extreame crueltie of Shylocke the Iewe towards the sayd Merchant, in cutting a iust pound of his flesh: and the obtayning of Portia by the choyse of three chests. As it hath beene diuers times acted by the Lord Chamberlaine his Seruants. Written by William Shakespeare. *At London, Printed by I. R. for Thomas Heyes, and are to be sold in Paules Church-yard, at the signe of the Greene Dragon.* 1600.
4°. (7 × 5⅛). S. 30. 4.

Collation: A–I[4]K[2], unpaged. Second edition.
Sinker 476. BM 1390.

The most excellent Historie of the Merchant of Venice. With the extreame crueltie of Shylocke the Iewe towards the said Merchant, in cutting a just pound of his flesh: and the obtaining of Portia by the choice of three Chests. As it hath beene divers times acted by the Lord Chamberlaine his Servants. Written by William Shakespeare. *London, Printed by M. P. for Laurence Hayes, and are to be sold at his Shop in Fleetbridge.* 1637. 4°. (7⅛ × 5⅛). S. 31. 3.

Collation: A–I[4], unpaged. Third edition.
BM 1390.

The most excellent Historie of the Merchant of Venice: With the extreame cruelty of Shylocke the Jew towards the said Merchant, in cutting a just pound of his flesh: and the obtaining of Portia by the choyce of three Chests. As it hath been diverse times acted by the Lord Chamberlaine his Servants. Written by William Shakespeare. *London: Printed for William Leake, and are to be solde at his shop at the signe of the Crown in Fleetstreet, between the two Temple Gates.* 1652. 4°. ($7\frac{1}{4} \times 5\frac{3}{8}$). S. 27. 5.

This is a re-issue of the edition of 1637 with a new titlepage having personae and stationer's advertisement on the verso.

A Most pleasaunt and excellent conceited Comedie, of Syr Iohn Falstaffe, and the merrie Wiues of Windsor. Entermixed with sundrie variable and pleasing humors, of Syr Hugh the Welch Knight, Iustice Shallow, and his wise Cousin M. Slender. With the swaggering vaine of Auncient Pistoll, and Corporall Nym. By William Shakespeare. As it hath bene diuers times Acted by the right Honorable my Lord Chamberlaines seruants. Both before her Maiestie, and else-where. *London Printed by T. C. for Arthur Iohnson, and are to be sold at his shop in Powles Church-yard, at the signe of the Flower de Leuse and the Crowne.* 1602. 4°. ($6\frac{5}{8} \times 4\frac{3}{4}$). W. 5. 5.

Collation: A–G[4], unpaged. A 1 blank but for signature. First edition.

A Most pleasant and excellent conceited Comedy, of Sir Iohn Falstaffe, and the merry Wiues of Windsor. With the swaggering vaine of Ancient Pistoll, and Corporall Nym. Written by W. Shakespeare. *Printed for Arthur Johnson,* 1619. 4°. ($7\frac{1}{2} \times 5\frac{5}{8}$). Q. 11. 2.

Collation: A–G[4], unpaged. Second edition.
BM 1390.

The Merry Wives of Windsor. With the humours of Sir Iohn Falstaffe, As also the swaggering vaine of Ancient

Pistoll, and Corporall Nym. Written by William Shake-Speare. Newly corrected. *London: Printed by T. H. for R. Meighen, and are to be sold at his Shop, next to the Middle-Temple Gate, and in S. Dunstans Church-yard in Fleet-street,* 1630. 4°. ($6\frac{7}{8} \times 5\frac{1}{4}$). T. 7. 6.

Collation: A–K⁴, unpaged. K 4 blank. Third edition.

BM 1390.

A Midsommer nights dreame. As it hath beene sundry times publickely acted, by the Right honourable, the Lord Chamberlaine his seruants. Written by William Shakespeare. *Imprinted at London, for Thomas Fisher, and are to be soulde at his shoppe, at the Signe of the White Hart, in Fleetestreete.* 1600. 4°. ($7\frac{1}{8} \times 5\frac{5}{8}$). S. 27. 3.

Collation: A–H⁴, unpaged. First edition. On the priority of the two editions of this year see Ebsworth's Introduction to the facsimile edition (1880) and the preface to the second volume of the Cambridge Shakespeare. The present copy belonged to Theobald, who has written the following note on the titlepage: 'Collated with the other Old Quarto, with the same Title, printed by James Roberts in 1600. L. T.' The collations are entered in the margin.

Sinker 822. BM 1390.

A Midsommer nights dreame. As it hath beene sundry times publikely acted, by the Right Honourable, the Lord Chamberlaine his seruants. Written by William Shakespeare. *Printed by Iames Roberts,* 1600. 4°. ($7\frac{1}{2} \times 5\frac{5}{8}$). Q. 11. 3.

Collation: A–H⁴, unpaged. Second edition.

Sinker 474. BM 1390.

Much adoe about Nothing. As it hath been sundrie times publikely acted by the right honourable, the Lord Chamberlaine his seruants. Written by William Shakespeare. *London Printed by V. S. for Andrew Wise, and William Aspley.* 1600. 4°. (7×5). S. 34. 3.

Collation: A–I⁴, unpaged.

Sinker 806. BM 1390.

The Tragœdy of Othello, The Moore of Venice. As it hath beene diuerse times acted at the Globe, and at the Black-Friers, by his Maiesties Seruants. Written by William Shakespeare. *London, Printed by N. O. for Thomas Walkley, and are to be sold at his shop, at the Eagle and Child, in Brittans Bursse.* 1622. 4°. ($7\frac{1}{8} \times 5\frac{5}{8}$). S. 27. 2.

Collation: $A^2B–M^4N^2$, paged. Stationer's address to the reader, signed Thomas Walkley. The portion from sheet I onwards has been supplied from a narrower copy. It is however of the same edition although the last line on H 4v is repeated at the head of I 1, this peculiarity occurring in the other known copies of the first edition.

BM 1390.

The Tragœdy of Othello, The Moore of Venice. As it hath beene diuerse times acted at the Globe, and at the Black-Friers, by his Maiesties Seruants. Written by William Shakespeare. *London, Printed by A. M. for Richard Hawkins, and are to be sold at his shoppe in Chancery-Lane, neere Sergeants-Inne.* 1630. 4°. ($7\frac{1}{8} \times 5$). S. 34. 5.

Collation: $A–M^4$, paged. Second edition.

BM 1390.

The Tragœdy of Othello, The Moore of Venice As it hath beene divers times Acted at the Globe, and at the Black-Friers, by his Majesties Servants. Written by William Shakespeare. The fourth Edition. *London, Printed for William Leak at the Crown in Fleet-street, between the two Temple Gates,* 1655. 4°. ($7\frac{1}{8} \times 5\frac{1}{8}$). R. 22. 1.

Collation: $A–M^4$, paged. Advertisement of books at end. Third edition.

The Tragedie of King Richard the second. As it hath beene publikely acted by the right Honourable the Lorde Chamberlaine his Seruants. *London Printed by Valentine Simmes for Androw Wise, and are to be sold at his shop in Paules church yard at the signe of the Angel.* 1597. 4°. ($6\frac{7}{8} \times 4\frac{3}{4}$). S. 35. 4.

Collation: $A–I^4K^2$, unpaged. First edition.

Sinker 804.

The Tragedie of King Richard the second. As it hath beene publikely acted by the Right Honourable the Lord Chamberlaine his seruants. By William Shake-speare. *London Printed by Valentine Simmes for Andrew Wise, and are to be sold at his shop in Paules churchyard at the signe of the Angel.* 1598. 4°. ($7\frac{1}{4} \times 5\frac{1}{4}$). R. 22. 5.

Collation: A–I⁴, unpaged. Second edition.

Sinker 805. BM 1388.

The Tragedie of King Richard the Second: With new additions of the Parliament Sceane, and the deposing of King Richard. As it hath been lately acted by the Kinges Maiesties seruants, at the Globe. By William Shake-speare. *At London, Printed for Matthew Law, and are to be sold at his shop in Paules Church-yard, at the signe of the Foxe.* 1615. 4°. ($7\frac{1}{4} \times 5\frac{1}{4}$). R. 19. 2.

Collation: A–K⁴, unpaged. Wanting K4 (? blank). Fourth edition. The 'additions' first appeared in 1608, in the third edition, with which the present copy has been throughout collated in Capell's hand.

BM 1389.

The Life and Death of King Richard the second. With new Additions of the Parliament Scene, and the Deposing of King Richard. As it hath beene acted by the Kings Majesties Servants, at the Globe. By William Shakespeare. *London, Printed by Iohn Norton.* 1634. 4°. ($7\frac{1}{8} \times 5\frac{3}{8}$). R. 20. 5.

Collation: A–K⁴, unpaged. Fifth edition.

BM 1389.

The Tragedie of King Richard the third. Conteining his treacherous Plots against his brother Clarence: the pitiful murther of his innocent Nephewes: his tyrannicall vsurpation: with the whole course of his detested life, and most deserued death. As it hath beene lately Acted by the Right honourable the Lord Chamberlaine his seruants. By William Shake-speare. *London Printed by Thomas Creede, for Andrew Wise, dwelling in Paules Church-yard, at the signe of the Angell.* 1598. 4°. ($7\frac{1}{4} \times 5\frac{1}{4}$). R. 22. 4.

Collation: A–M[4], unpaged. Wanting M 4 (? blank). Second edition, the first having appeared in 1597.

Sinker 655. BM 1389.

The Tragedie of King Richard the third. Conteining his treacherous Plots against his brother Clarence: the pittifull murther of his innocent Nephewes: his tyrannicall vsurpation: with the whole course of his detested life, and most deserued death. As it hath bene lately Acted by the Right Honourable the Lord Chamberlaine his seruants. Newly augmented, By William Shakespeare. *London Printed by Thomas Creede, for Andrew Wise, dwelling in Paules Church-yard, at the signe of the Angell.* 1602.

4°. (7×5). S. 30. 1.

Collation: A–L[4] M[2], unpaged. Third edition.

BM 1389.

The Tragedie of King Richard the third. Containing his treacherous Plots against his brother Clarence: the pittifull murther of his innocent Nephewes: his tyrannicall vsurpation: with the whole course of his detested life, and most deserued death. As it hath beene lately Acted by the Kings Maiesties seruants. Newly augmented, By William Shake-speare. *London, Printed by Thomas Creede, and are to be sold by Mathew Lawe, dwelling in Pauls Church-yard, at the Signe of the Foxe, neare S. Austins gate,* 1612.

4°. ($7\frac{1}{4} \times 5\frac{1}{4}$). R. 19. 3.

Collation: A–L[4] M[2], unpaged. Sheets I—M have been supplied from a shorter copy. Fifth edition, the fourth having appeared in 1605.

BM 1389.

The Tragedie of King Richard the third. Contayning his treacherous Plots against his brother Clarence: The pittifull murder of his innocent Nephewes: his tyrannicall Vsurpation: with the whole course of his detested life, and most deserued death. As it hath been lately Acted by the Kings Maiesties Seruants. Newly augmented. By William

Shake-speare. *London, Printed by Thomas Purfoot, and are to be sold by Mathew Law, dwelling in Pauls Church-yard, at the Signe of the Foxe, neere S. Austines gate*, 1622.

4°. ($7\frac{1}{8} \times 5$). S. 34. 2.

Collation: A–L⁴M², unpaged. Sixth edition.

BM 1389.

The Tragedie of King Richard the third. Contayning his trecherous Plots, against his brother Clarence: The pittifull murther of his inocent Nepthewes [*sic*]: his tiranous vsurpation: with the whole course of his detested life, and most deserued death. As it hath beene lately Acted by the Kings Maiesties Sernauts [*sic*]. Newly agmented. By William Shake-speare. *London. Printed by Iohn Norton, and are to be sold by Mathew Law, dwelling in Pauls Church-yeard, at the Signe of the Foxe, neere St. Anstines* [*sic*] *gate*, 1629.

4°. ($6\frac{3}{4} \times 5$). T. 8. 5.

Collation: A–L⁴M², unpaged. Seventh edition.

BM 1389.

⌜The Tragedie of King Richard the third. Contayning his treacherous Plots, against his brother Clarence: The pitifull murder of his innocent Nephewes: his tyranous vsurpation: with the whole course of his detested life, and most deserued death. As it hath beene Acted by the Kings Maiesties Seruants. Written by William Shake-speare. *London, Printed by Iohn Norton.* 1634.⌟

4°. ($7\frac{1}{4} \times 5\frac{1}{4}$). R. 21. 4.

Collation: A–L⁴M², unpaged. Wanting A 1, containing titlepage. Eighth edition.

BM 1389.

An excellent conceited Tragedie of Romeo and Iuliet. As it hath been often (with great applause) plaid publiquely, by the right Honourable the L. of Hunsdon his Seruants. *London, Printed by Iohn Danter.* 1597.

4°. ($7\frac{1}{8} \times 5\frac{1}{4}$). R. 20. 2.

Collation: A–K⁴, unpaged. Wanting A 1 (? blank). Prologue. From sheet E onwards a smaller type has been used. First edition.

Sinker 781. BM 1391.

The most Excellent and Lamentable Tragedie, of Romeo and Juliet. As it hath beene sundrie times publiquely Acted, by the Kings Maiesties Seruants at the Globe. Newly corrected, augmented, and amended: *London Printed for Iohn Smethwick, and are to be sold at his Shop in Saint Dunstanes Church-yard, in Fleetestreete vnder the Dyall.* 1609. 4°. ($6\frac{3}{4} \times 5$). T. 8. 2.

Collation: A–L^{4}M^2, unpaged. Prologue. The third edition, the second having appeared in 1599.

BM 1391.

[The most Excellent and Lamentable Tragedie of Romeo and Juli]et. As it hath beene sundrie times publikely Acted, by the Kings Maiesties Seruants at the Globe. Written by W. Shake-speare. Newly Corrected, augmented, and amended. *London, Printed for Iohn Smethwicke, and are to be sold at his Shop in Saint Dunstanes Church-yard, in Fleetstreete vnder the Dyall.* 4°. ($7 \times 5\frac{1}{8}$). S. 37. 5.

Collation: A–L^4, unpaged. Prologue pasted over. The copy in the BM has a different titlepage, without the author's name, but is otherwise identical. The fourth edition, printed between 1609 and 1637, not in 1607 as stated in BM catalogue.

BM 1391.

The most Excellent And Lamentable Tragedie of Romeo and Juliet. As it hath been sundry times publikely Acted by the Kings Majesties Servants at the Globe. Written by W. Shake-speare. Newly corrected, augmented, and amended. *London, Printed by R. Young for John Smethwicke, and are to be sold at his Shop in St. Dunstans Church-yard in Fleetstreet, under the Dyall.* 1637. 4°. ($7\frac{1}{8} \times 5$). S. 34. 1.

Collation: A–L^4, unpaged. The fifth edition.

BM 1391.

A Wittie and pleasant Comedie Called The Taming of the Shrew. As it was acted by his Maiesties Seruants at the Blacke Friers and the Globe. Written by Will. Shakespeare. *London, Printed by W. S. for Iohn Smethwicke, and are to be sold at his Shop in Saint Dunstones Church-yard vnder the Diall.* 1631. 4°. ($7\frac{5}{8} \times 5\frac{3}{8}$). Q. 10. 5.

Collation: A–I[4], unpaged.

BM 1392.

The most lamentable Tragedie of Titus Andronicus. As it hath sundry times beene plaide by the Kings Maiesties Seruants. *London, Printed for Eedward* [*sic*] *White, and are to be solde at his shoppe, nere the little North dore of Pauls, at the signe of the Gun.* 1611. 4°. ($7\frac{1}{4} \times 5\frac{1}{4}$). R. 19. 4.

Collation: A–K[4], unpaged. Second edition, the first having appeared in 1600.

BM 40.

The Famous Historie of Troylus and Cresseid. Excellently expressing the beginning of their loues, with the conceited wooing of Pandarus Prince of Licia. Written by William Shakespeare. *London Imprinted by G. Eld for R. Bonian and H. Walley, and are to be sold at the spred Eagle in Paules Church-yeard, ouer against the great North doore.* 1609. 4°. ($6\frac{7}{8} \times 5$). T. 7. 1.

Collation: ¶[2]A 2–4 B–L[4]M[2], unpaged. Wanting M2 (? blank). Addrèss to the reader. This is the second issue of the first edition, the original titlepage (A 1) being replaced by a half-sheet (¶) containing titlepage and address to the reader.

Lucrece. *At London, Printed by P. S. for Iohn Harrison.* 1598. 8°. ($4\frac{7}{8} \times 3\frac{1}{8}$). *. 19. 1.

Collation: A–D[8]E[4], unpaged. Epistle dedicatory to Henry Wriothesley, Earl of Southampton, signed William Shakespeare. Argument. Collated throughout by Capell with the ed. of 1594. No other copy of this, the second, edition is known.

Sinker 774.

Lucrece. *At London, Printed be* [sic] *N. O. for Iohn Harison.* 1607. 8°. ($5\frac{1}{8} \times 3\frac{1}{4}$). *. 9.

Collation: A–D[8], unpaged. (A 4 is misprinted B 4). Epistle dedicatory to Henry Wriothesley, Earl of Southampton, signed, William Shakespeare. Argument. This is the fourth edition, the third having appeared in 1600.

The Passionate Pilgrime. By W. Shakespeare. *At London Printed for W. Iaggard, and are to be sold by W. Leake, at the Greyhound in Paules Churchyard.* 1599.

8°. ($4\frac{1}{2} \times 3\frac{1}{4}$). *. 22. 1.

Collation: A–D⁸, unpaged. A 1 and D 8 blank. Printed on the recto of leaves only, except in sigs. D 5–7. Ornament at head and foot of each printed page. At sig. C 3 is a separate titlepage: 'Sonnets To sundry notes of Musicke' with same imprint as above, (in the present copy the date has been cut away by the binder). The only other copy known which was formerly at Lamport Hall is now at Britwell Court. First edition.

Sinker 801.

Poems: written by Wil. Shake-speare. Gent. *Printed at London by Tho. Cotes, and are to be sold by Iohn Benson dwelling in S^t^. Dunstans Church-yard.* 1640.

8°. ($5\frac{1}{4} \times 3\frac{3}{8}$). *. 10.

Collation: Portrait unsigned, $*^4$A–L^{8}M^4, unpaged. Engraved portrait after that by Droeshout, signed W. M. with verses below. Address to the reader signed I. B. (*i.e.* John Benson). Commendatory verses signed Leon. Digges and Iohn Warren. Duplicate titlepage, as above but without date. At the end of the poems purporting to be by Shakespeare appear commendatory verses signed I. M. (Milton's lines from the second folio), W. B. (*i.e.* William Basse; the lines first appeared in Donne's poems in 1633), and one copy unsigned; after which is 'An Addition of some Excellent Poems, to those precedent, of Renowned Shakespeare, By other Gentlemen,' of which two are signed B. I. (*i.e.* Ben Jonson), one F. B. (*i.e.* Francis Beaumont), and one I. G.

BM 1392.

⌜Shake-speares Sonnets. Neuer before Imprinted. *At London By G. Eld for T. T. and are to be solde by Iohn Wright, dwelling at Christ Church gate.* 1609.⌝

4°. (7 × 5). S. 36. 5.

Collation: A^{2}B–K^{4}L^2, unpaged. Wanting A 1–2, B 1, K 2–L 2, supplied in manuscript by Capell. Dedication to 'Mr. W. H.' signed T. T. (*i.e.* Thomas Thorpe the publisher). 'A Lovers complaint' begins on K 1^v. Some copies bear in the imprint the name of William Aspley in place of Wright's name and address.

BM 1392.

Venus and Adonis.

Vilia miretur vulgus, mihi flauus Apollo
Pocula Castalia plena ministret aqua.

London, Printed for I. P. 1620. 8°. ($4\frac{1}{2} \times 3\frac{1}{4}$). *. 22. 2.

Collation: A–C⁸D⁴, unpaged. Wanting D 4 (? blank), sig. C 7 slightly defective. Epistle dedicatory to Henry Wriothesley, Earl of Southampton, signed, William Shakespeare. The only other copy of this edition which has been traced was purchased for the Bodleian, but cannot now be found. The ninth edition, the first having appeared in 1593. At the end of this volume, which also contains the 'Passionate Pilgrim' of 1599 is a note in an old handwriting 'Not quite perfect, see 4 or 5 Leaves back; so it cost me but 3 Halfpence'.

SHAKESPEARIAN PLAYS, PSEUDO.

The True Chronicle Historie of the whole life and death of Thomas Lord Cromwell. As it hath beene sundry times publikely Acted by the Kings Maiesties Seruants. Written by W. S. *London: Printed by Thomas Snodham.* 1613.

4°. ($7 \times 5\frac{1}{8}$). S. 37. 1.

Collation: A–G⁴, unpaged. Wanting G 4 (? blank). Second edition, the first having appeared in 1602.

BM 1344.

The Lamentable Tragedie of Locrine, the eldest sonne of King Brutus, discoursing the warres of the Britaines, and Hunnes, with their discomfiture: The Britaines victorie with their Accidents, and the death of Albanact. No lesse pleasant then profitable. Newly set foorth, ouerseene and corrected, By W. S. *London Printed by Thomas Creede.* 1595.

4°. ($6\frac{7}{8} \times 5\frac{1}{8}$). S. 37. 2.

Collation: A–K, unpaged. Wanting A 1 (? blank).

Sinker 651. BM 1343.

The London Prodigall. As it was plaide by the Kings Maiesties seruants. By William Shakespeare, *London. Printed by T. C. for Nathaniel Butter, and are to be sold neere S. Austins gate, at the signe of the pyde Bull.* 1605.

4°. (7×5). S. 34. 4.

Collation: A–G⁴, unpaged.

BM 1393.

The first part Of the true & honorable history, of the Life of Sir Iohn Old-castle, the good Lord Cobham. As it hath bene lately acted by the Right honorable the Earle of Notingham Lord High Admirall of England, his Seruants. Written by William Shakespeare. *London printed for T. P.* 1600. 4°. ($7\frac{1}{2} \times 5\frac{5}{8}$). Q. 12. 1.

Collation: A–K[4], unpaged. Prologue. Two editions appeared in this year, the other without author's name and printed by V. S. for Thomas Pavier. The play was the work of Drayton, Hathway, Munday, and Wilson.

Sinker 823. BM 1394.

The late, And much admired Play, Called Pericles, Prince of Tyre. With the true Relation of the whole Historie, aduentures, and fortunes of the said Prince: As also, The no lesse strange, and worthy accidents, in the Birth and Life, of his Daughter Mariana. As it hath been diuers and sundry times acted by his Maiesties Seruants, at the Globe on the Banck-side. By William Shakespeare. *Imprinted at London for Henry Gosson, and are to be sold at the signe of the Sunne in Pater-noster row, &c.* 1609.

4°. ($7\frac{1}{4} \times 5\frac{1}{4}$). R. 21. 3.

Collation: A–I[4], unpaged. Wanting I 4 (? blank). This is the first edition. Another edition appeared later in the same year with identically the same titlepage, but it can be distinguished from the present by having the stage-direction on A 2 misprinted 'Eneer Gower'. On the question of priority see the preface to the ninth volume of the Cambridge Shakespeare.

BM 1391.

The Late, And much admired Play, called, Pericles, Prince of Tyre. With the true Relation of the whole History, aduentures, and fortunes of the saide Prince. Written by W. Shakespeare. *Printed for T. P.* 1619:

4°. ($7\frac{1}{2} \times 5\frac{5}{8}$). Q. 12. 3.

This forms the third part of the volume, of which 'The Whole Contention' (*q.v.*) forms the first two. The signatures are continuous throughout the volume and this is the only titlepage which is dated. Fourth edition, the third having appeared in 1611.

BM 1391.

The late, And much admired Play, called Pericles, Prince of Tyre. With the true Relation of the whole History, aduentures, and fortunes of the sayd Prince: Written by Will. Shakespeare: *London, Printed by I. N. for R. B. and are to be sould at his shop in Cheapside, at the signe of the Bible.* 1630.

4°. ($7\frac{1}{8} \times 5\frac{1}{4}$). R. 22. 2.

Collation: A–$H^4 I^2$, unpaged. The fifth edition. There was another issue of this edition the same year, with a different titlepage in which the imprint occupies only two lines instead of four.

BM 1391.

The late, And much admired Play, called Pericles, Prince of Tyre. With the trùe Relation of the whole History, adventures, and fortunes of the said Prince. Written by W. Shakespeare. *Printed at London by Thomas Cotes,* 1635.

4°. ($7\frac{1}{4} \times 5$). R. 23. 4.

Collation: A–$H^4 I^2$, unpaged. Sixth edition.

BM 1391.

The Puritaine Or the Widdow of Watling-streete. Acted by the Children of Paules. Written by W. S. *Imprinted at London by G. Eld.* 1607. 4°. ($7\frac{1}{4} \times 5\frac{1}{2}$). R. 23. 3.

Collation: A–H^4, unpaged. Wanting A 1 (? blank).

BM 1344.

A Yorkshire Tragedie. Not so New, as Lamentable and True. Written by W. Shakespeare. *Printed for T. P.* 1619:

4°. ($7\frac{1}{2} \times 5\frac{5}{8}$). Q. 11. 1.

Collation: titlepage unsigned, A–$C^4 D^2$, unpaged. The head-title runs 'All's One, or, One of the four Plaies in one, called a Yorkshire Tragedy. As it was plaid by the Kings Maiesties Players.' Second edition, the first having appeared in 1608.

BM 1394.

SHELTON, Thomas.

The History of Don-Quichote.... n. d. The Second Part of the History of...Don Quixote.... 1620. *See* CERVANTES SAAVEDRA, Miguel de.

SHIRLEY, James.

The Coronation.... 1640. *See* BEAUMONT, Francis, and FLETCHER, John.

SIDNEY, *Sir* PHILIP.

⌜An Apologie for Poetrie. Written by the right noble, vertuous, and learned, Sir Phillip Sidney, Knight. Odi profanum vulgus, et arceo. *At London, Printed for Henry Olney, and are to be sold at his shop in Paules Church-yard, at the signe of the George, neere to Cheap-gate. Anno* . 1595 .⌟

4°. (7 × 5). S. 18. 2.

Collation: A–L⁴, unpaged. Wanting sig. A and L 4 (A 1 and L 4 ? blank). The two leaves after the titlepage contain address to the reader signed Henry Olney, list of errata, and four sonnets by Henry Constable. There appears to have been another issue the same year differing in titlepage and preliminary matter only. It is entitled 'The Defence of Poesie', is printed for William Ponsonby and does not contain the Constable sonnets. It was under this title and without the sonnets that it was included among the collected works in the 'Arcadia'.

Sinker 814. BM 1405.

The Countesse of Pembrokes Arcadia, written by Sir Philippe Sidnei. *London Printed by Iohn Windet, for william Ponsonbie. Anno Domini*, 1590. 4°. ($7\frac{1}{4} \times 5\frac{1}{4}$). R. 10.

With the Sidney arms on the titlepage. Collation: A⁴ B–2Z⁸, folios numbered. Wanting A 1 (? blank). Epistle dedicatory to the Countess of Pembroke, signed. Printer's note. This first edition is imperfect, breaking off in the middle of the third book. The division into chapters and the arrangement of the verse was the work of the 'ouer-seer of the print'. The edition seems probably to have been printed from a corrected copy of the first portion of the romance left by Sidney in the hands of Fulke Greville, afterwards Lord Brooke (see Greville to Walsingham, August 23, 1586, in the State Papers, quoted by O. Sommer in Introd. to facsimile edition, 1891). The remainder of the romance was made up by the Countess of Pembroke from Sidney's loose papers, and published by Ponsonby in 1593. The rarity of the present edition suggests that the publication of the complete work was intrusted to Ponsonby on condition of his recalling the earlier issue. The 1590 edition cannot be regarded as surreptitious, but there was an attempt at a surreptitious edition in 1586, of which Ponsonby gave warning to Greville. This seems to be the only recorded copy having the printer's name on the titlepage, which is otherwise printed from the same setting up of the type. The text is identical, but slight differences in the type seem to point to the present being the earlier issue.

Sinker 634. BM 1405.

The Countesse Of Pembrokes Arcadia. Written by Sir Philip Sidney Knight. Now the sixt time published, with some new Additions. Also a supplement of a defect in the third part of this Historie, By Sir W. Alexander. *London, Printed by W. S. for Simon Waterson.* 1627.

F°. ($11\frac{1}{4} \times 7\frac{1}{2}$). F. 7.

Title within ornamental border. Collation: three leaves unsigned, A–3F^6, paged. Epistle dedicatory to the Countess of Pembroke, signed. Address to the reader signed H. S. Alexander's addition occupies sigs. 2E 2–2F 5, and at the end is a note signed S. W. A. At sig. 2S 2 begins a sixth book with separate titlepage: 'A sixth Booke, to the Countesse of Pembrokes Arcadia: Written by R. B. of Lincolnes Inne Esquire. Sat, si bene; si male, nimium. London, Printed by H. L. and R. Y. 1628.'. Address to the reader signed R. B. (*i.e.* Richard Beling). At the end of the 'Arcadia' are Sidney's miscellaneous poems, 'Defence of Poesie', 'Astrophel and Stella' and the entertainment at Wansted ('The Lady of May'). This is in reality the ninth edition.

SKELTON, John.

⌜Pithy pleasaunt and profitable workes of maister Skelton, Poete Laureate. Nowe collected and newly published. *Anno* 1568. *Imprinted at London in Fletestreate, neare vnto saint Dunstones churche by Thomas Marshe.*⌝

B. L. 8°. ($5\frac{1}{2} \times 3\frac{5}{8}$). *. 3.

Collation: four leaves unsigned (except the third, signed A 4 on verso), A–Z^8 2A^4, unpaged. Wanting all before C 7, D 3 and 6, F 1, 2, 7, K 1–3, L 2, M 1 and 8, N 1–3 and 6, Y 1–5, Z 2–8. (In Dr Sinker's catalogue the defect in sig. Y is erroneously given as 1–4 and 7.) Latin verses on verso of title. Commendatory verses by Churchyard. Table of contents. Three collections under the title of 'certayne bokes cōpyled by Mayster Skelton' had already appeared without date.

Sinker 315. BM 1409.

SKINNER, Stephen.

Etymologicon Linguæ Anglicanæ, Seu Explicatio vocum Anglicarum Etymologica ex propriis fontibus, scil. ex Linguis duodecim; Anglo-Saxonica seu Anglica prisca, notata AS. Runica, Gothica, Cimbrica, seu Danica antiqua, notata Run. Dan. Franco-Theotisca, seu Teutonica vetere, notata Fr. Th. Danica recentiori, notata Dan. rec. Belgica, notata Belg. Teutonica recentiori, notata Teut. Cambro-Britanica, notata C. Br. Franco-Gallica, notata Fr. Italica, notata It. Hispanica, notata Hisp. Latina, notata Lat. Græca, notata Gr.... Accedit Etymologicon Botanicum,.... Accedit & tertio vocum Forensium.... Etymologica expositio,.... Quarto adjectæ sunt Originationes omnium vocum antiquarum Anglicarum,... Tandem ultimo Etymologicon Onomasticon,... Omnia Alphabetico ordine in quinque distinctas Classes digesta.... Authore Stephano Skinner, M.D. *Londini, Typis T. Roycroft, & prostant venales apud H. Brome sub signo Bombardæ ad occidentale Sancti Pauli latus, R. Clavel, B. Tooke sub signo Navis Cœmeterio Divi Pauli, & T. Sawbridge sub signo trium Iridum in Parva Britannia.* M DC LXXI.

F°. (12 × 8). C. 3.

Collation: $A^2a^2B–D^4E–V^2 2A–5V^4 5X^2$, unpaged. License on verso of leaf before titlepage, signed Jo. Cooke and dated Sept. 7, 1668. Address to the reader. Præfatio. Prolegomena Etymologica. Each part begins with a head-title.

SMITH, *Sir* Thomas.

De recta & emendata Linguæ Anglicæ Scriptione, Dialogus, Thoma Smitho Equestris ordinis Anglo authore. *Lutetiæ, Ex officina Roberti Stephani Typographi Regij.* M. D. LXVIII. *Cum Priuilegio Regis.* [Colophon] *Excudebat Robertus Stephanus Typographus Regius, Lutetiae Parisiorum Idib. Nouembris, Ann.* M. D. LXVII. 4°. (8¾ × 6¼). M. 2. 1.

Collation: $*^2a–l^4$, folios numbered.

De recta & emendata Linguæ Græcæ Pronuntiatione, Thomæ Smithi Angli, tunc in Academia Cantabrigiensi publici prælectoris, ad Vintoniensem Episcopum Epistola. *Lutetiæ, Ex officina Roberti Stephani Typographi Regij.* M. D. LXVIII. *Cum Priuilegio Regis.*

4°. ($8\frac{3}{4} \times 6\frac{1}{4}$). M. 2. 2.

Collation: 2 leaves unsigned (second blank) A–M[4]; folios numbered. Signed at the end: 'Cantabrigiæ 12. Augusti. 1542. Tho. Smithus.'

SOLINUS, Julius.

The excellent and pleasant worke of Iulius Solinus Polyhistor. Contayning the noble actions of humaine creatures, the secretes & prouidence of nature, the description of Countries, the maners of the people: with many meruailous things and strange antiquities, seruing for the benefitt and recreation of all sorts of persons. Translated out of Latin into English, by Arthur Golding, Gent. *At London Printed by I. Charlewoode for Thomas Hacket.* 1587.

B. L. 4°. ($7 \times 5\frac{1}{4}$). T. 1. 3.

Collation: A–2F[4]2G[2] (without Z), unpaged. Life of Solinus by Iohn Camertes. Solinus' address to Autius. Epistle dedicatory to the same.

Sinker 366. BM 1425.

SOUTHWELL, Robert.

Saint Peters Complaint, With other Poemes. *London Imprinted by Iohn Wolfe.* 1595. 4°. ($7\frac{1}{4} \times 5\frac{3}{8}$). R. 18. 1.

Collation: A–I[4]K[2], paged. Epistle dedicatory 'The Author to his louing Cosen'. Verses to the reader (two copies). 'Saint Peter's Complaint' ends sheet E, after which follow the miscellaneous poems. By Robert Southwell whose initials appear on the titlepage of some of the later editions. The first edition was probably that published the same year as printed by I[ames]. R[oberts]. for G[abriel]. C[awood]. and of which the present appears to be a piratical reprint.

Sinker 608.

Mœoniæ. Or, certaine excellent Poems and spirituall Hymnes: Omitted in the last Impression of Peters Complaint; being needefull thereunto to be annexed, as being both Diuine and Wittie. All composed by R. S. *London Printed by Valentine Sims, for Iohn Busbie* 1595.

4°. ($7\frac{1}{4} \times 5\frac{3}{8}$). R. 18. 2.

Collation: A^2B–E^4, paged. Ornament at the foot of each page. Address to the reader, signed I. B. (*i.e.* John Busbie). By Robert Southwell. The poems in this volume were added to the later editions of 'Saint Peter's Complaint'.

Sinker 802. BM 1341.

SPENSER, EDMUND.

Amoretti and Epithalamion. Written not long since by Edmunde Spenser. *Printed for William Ponsonby.* 1595. [Colophon] *Imprinted by P. S. for William Ponsonby.*

8°. ($4\frac{7}{8} \times 3$). *. 18.

Collation: A–H^8, unpaged. Ornament at head and foot of each page. Part ii. has a separate titlepage with the word 'Epithalamion' and printer's device but no imprint, at sig. G 3. Certain copies have a half-sheet (4 leaves) with sig. ¶ inserted between A 1 and 2, but it is possible that some were issued without this addition. The half-sheet contains an epistle dedicatory to Sir Robert Needham Knight, signed with the stationer's initials and commendatory verses from G. W. senior and G. W. I[unior].

Sinker 770. BM 1438.

Colin Clouts Come home againe. By Ed. Spencer. *London Printed for William Ponsonbie.* 1595.

4°. ($7\frac{3}{4} \times 5\frac{1}{2}$). Q. 10. 2.

Collation: A–H^4, unpaged. Epistle dedicatory to Sir Walter Raleigh, signed Ed. Sp. and dated, Kilcolman, Dec. 27, 1591. 'Astrophel', with half-title and dedicated to the Countess of Essex, begins on sig. E 4.

Sinker 650. BM 1438.

Complaints. Containing sundrie small Poemes of the Worlds Vanitie. Whereof the next Page maketh mention. By Ed. Sp. *London. Imprinted for William Ponsonbie, dwelling in Paules Churchyard at the signe of the Bishops head.* 1591. 4°. ($7\frac{1}{8} \times 4\frac{3}{4}$). S. 29. 1.

Title within woodcut border. Collation: A–Z[4], unpaged. Z 4 blank. List of contents on verso of general titlepage. Printer's address to the reader. Epistle dedicatory to the Countess of Pembroke, signed E. S. 'The Ruines of Time'. 'The Teares of the Muses' with separate title dated 1591 within same border. Epistle dedicatory to Lady Strange, signed Ed. Sp. 'Vergils Gnat' with dedicatory verses to the Earl of Leicester. 'Prosopopoia. Or Mother Hubberds Tale', with separate title dated 1591 within same border. Epistle dedicatory to Lady Compton and Mountegle, signed Ed. Sp. 'The Ruines of Rome: by Bellay'. 'Muiopotmos, Or The Fate of the Butterflie' with separate title dated 1590 within same border. Epistle dedicatory to Lady Carey, signed E. S. 'Visions of the worlds vanitie'. 'The Visions of Bellay'. 'The Visions of Petrarch formerly translated'.

Sinker 724. BM 1429.

The Faerie Queene. Disposed into twelue books, Fashioning XII. Morall vertues. *London Printed for William Ponsonbie.* 1590. 4°. (7 × 5). S. 19.

Collation: A–2P[8]2Q[4], paged. Dedication to Queen Elizabeth signed Ed. Spenser, on verso of titlepage. Books I–III. Letter to Raleigh signed and dated Jan. 23, 1589. Commendatory verses signed W. R. (*i.e.* Walter Raleigh), Hobynoll (*i.e.* Gabriel Harvey), R. S., H. B., W. L., Ignoto. Dedicatory verses from the author to Sir Christopher Hatton, the Earl of Essex, the Earl of Oxford, the Earl of Northumberland, the Earl of Ormond and Ossory, Lord Charles Howard, Lord Grey of Wilton, Sir Walter Raleigh, Lady Carew, 'To all the gracious and beautifull Ladies in the Court', the last two only signed E. S. Errata. More dedicatory verses (mostly duplicates of the above) to Hatton (dupl.), Lord Burleigh (signed E. S.), Oxford (dupl.), Northumberland (dupl.), Earl of Cumberland (signed E. S.), Essex (dupl.), Ormond (dupl.), Howard (dupl.), Lord Hunsdon (signed E. S.), Grey (dupl.), Lord Buckhurst, Sir Fr. Walsingham, (signed E. S.), Sir John Norris (signed E. S.), Raleigh (dupl. signed E. S.), Countess of Pembroke (signed E. S.). On M 5[v] is a large woodcut of St George and the dragon at beginning of Book II. On X 7[v] spaces have been left for the insertion of some Welsh words. These were filled up in the later copies and in the edition of 1596. The printer was John Wolfe, whose device appears on the titlepage. The first edition of Books I–III.

Sinker 598. BM 1438.

The Faerie Queene. Disposed into twelue bookes, Fashioning XII. Morall vertues. *London Printed for William Ponsonbie.* 1596. 4°. (7⅜ × 5¼). R. 6.

Collation: A–2O[8], paged. Dedication to Queen Elizabeth on verso of titlepage. At the end of the volume are verses signed W. R. (*i.e.* Walter Raleigh) and Hobynoll (*i.e.* Gabriel Harvey). Large woodcut of St George and the dragon on M 5[v] at beginning of Book II, as in the former edition. The printer was Richard Field, whose device appears on the titlepage. The second edition of Books I–III.

Sinker 747. BM 1438.

The second Part of the Faerie Queene. Containing The Fourth, Fifth, and Sixth Bookes. By Ed. Spenser. *Imprinted at London for William Ponsonby.* 1596. 4°. (7⅜ × 5¼). R. 7.

Collation: A–2I[8]2K[4], paged. Printed by Richard Field, with his device on the titlepage. The first edition of Books IV–VI.

Sinker 748. BM 1438.

[Another copy.] (7 × 5). S. 18. 1.

The Faerie Queene, disposed into XII. Bookes, Fashioning twelue Morall Vertues. *At London. Printed by H. L. for Mathew Lownes.* 1609. F°. (10½ × 7¼). G. 3. 1.

Collation: A–2H[6]2I[4], paged. 2I 4 blank. Double columns. Dedication to Queen Elizabeth on verso of titlepage. Bks. I–III. Commendatory verses signed W. R. (*i.e.* Walter Raleigh) and Hobynoll (*i.e.* Gabriel Harvey). 'The Second Part of the Faery Queene', containing Bks. IV–VI, begins at sig. Q 5 with separate titlepage 'Imprinted at London for Mathew Lownes. 1609.'. The fragment of the seventh book 'Of Mutability' first appears in this edition with head-title at sig. 2H 4. The copy described in the Huth catalogue, which has the date in the colophon printed '16012' belongs, as the collation shows, to the edition of 1611, and can only have the earlier titlepage prefixed. The copy of the 'Faery Queen' on the other hand in the collected edition of 1611, there described, is properly that of 1609.

BM 1439.

The Faerie Queen: The Shepheards Calendar: Together with the other Works of England's Arch-Poët, Edm. Spenser: Collected into one Volume, and carefully corrected. *Printed by H. L. for Mathew Lownes. Anno Dom.* 1611.

F°. ($11\frac{1}{4} \times 7\frac{1}{4}$). F. 5.

Title within woodcut border originally used in 1593 for Sidney's 'Arcadia'. Collation: A^6, with two unsigned leaves inserted after A 1, $B–P^6Q^4R–2H^6$; $¶^8$; $A–E^6F^4$; A^8; $A–L^6M^2$; first alphabet only paged. 2H 6, ¶ 8 and F 4 (second alphabet) blank. Wanting A 1 (first alphabet) (? blank). Double columns. Titlepage and dedication to Queen Elizabeth occupying unsigned sheet. 'Faery Queen' Bks I–III, with commendatory verses signed W. R. (*i.e.* W. Raleigh) and Hobynoll (*i.e.* G. Harvey) at the end. Bks IV–VI, with separate titlepage 'Imprinted at London for Mathew Lownes. Anno Dom. 1613.' (Some copies, *vide infra*, have the date 1612, but the difference is in the last figure alone). Bk VII begins with head-title at sig. 2G 6. At the end of this portion appears a colophon with the date printed '16012', followed by one blank leaf. The quire signed ¶ containing letter to Sir Walter Raleigh signed Edm. Spenser and dated Jan. 23, 1589, followed by commendatory verses signed W. R., Hobbynoll (these two same as above), R. S., H. B., W. L., and Ignoto. Also dedicatory verses to Sir Christopher Hatton, Lord Burleigh, Earl of Oxford, Earl of Northumberland, Earl of Cumberland, Earl of Essex, Earl of Ormond and Ossory, Lord Ch. Howard, Lord Hunsdon, Lord Grey of Wilton, Lord Buckhurst, Sir Fr. Walsingham, Sir Joh. Norris, Sir Wal. Raleigh and the Countess of Pembroke, each signed E. S., followed by one blank leaf. The second alphabet contains the 'Shepherds Calender'. Separate titlepage with imprint 'At London, Printed by H. L. for Mathew Lownes, and are to be sold at the signe of the Bishops head in Paules Church-yard. 1611'. Contents as in separate edition, with same woodcuts. One leaf blank at end. The single quire A contains 'Prosopopoia' with separate titlepage bearing imprint 'At London, Printed by H. L. for Mathew Lownes. Anno Dom. 1613'. Epistle dedicatory to Lady Compton and Mountegle, signed Ed: Sp. The signatures are continuous throughout the remainder of the volume. 'Colin Clout' with separate titlepage having imprint without date. Epistle dedicatory to Sir W. Raleigh signed Ed. Sp. and dated, Kilcolman, Dec. 27, 1591. 'Astrophel' follows with head-title only. 'Prothalamion' 'Amoretti' 'Epitalamion' 'Hymnes' 'Daphnaida' 'Complaints' and 'Muiopotmos' have each a separate titlepage with imprint dated 1611. Some copies of the present volume appear to have been issued containing the 1609 edition of the 'Faery Queen';

copies in this state are in the Cambridge University and Huth Libraries.

BM 1438.

The Faerie Queen : The Shepheards Calendar : Together with the other Works of England's Arch-Poët, Edm. Spenser : Collected into one Volume, and carefully corrected. *Printed by H. L. for Mathew Lownes. Anno Dom.* 1617.

F°. (11 × $7\frac{3}{8}$). F. 6.

Title within woodcut border as above. Collation : A^6, with two unsigned leaves inserted after A 1, $B–P^6Q^4R–2H^6$; ¶^{8}; $A–E^6F^4$; A^8; $A–L^6M^2$, paged in first alphabet only. A 1, 2H 6 (first alphabet), ¶ 8 and F 4 (second alphabet), blank. Double columns. In this copy the quire signed ¶ is misplaced after the second alphabet, an arrangement also found in the copy in the Cambridge University Library. It is sometimes found at the end of the volume. The inserted sheet contains titlepage and dedication to Queen Elizabeth. The 'Faery Queen' is the same edition as above (1611), but has the date 1612 on the titlepage to Part II; so also is sig. ¶ and the single quire A containing the 'Prosopopoia'. The remainder is a very close reprint, the contents and collation being identical. The separate titlepages have dates as follows (they are all printed 'by H. L. for Mathew Lownes' except the first) : 'Shepheards Calender' with imprint 'London, Printed by Bar: Alsop for Iohn Harrison the elder, and are to bee solde at his shop at the signe of the golden Anker in Pater Noster Row, 1617.'; 'Colin Clout' undated, 'Prothalamion' etc. 1617. The peculiarities observable in the various copies of the collected editions of 1611 and 1617 are best explained on the following hypothesis. On Sept. 3, 1604 W. Ponsonby assigned his right in both parts of the 'Faery Queene' to S. Waterson, who on Nov. 5 in the same year passed it on to M. Lownes, who published an edition in 1609. Two years later the question of a collected edition of Spenser's works arose. Lownes caused a complete edition to be printed, and at the same time determined to use up the remaining copies of the 1609 'Faery Queen'. Instead however of printing the new titlepage on A 1 he caused a single sheet to be printed containing title and dedication, which could be substituted for the 1609 title. A 1 consequently remained blank in the new edition as it is found in the present copy, and the title-sheet was inserted after it. The result of using up the 1609 edition was that the stock of some of the additional matter in the 1611 edition was exhausted before the stock of the 'Faery Queen'. In 1617 a new title-sheet was printed and prefixed to the remainder stock, the additional pieces being reprinted when necessary. Even now some of the original copies of 1609 remained and were issued with the general title and additional matter dated 1617. A copy in this state is in the Library. The first part to run out was the fourth alphabet containing 'Colin Clout' etc., which is always found reprinted in copies having the 1617 titlepage. Perhaps the next was the 'Prosopopoia' which is found dated 1613 in the present copy, but which is undated in the copy in the Cambridge University Library. This last-mentioned copy however has the original edition of the 'Shepherds Calender' dated 1611, while the present copy has the reprint of 1617. How this came to bear the imprint given above requires explanation. The editions of the 'Calender' of 1581 to 1597 were all printed for John Harrison the younger (*i.e.* John Harrison II) and he probably objected when Lownes issued the work with his own name as publisher in the collected edition of 1611. Before the reprint however was required John Harrison the elder (*i.e.* John Harrison I) either died or retired from business (1616), whereupon John Harrison II assumed the style of 'the elder' to distinguish himself from a John Harrison IV who had started business in 1603.

BM 1438.

The Shepheardes Calender Conteyning twelue Æglogues proportionable to the twelue monethes. Entitled to the noble and vertuous Gentleman most worthy of all titles both of learning and cheualrie M. Philip Sidney. *At London. Printed by Hugh Singleton, dwelling in Creede Lane neere vnto Ludgate at the signe of the gylden Tunne, and are there to be solde.* 1579. **B. L.** 4°. ($6\frac{3}{4} \times 4\frac{5}{8}$). T. 9. 1.

Collation: ¶⁴A–N⁴, folios numbered. Verses 'To his Booke', signed Immeritô, on verso of title. Epistle to Gabriel Harvey, signed E. K. (*i.e.* Edward Kirke?), with postscript dated April 10, 1579. General argument. Twelve eclogues with arguments and glosses by E. K. and woodcut to each. First edition.

Sinker 293. BM 880.

The Shepheardes Calender Conteining twelue Æglogues proportionable to the twelue Monethes. Entitled to the noble and vertuous Gentleman most worthy of all titles, both of learning and cheualrie M. Philip Sidney. *Imprinted at London for Iohn Harison the younger, dwelling in Pater noster Roe, at the signe of the Anker, and are there to be solde.*

[Colophon] *Imprinted at London by Thomas East, for Iohn Harrison the younger, dwelling in Pater noster Roe, at the signe of the Anker, and are there to bee solde.* 1581.

B. L. 4°. ($6\frac{7}{8} \times 5\frac{1}{4}$). T. 6.

Collation: ✱✱⁴A–N⁴, folios numbered. Contents as before. Second edition.

Sinker 427.

The Shepheardes Calender, Conteining twelue Æglogues proportionable to the twelue Monethes. Entitled to the noble and vertuous Gentleman most worthie of all titles, both of learning and chiualry, Maister Philip Sidney. *Imprinted at London by Iohn Wolfe for Iohn Harrison the yonger, dwelling in Pater noster Roe, at the signe of the Anker.* 1586. [Colophon] *Imprinted at London by Thomas East, for Iohn Harrison the younger, dwelling in Pater noster Roe, at the signe of the Anker, and are there to be sold.* 1586.

B. L. 4°. ($7\frac{3}{4} \times 5\frac{3}{4}$). Q. 9. 2.

Title within woodcut border. Collation: four leaves unsigned, A–N⁴, folios numbered. Contents as before. Third edition.

Sinker 589.

The Shepheards Calender. Conteining twelue Aeglogues proportionable to the twelue Monethes. Entituled, To the noble and vertuous Gentleman most worthie of all titles, both of learning and chiualry Maister Philip Sidney. *London Printed by Iohn Windet, for Iohn Harrison the yonger, dwelling in Pater noster Roe, at the signe of the Anger* [sic]. 1591.

B. L. 4°. ($7\frac{1}{8} \times 5$). S. 29. 3.

Title within woodcut border. Collation: ✱⁴A–N⁴, folios numbered. Contents as before. Fourth edition.

Sinker 636. BM 880.

STEPHENS, John.

Satyrical Essayes Characters and others. Or Accurate and quick Descriptions, fitted to the life of their Subiects.

τῶν ἠθῶν δὴ φυλαττεσθαι μάλλον δεῖ ἢ τοὺς ἐχεις [*sic*].
Theophras.

Aspice & hæc: si fortè aliquid decoctius audis.
Inde vaporata Lector mihi ferueat aure: Iuuen.
Plagosus minimè Plagiarius.

Iohn Stephens. *London, Printed by Nicholas Okes, and are to be sold by Roger Barnes, at his Shop in Saint Dunstanes Church-yard.* 1615. 8°. ($5\frac{3}{4} \times 3\frac{5}{8}$). Z. 3. 1.

Collation: A–X[8], paged. Wanting A 1 (? blank). Epistle dedicatory to Thomas Turner Esquire, signed I. S. Address 'To the People'. Table of Contents. Verses headed 'A Caution'. Commendatory verses signed Antho. Croftes. First edition; a second appearing the same year. The author's 'New Essayes and Characters' appeared in 1631.

BM 1447.

STOW, John.

The Annales of England, faithfully collected out of the most autenticall Authors, Records, and other Monuments of Antiquitie, from the first inhabitation vntill this present yeere 1592 By Iohn Stow citizen of London. *Imprinted at London by Ralfe Newbery. Cum priuilegio Regiæ maiestatis.*

B. L. 4°. (8 × 6). P. 5.

Title within woodcut border representing a genealogical tree of the sovereigns of England from Edward III to Elizabeth. Collation: a–c[4] A–4P[8] 4Q[6] (omitting all Z's), paged. Wanting 4Q 6 (? blank). Author's epistle dedicatory to the Archbishop of Canterbury dated May 26, 1592. Preface to the reader. List of authorities. Alphabetical table. Erratum concerning Oxford colleges. Annals, preceded by description of England etc., and followed by description of the Universities and list of errata. The first quarto edition appeared under the title of the 'Chronicles of England' in 1580, enlarged apparently from the 'Summarie of Englyshe Chronicles' first printed in octavo in 1565. The present is the second edition in quarto.

Sinker 355. BM 1453.

The Annales of England, Faithfully collected out of the most autenticall Authors, Records, and other Monuments of

Antiquitie, lately corrected, encreased, and continued, from the first inhabitation vntill this present yeere 1601. By Iohn Stow citizen of London. *Imprinted at London by Ralfe Newbery. Cum priuilegio Regiæ maiestàtis.*

𝔅. 𝔏. 4°. ($9\frac{1}{4} \times 6\frac{3}{4}$). M. I.

Title within woodcut border as above. Collation: a–c^4A–$4Q^8 4R^4$ (omitting all Z's), paged. Contents as before, omitting the two errata. The Epistle dedicatory to the Archbishop of Canterbury is dated November 24, 1600.

Annales, or, a generall Chronicle of England. Begun by Iohn Stow: Continued and Augmented with matters Forraigne and Domestique, Ancient and Moderne, vnto the end of this present yeere, 1631. By Edmund Howes, Gent. *Londini, Impensis Richardi Meighen*, 1631. [Colophon] *London, Printed by A. M. for Richard Meighen, and are to bee sold at his Shop at the Middle Temple Gate, neere Templebarre in Fleetstreet.* 1632. 𝔅. 𝔏. F°. ($12\frac{3}{4} \times 8\frac{1}{2}$). B. 3.

Title within woodcut border (the date cut, not printed). Collation: $*^2$¶^{8}A–$4M^6 4N^2 4n^4 4O$–$4P^6 4Q^4 4R^6 4S^8$, paged. Double columns. Wanting 4S 8 (? blank). Epistle dedicatory to the King (*i.e.* Charles I.), signed Edmond Howes. Epistle to the reader signed by the same. 'An Historical Preface'. At sig. 4n 1 is a separate titlepage to an Appendix on the Universities of Cambridge, Oxford and London, the two former by Stow, the last 'Collected and Written by Sir George Buck'. This titlepage has the imprint 'London: Printed by Aug. Matthewes, for Richard Meighen. 1632'. Then follows an address to the reader signed by Howes. The account of 'The Third Vniversitie of England' again has a separate titlepage on 4O 1, with a similar imprint, dated 1631. Then follow: Latin verses on London; Epistle dedicatory to Sir Edward Coke signed George Buc, and dated 'his Maiesties Office of the Reuels, vpon Saint Peters hill', Aug. 24, 1612; and a catalogue of all the subjects taught at the University of London. At the end is a passage from Drayton's 'Poly-olbion', a letter to the Lord Mayor and Aldermen of London signed Edmond Howes, and an alphabetical Table. This appears to be the fifth and last edition.

BM 1454.

A Suruay of London. Contayning the Originall, Antiquity, Increase, Moderne estate, and description of that Citie, written in the yeare 1598. by Iohn Stow Citizen of London. Also an Apologie (or defence) against the opinion of some men, concerning that Citie, the greatnesse thereof. With an Appendix, containing in Latine, Libellum de situ & nobilitate Londini: Written by William Fitzstephen, in the raigne of Henry the second. *Imprinted by Iohn Wolfe, Printer to the honorable Citie of London: And are to be sold at his shop within the Popes head Alley in Lombard street.* 1598.

B. L. 4°. ($7\frac{3}{8} \times 5\frac{5}{8}$). S. 21.

Collation: A^4B–$2G^8 2H^{10}$; paged. Epistle dedicatory by Stow to the Lord Mayor (*i.e.* Stephen Some) and citizens of London. Table of contents. List of errata at the end.

Sinker 613. BM 1454.

A Suruay of London.... 1599.

B. L. 4°. ($7\frac{3}{8} \times 5\frac{5}{8}$). R. 4.

A duplicate of the above except for the alteration in the date.

Sinker 614.

STRAPAROLA, Giovanni Francesco.

Le piaceuoli Notti di M. Giouanfrancesco Straparola da Carauaggio. Nelle quali si contengono le Fauole con i loro Enimmi da dieci donne, & duo giouani raccontate. Nuouamente ristampate, & con diligenza rauuedute. Libro primo. [Libro secondo.] *In Venetia, Appresso Iseppo di Mantelli* M. D. LXVII. 2 vols. 8°. ($5\frac{7}{8} \times 3\frac{5}{8}$). Z. 1.

Collation: vol. I, A–X^8, folios numbered; vol. II, 2A–$2T^8 2V^2$, folios numbered. 'Proemio' to vol. I. The first edition appeared in 1550–53. The present is about the ninth.

SYLVESTER, Josuah.

Du Bartas his Deuine Weekes, and Workes.... 1641. *See* Du Bartas, Guillaume de Saluste.

TASSO, Torquato.

Godfrey of Bulloigne, or The Recouerie of Ierusalem. Done into English Heroicall verse, by Edward Fairefax Gent.

Imprinted at London by Ar. Hatfield, for I. Iaggard and M. Lownes. 1600 F°. (10 × 6¼). H. 4.

Collation: A⁴B–2K⁶2L⁴, paged. Dedicatory verses to Queen Elizabeth signed by the translator. 'The Allegorie of the Poem'. A cancel slip is inserted on B 1, containing a different rendering of the first stanza. First edition of the translation by Fairfax. The second edition, 1624, follows the original, not the cancel, in the rendering of the first stanza. A translation of cantos i–v by Richard Carew had appeared in 1594. At the end of the 'Allegory' in the present copy are six lines of blank verse in Capell's handwriting and subscribed with his initials. They are a translation of the second stanza of the first book.

Sinker 666. BM 700.

TAVERNER, RICHARD.

Prouerbes or Adagies, gathered oute of the Chiliades of Erasmus.... 1552. *See* ERASMUS, Desiderius.

TAYLOR, JOHN.

Taylor's Motto. Et habeo, Et Careo, Et Curo. *London Printed for I T & H G*, 1621. 8°. (6½ × 4¼). X. 4. 3.

Titlepage engraved. Collation: A⁸ with titlepage inserted after A 2, B–D⁸E⁴, unpaged. A 1 blank. Explanation of titlepage in verse, signed Iohn Taylor on A 2ᵛ. Verses 'To Euery Body', signed. According to Mr Hazlitt at least three editions appeared during the year.

BM 1484.

THOMAS, WILLIAM.

The Historye of Italye. A booke exceding profitable to be red: because it intreateth of the astate of many and dyuers common weales, how they haue bene, and now be gouerned. *Imprinted at London in Fletestrete nere to Saicnt* [sic] *Dunstons Church by Thomas Marshe.* [Colophon adds] *Anno Domini*. 1561. 𝔅. 𝔏. 4°. (7 × 5⅛). S. 7. 1.

Title within woodcut border. Collation: A⁴𝔄⁴A–3I⁴, folios numbered, except in sheet T which contains Table of Popes and of which the last leaf is blank. Wanting A 4 of preliminary sheet (? blank). Table of contents. Epistle dedicatory to Iohn Erle of Warrewicke, signed by the author Wylliam Thomas and dated

London Sept. 20, 1549. Alphabetical table. 'Conclusion' at the end. Thomas was clerk of the Council to Edward VI. Second edition, the first having appeared in 1549.

Sinker 308. BM 1494.

TOFTE, ROBERT.

Ariostos seuen Planets Governing Italie... 1611. *See* ARIOSTO, Lodovico.

TOM TYLER.

Tom Tyler and His Wife. An excellent old play, as It was Printed and Acted about a hundred Years ago. The second Impression. *London, Printed in the Year,* 1661.

4°. ($7\frac{1}{4} \times 5\frac{3}{8}$). R. 23. I.

Collation: A–C[4]D[2]; A–B[8], paged. Personae. Prologue. A Catalogue of Plays with fresh pagination occupies last two sheets. No earlier edition is known.

TURBERVILLE, GEORGE.

The Heroycall Epistles of...Publius Ouidius Naso... 1567. *See* OVIDIUS NASO, Publius.

⌈Epitaphes, Epigrams, Songs and Sonets, with a Discourse of the Friendly affections of Tymetes to Pyndara his Ladie. Newly corrected with additions, and set out by George Turberuile Gentleman. *Imprinted at London by Henrie Denham, dwelling in Pater Noster Row at the signe of the Starre.*⌉ [Colophon adds] *Anno Domini.* 1570. *Cum Priuilegio.* 8°. B. L. ($5\frac{1}{2} \times 3\frac{7}{8}$). Z. 10.

Collation: A–V[8], folios numbered. Wanting sig. A, containing titlepage; epistle dedicatory to Anne, Countess of Warwick, signed; address to the reader, signed; and verses 'To the Rayling Route of Sycophants.' Table of contents beginning on B 1[v]. Dudley crest within garter of the order (for Ambrose, Earl of Warwick) with date 1570; below a lion passant charged with a crescent for difference. Verses subscribed. Verses on Anne Countess of Warwick. Argument in verse. At end, 'The Authours Epilogue'. Of the first edition, before 1567, only a fragment is known; of the second, 1567, an imperfect copy is preserved in the Bodleian; the present is the third.

Sinker 335.

TWYNE, Thomas.

The .xiii. Bookes of Æneidos.... 1584. *See* Vergilius Maro, Publius.

VERGILIUS MARO, Publius.

The .xiii. Bukes of Eneados of the famose Poete Virgill Translatet out of Latyne verses into Scottish metir, bi the Reuerend Father in God, Mayster Gawin Douglas Bishop of Dunkel & vnkil to the Erle of Angus. Euery buke hauing hys perticular Prologe. *Imprinted at Londo* 1553.

B. L. 4°. ($8\frac{3}{8} \times 6$). O. 2.

Title within woodcut border. Collation: $A^2B\text{–}Z^8a\text{–}z^82a\text{–}2b^8$; with one unsigned leaf inserted after X 3. A 1 and 2b 8 wanting (? blank). Printed by William Copeland.

Sinker 198. BM 1544.

The .xiii. Bookes of Æneidos. The first twelue beeinge the woorke of the diuine Poet Virgil Maro, and the thirtenth the supplement of Maphæus Vegius. Translated into English verse to the fyrst thirdpart of the tenth Booke, by Thomas Phaër Esquire: and the residue finished, and now the second time newly set forth for the delite of such as are studious in Poetrie: By Thomas Twyne, Doctor in Physicke. *Imprinted at London by William How, for Abraham Veale, dwelling in Paules Church yeard, at the signe of the Lambe.* 1584.

B. L. 4°. ($7 \times 5\frac{1}{4}$). S. 26.

Collation: four leaves unsigned, $A\text{–}V^8X^4$, unpaged. Wanting X 4 (? blank). Epistle dedicatory to Robert Sackevill son of Lord Buckhurst, signed Thomas Twyne, and dated Lewis, Jan. 1, 1584. Address to the readers, signed. Life of Vergil translated from Aelius Donatus. Arguments to the thirteen books in verse. General summary. At the end of Book xii is Phaer's prose conclusion. Each book is signed and dated by the translator, the work being concluded on July 6, 1573. The 'seuen first bookes' appeared in 1558, the 'nyne fyrst Bookes' in 1562, the 'whole xii. Bookes' in 1573, the thirteenth book was first added in the edition of 1583, having been finished by Twyne on Oct. 26 of that year. The present is the second edition of the completed work.

Sinker 438. BM 1545.

UGUBIO, ANDREA ZENOPHONTE DA.

Formulario nuouo da dittar Lettere amorose messiue & responsiue. Composto per Andrea Zenophonte da Vgubio. Opera nuoua intitolata Flos Amoris. M D XLIIII. [Colophon] *In Vinegia per Francesco Bindoni & Mapheo Pasini compagni.* 1544. 8°. ($5\frac{1}{2} \times 3\frac{3}{4}$). Z. 7. 3.

Title within woodcut border. Collation: A–C[8], unpaged. There was a previous edition in 1531.

UNDERDOWNE, THOMAS.

An Æthiopian Historie.... 1587. *See* HELIODORUS.

UPTON, JOHN.

Critical Observations on Shakespeare. By John Upton Prebendary of Rochester.... *London: Printed for G. Hawkins, in Fleet-street.* M, DCC, XLVI. 8°. ($8\frac{1}{8} \times 4\frac{7}{8}$). P. 16.

Dedicated to the Earl of Granville. Reprinted with omission of the 'Reverie' (pp. 139–48) in 1748.

URQUART, *Sir* THOMAS.

Epigrams, Divine and Morall. By Sir Thomas Vrchard, Knight. *London, Printed for William Leake, and are to be sold at his Shop in Chancery Lane neere the Roules.* 1646. 4°. ($7 \times 5\frac{1}{4}$). S. 32. 1.

Collation: A–I[4], paged. Wanting A 1 (Portrait by Glover) and I 4 (? blank). Epistle dedicatory to Iames, Marques of Hamilton, signed by the author. Text in three books. Doxology. Errata. Printer's address to the reader. Imprimatur signed Johannes Hansley, March 15, 1646. At the end of the text is the note 'Here end the first three Bookes of Sir Thomas Vrchards Epigrams'. No more however appeared. This is said to be a re-issue of an edition of 1641, but if so the last leaf as well as the titlepage must be a cancel.

WALPOLE, Horace.

Historic Doubts on the Life and Reign of King Richard the Third. By Mr. Horace Walpole.... *London: Printed for J. Dodsley in Pall-Mall.* M.DCC.LXVIII.

4°. (9½ × 7⅜). I. 3. I.

With portraits of Richard and his Queen engraved by Grignion after Vertue.

WARNER, William.

Albions England. A Continued Historie of the same Kingdome, from the Originals of the first Inhabitants thereof: With most the chiefe Alterations and Accidents theare hapning, vnto, and in the happie Raigne of our now most gracious Soueraigne, Queene Elizabeth: Not barren in varietie of inuentiue and historicall Intermixtures: First penned and published by William Warner: and now reuised, and newly inlarged by the same Author: Whereunto is also newly added an Epitome of the whole Historie of England. *London, Printed by Edm. Bollifant for George Potter, and are to be sold at his shop in Paules Church-yard, at the signe of the Bible.* 1602. 4°. (7¼ × 5¼). R. 9.

Collation: A–2C^8, paged. Wanting 2C 8 (? blank). Epistle dedicatory to Henry Carey, Baron of Hunsdon, signed. Address to the reader signed W. W. Table of contents. Text in thirteen books. 'A Breuiate of the true Historie of Æneas' in prose as an addition to Bk. ii. Epitome of the history of England with address to the reader. The first part originally appeared in 1586. In the second edition, 1589, a second part was added. The third edition with continuation appeared in 1592. In 1596 appeared a fourth, revised and enlarged, which was re-issued with a new titlepage the following year. The present edition of 1602 was the fifth and was the first one containing all thirteen books. A 'Continuance' appeared in 1606 and was incorporated in the final edition of 1612, making sixteen books in all.

BM 1570.

WATSON, Thomas.

An Ould facioned Loue. Or a loue of the Ould facion. By I. T. gent. *At London Printed by P. S. for William*

Mattes, dwelling in fleetstrete at the signe of the hand and plough. 1594. 4°. ($7\frac{1}{4} \times 5\frac{1}{2}$). R. 23. 2.

Collation: A–F[4], paged. Wanting A 1 (? blank). Epistle dedicatory to Mistres Anne Roberts, signed I. T. Address to the reader. As appears from this address the work is a translation of Thomas Watson's Latin 'Amyntae Gaudia'. It consists of five 'Epistles', some in four-line, some in six-line stanzas, with a final 'Answer of Phillis to Amintas by the Translator' in six-line stanzas. Watson's work contained eighteen epistles in all, of which only the first five are here translated. Watson's work appeared in 1592.

Sinker 768.

WHETSTONE, George.

The Right Excellent and famous Historye, of Promos and Cassandra: Deuided into two Commicall Discourses. In the fyrste parte is showne, the vnsufferable abuse, of a lewde Magistrate: The vertuous behauiours of a chaste Ladye: The vncontrowled leawdenes of a fauoured Curtisan. And the vndeserued estimation of a pernicious Parasyte. In the second parte is discoursed, the perfect magnanimitye of a noble Kinge, in checking Vice and fauouringe Vertue: Wherein is showne, the Ruyne and ouerthrowe, of dishonest practises: with the aduauncement of vpright dealing. The worke of George Whetstones Gent. Formæ nulla fides. [Colophon] *Imprinted at London by Richarde Ihones, and are to be solde ouer agaynst Saint Sepulchres Church, without Newgate. August*. 20. 1578.

𝔅. 𝔏. 4°. ($6\frac{5}{8} \times 4\frac{7}{8}$). T. 9. 2.

Collation: A–M[4], unpaged. Wanting M 4 (? blank). Epistle dedicatory to William Fleetwoode, signed George Whetstone and dated July 29, 1578. Printer's address to the reader, signed R. I. Argument. Part II has a separate titlepage within woodcut border, 'The seconde part of the Famous Historie of Promos and Cassandra. Set forth in a Comical Discourse by George Whetstone Gent. Formæ nulla fides.'

Sinker 466. BM 1584.

The Rocke of Regard, diuided into foure parts. The first, the Castle of delight: Wherin is reported, the wretched end of wanton and dissolute liuing. The second, the Garden of Vnthriftinesse: Wherein are many sweete flowers, (or rather fancies) of honest loue. The thirde, the Arbour of Vertue: Wherein slaunder is highly punished, and vertuous Ladies and Gentlewomen, worthily commended. The fourth, the Ortchard of Repentance: Wherein are discoursed, the miseries that followe dicing, the mischiefes of quareling, the fall of prodigalitie: and the souden ouerthrowe of foure notable cousners, with diuers other morall, natural, & tragical discourses: documents and admonitions: being all the inuention, collection and translation of George Whetstons Gent. Formæ nulla fides. [Colophon] *Imprinted at London for Robert Waley. Anno.* 1576.

B. L. 4°. ($7\frac{1}{4} \times 5\frac{3}{8}$). R. 12. 2.

Collation: ¶[4]2¶[2]A–G[8]H–I[4]K–Q[8]R[4], paged in two portions beginning with sigs. A and K respectively. Epistle dedicatory from the author 'To all the young Gentlemen of England', dated 'From my lodging in Holborne', October 15, 1576. Address to the reader. Commendatory verses from Nicholas Bowyer, R. C., Humphrey Turner, Abraham Fleming, John Wytton. Argument to 'the Countesse of Celants complaint', the first poem in 'The Castle of Delight'. The four parts begin each with separate half-title, at sigs. A 1, D 8, G 4 and K 1 respectively. Each part has an epilogue in verse. Part III has an epistle dedicatory to Lady Iana Sibilla Greye; Part IV, to Sir Thomas Cecill, each signed and dated as before. Part IV contains three poems by R. C., who may have been Robert Cudden of Gray's Inn, a kinsman of Whetstone, at whose request one of his poems in this part was written. On the verso of the titlepage and on several other leaves is writing in an early English hand.

Sinker 545. BM 1584.

WHITNEY, GEFFREY.

A Choice of Emblemes, and other Deuises, For the moste parte gathered out of sundrie writers, Englished and Moralized. And diuers newly deuised, by Geffrey Whitney. A worke adorned with varietie of matter, both pleasant and profitable: wherein those that please, maye finde to fit their fancies: Bicause herein, by the office of the eie, and the eare, the minde maye reape dooble delighte throughe holsome preceptes, shadowed with pleasant deuises: both fit for the vertuous, to their incoraging: and for the wicked, for their admonishing and amendment.

To the Reader.

Peruse with heed, then frendlie iudge, and blaming rashe refraine:
So maist thou reade vnto thy good, and shalt requite my paine.

Imprinted at Leyden, In the house of Christopher Plantyn, by Francis Raphelengius. M. D. LXXXVI. 4°. ($8\frac{1}{4} \times 6$). P. I.

Collation: *[4]2*[4]3*[2]A–Z[4]a–f[4], paged. Wanting f 4 (? blank). Large woodcut of the achievement of Robert, Earl of Leicester, on verso of titlepage. Epistle dedicatory to the same, signed and dated London, Nov. 28, 1585. Address to the reader, signed and dated Leyden, May 4, 1586. Commendatory verses in Latin from Ianus Dousa à Noortwijck, Bonaventura Vulcanius Brugensis, Petrus Colvius Brugensis, Stephanus Limbertus Anglus Nordovicensis, and in English from Arthur Bourchier. Verses of the author, headed 'D. O. M.' and list of errata. Part ii begins with a separate titlepage, without imprint but bearing Leicester's crest, on sig. O 1, followed by verses on Warwick and Leicester. Woodcuts in the text throughout.

Sinker 998. BM 1591.

WOTTON, *Sir* HENRY.

Reliquiæ Wottonianæ: or, a Collection Of Lives, Letters, Poems; with Characters of Sundry Personages: And other Incomparable Pieces of Language and Art. Also Additional Letters to several Persons, not before Printed. By the Curious Pencil of the ever Memorable Sir Henry Wotton, K[t.] Late Provost of Eaton Colledge. The Third Edition, with large Additions. *London, Printed by T. Roycroft, for R. Marriott, F. Tyton, T. Collins, and J. Ford,* 1672.

8°. ($6\frac{3}{4} \times 4\frac{1}{4}$). U. 5.

Collation: A[8]b–e[8]f[4]C–2Q[8], paged. Wanting 2Q 8 (? blank). Engraved portrait by Dolle. Epistle dedicatory to Philip, Earl of Chesterfield, signed Izaak Walton and dated Feb. 27, 1672. Address to the reader. 'An Account of the Work.' Life of Wotton signed Iz. Wa. Elegy on Wotton signed A. Cowley. Letter from Wotton to Marcus Velserus of Augsburg in Latin and same in English, dated

'London, Decemb. 2. after the Julian Accompt' 1612. Letter from Wotton to the Regius Professor of Divinity in Cambridge dated Jan. 17, 1637. Table of contents at the end. Contains an engraved portrait of Robert Devereux, Earl of Essex, at sig. K 2^v and of George Villiers, Duke of Buckingham, at sig. P 8^v, both signed by Dolle. The first edition appeared in 1651; this is the third.

YONG, BARTHOLOMEW.

Diana of George of Montemayor.... 1598. *See* MONTEMAYOR, Jorge de.

MANUSCRIPTS.

Catalogue of a Collection intitl'd Shakesperiana; comprehending All the several Editions of the Works of Shakespeare, old & new; divers rare old Editions of Writers, prose-men & verse-men; with a Variety of other Articles, chiefly such as tend to illustrate him;—made by his last Editor, E. C; and by him deposited in the Library of Trinity College in Cambridge, this eleventh Day of Iune in the Year 1779. large 4°. (11 × 9).

An alphabetical index to the books in the collection, in Capell's own handwriting. At the end is inserted a leaf containing a list of 'Quarto's wanted' to complete the collection of Shakespearian editions. Of this list thirty copies were privately printed by Steevens in 1780, and it was also reprinted in Hartshorne's 'Book Rarities of Cambridge' in 1829. The list is not very accurate and there are many omissions. It inserts, moreover, as if in the collection, many editions which it never contained, Capell having intended to make the list of Shakespearian quartos complete by reference to other collections when his own failed. In the inside of the cover is the following inscription: 'June 26. 1779. Ordered by the Master and Seniors, agreeably to the express Desire of M^r^. Capel, that the whole Collection given by him be kept together in the same Class; and that no Manuscript or Book belonging to it be taken out of the Library on any Pretence whatever. J. Peterborough M C.' There are also three documents inserted relating to articles in the collection. One of these runs 'Effigies William Shakespeare Britanni ad fidem tabellæ unicæ manu Richard Burbage depictæ (circa annum, ut videtur, 1609) per R. Barret Londinensem quam exactissimè expressa anno 1759, curantibus David Garrick et Edward Capell. Capell's Collection given to ye College 1779'. Another is headed 'Extract of a letter to M^r^. Capell, that accompany'd a Cast from the face of Shakespear's monument at Stratford, dated Decr. 13. 1780.'. The portrait and cast are both in the Library. The third is a list of certain books in Capell's handwriting. There has also been added to the collection a fine medallion head of Capell, engraved by Bartolozzi after a plaster model taken from life by Roubilliac in 1750.

Mr William Shakespeare his Comedies, Histories, and Tragedies, set out by himself in quarto, or by the Players his Fellows in folio, and now faithfully republish'd from those Editions in ten volumes octavo; with an Introduction: Whereunto will be added, in some other Volumes, Notes, criticall and explanatory, and a Body of Various Readings entire.

> Qui genus humanum ingenio superavit, et omneis
> Præstinxit, stellas exortus uti æthereus Sol.
>
> Lucr. Lib. 3. l. 1056.

London: Printed for &c. 1768.

6 vols. large 4°. ($11\frac{3}{4} \times 9\frac{1}{4}$). MS. I.

Epistle dedicatory to the Duke of Grafton, signed and dated 'Essex Court in the Temple. Nov. 9th. 1766', alterēd to 1767 as in printed edition. At the end of vol. vi is inserted a printed table as in MS. 3. The date at which Capell began and ended each play is entered, but these dates do not run consecutively through the volumes as finally bound up. The earliest date is that to the 'Merry Wives of Windsor', begun Nov. 25, 1749, and ended Jan. 18, 1750; the latest that to the 'Taming of the Shrew', begun July 4, 1766 and ended Aug. 1 of the same year. Whether these dates refer to the actual construction of the text or merely to the present transcript is not clear, but they certainly bear some relation to the latter as may be seen from the handwriting which gradually grows larger, heavier, and less easy to read, though always distinguished by copperplate regularity.

Notes and Various Readings to Shakespeare,....Volume the First. [Volume the Second.] *London: Printed by &c.*

Volume the Third. The School of Shakespeare: or, authentic Extracts from divers English Books, that were in Print in that Author's Time; evidently shewing from whence his several Fables were taken, and some Parcel of his Dialogue: Also, further extracts, from the same or like Books, which or contribute to a due Understanding of his Writings, or give Light to the History of his Life, or to the dramatic History of his Time. With a Preface, and an Index of Books extracted. *London: Printed by &c.*

3 vols. large 4°. ($11\frac{5}{8} \times 9\frac{3}{8}$). MS. 2.

The first vol. contains an address to the reader signed E. C., and a glossary to Shakespeare, after which come the notes and various readings to the different plays, which fill the remainder of vol. i and the whole of vol. ii. Vol. iii contains Preface signed E. C., 'Index of Books extracted', and Extracts. There follows 'Notitia Dramatica; or, Tables of Ancient Plays, (from their Beginning, to the Restoration of Charles the second) so many as have been printed, with their several Editions: faithfully compiled, and digested in quite new Method, by E. C. With a Preface.'. This is followed by a bibliographical appendix of titles, which was never printed. The 'School of Shakespeare' was begun Feb. 3, 1767 and ended Jan. 16, 1771. Part of the commentary was published in 1774 but was not well received and was recalled. The whole was then put forth in three quarto vols. in 1779–1783, the last of which appeared after Capell's death in 1781.

Paradise Lost a Poem in Twelve Books; written by Iohn Milton. *London: Printed for &c.* 4°. ($11\frac{3}{4} \times 9\frac{3}{8}$). MS. 3.

Epistle dedicatory to the Bishop of Rochester signed, and dated Essex Court in the Temple, Ian. 23, 1767. With List of editions and various readings at the end. The text was begun July 23, 1759 and ended Dec. 18, 1760. After this with separate titlepage 'Hermes, or, A Guide to the Elements; setting forth their just Number, and a Mode of representing with Certainty: For the Benefit of Youth, and of Foreigners. Fronte, exile negotium, Et dignum pueris putes; Aggressis, labor arduus. Ter. Mau. London: Printed for &c.' a treatise on phonetics with a folding leaf of sounds (printed), and a vocabulary to 'Paradise Lost'. Neither of the works in this volume was printed.

["Prolusions, or, select Pieces of ancient Poetry", by E. C. 2. Vol[s]. 4°. small.] MS. 4.

This entry is in Capell's MS catalogue but the book is not in the collection.

A Collection of Poems, In Two Volumes; Being all the Miscellanies of Mr. William Shakespeare, which were Publish'd by himself in the Year 1609. and now correctly Printed from those Editions. The First Volume contains, I. Venus and Adonis. II. The Rape of Lucrece. III. The Passionate Pilgrim. IV. Some Sonnets set to sundry Notes of Musick. The Second Volume contains One Hundred and Fifty Four

Sonnets, all of them in Praise of his Mistress. II. A Lover's Complaint of his Angry Mistress. *London: Printed for Bernard Lintott, at the Cross-Keys, between the Two Temple-Gates in Fleet-street.*

8°. 2 vols. in one. ($6\frac{5}{8} \times 4\frac{1}{4}$). MS. 5.

The second leaf, signed A 2, contains an 'Advertisement', at the end of which on A 2[v] is the MS note 'I gave M[r] Capell the Information of the opposite Page. R. Farmer'. Then follow two leaves containing a 'Preface' in Capell's handwriting. The next leaf is B 1. The text has been carefully corrected throughout by Capell, who has modernised the spelling. The volume apparently contains Capell's material for an edition of the Poems, which however were not included in his edition of Shakespeare's works. The collection was published in 1709. On the fly-leaf are the lines also in Capell's hand:

Βαια φαγων, και βαια πιων, και πολλα νοσησας,
Οψε μεν, αλλ' εθανον· Ερρετε παντες ομου!

Pain of all sorts to cure, Grief, Labour, Fast,
Death of the latest came, but came at last.

INDEX

LIST OF PRINTERS, STATIONERS, ETC.

CAMBRIDGE: PRINTED BY J. AND C. F. CLAY, AT THE UNIVERSITY PRESS.

For EU product safety concerns, contact us at Calle de José Abascal, 56–1°, 28003 Madrid, Spain or eugpsr@cambridge.org.

www.ingramcontent.com/pod-product-compliance
Ingram Content Group UK Ltd.
Pitfield, Milton Keynes, MK11 3LW, UK
UKHW010047140625
459647UK00012BB/1668

* 9 7 8 1 1 0 8 0 0 4 4 0 4 *